La Revolución

MEXICO'S GREAT REVOLUTION

AS MEMORY, MYTH, & HISTORY

THOMAS BENJAMIN

UNIVERSITY OF TEXAS PRESS   AUSTIN

FIRST EDITION, 2000

Requests for permission to reproduce material from this
work should be sent to Permissions, University of Texas
Press, Box 7819, Austin, TX 78713-7819.

∞ The paper used in this book meets the minimum
requirements of ANSI/NISO Z39.48-1992 (R1997)
(Permanence of Paper).

Library of Congress Cataloging-in-Publication Data

Benjamin, Thomas, 1952–
    La Revolución : Mexico's great revolution as memory,
    myth, and history / Thomas Benjamin.
            p.   cm.
    Includes bibliographical references (p.   ) and index.
    ISBN 0-292-70880-7 (cloth : alk. paper)—
      ISBN 0-292-70882-3 (pbk. : alk. paper)
    1. Mexico—History—Revolution, 1910–1920—
    Historiography. 2. Mexico—History—
    1910–1946—Historiography. 3. Myth.
    I. Title.
    F1234.B465 2000
    972.08'16 21—dc21   99-046431

Cover photo by Sharon Lee House

It is the beginning of a great history
I undertake to relate to you.
Register it, all of you, and let your memory
never permit it to be forgotten.

Revolutionary Ballad

For Sharon

Contents

Preface

I HAVE BEEN READING the Mexican revolution for more than twenty-five years. During the 1980s I summarized what I was beginning to learn in historiographical essays. Historiography led me back through the few generations of historians who have narrated, researched, and interpreted Mexico's great revolution of the twentieth century. I noticed how historians often mirrored, and influenced, the political presumptions of their time. Historians of the Mexican revolution in the post-Tlatelolco era were heirs of a vast historiography that many believed required drastic revision. Revisionists attacked official and prorevolutionary history and the "myth of the revolution" fell before their archival research and scholarship. In my wandering through revolutionary historiography, I started to think about official memory, myth, and history. Was there an Ur-revolutionary historiography and, if so, when did it arise, how and why did it appear, and what did it look like?

This volume is my attempt to answer those questions. The Mexican revolution discussed in these pages exists only in words and on paper: a discourse of memory. The events created by Mexicans during the 1910s through the 1930s to transform their society and rebuild their nation are also the Mexican revolution. The Mexican revolution was not, I hasten to add, fundamentally a logomachy, merely a struggle in words. Attention to words implies no dismissal of acts. Revolutionaries made a revolution, or perhaps revolutions, by their actions; they also invented one through their words. Many hundreds of historians have studied the former. I think it is time to look more closely at the latter.

I am not the first to do so, which means this book is written on the foundation of at least two others. The first is Guillermo Palacios's thesis, "La Idea de la Revolución Mexicana," written at El Colegio de México in 1969. I took from his work the basic idea of "the idea of the Revolution," which I call *la Revolución*. The second is Ilene O'Malley's *The Myth of the Mexican Revolution: Hero Cults and the Institutionalization of the Mexican State, 1920–*

1940, published in 1986. This excellent book demonstrates how and why the postrevolutionary state transformed Francisco I. Madero, Emiliano Zapata, Venustiano Carranza, and Francisco Villa into official heroes, myths, and symbols. Both of these studies helped to guide me during my research and writing.

Over the past ten years I have been reading this particular Mexican revolution. Research for this book is based primarily on the kind of minor political writings historians have often ignored or disregarded (at least I did so for a long time). The Colección de Folletos de la Revolución Mexicana—the pamphlet collection—of the Biblioteca Lerdo de Tejada in Mexico City, is a treasure trove of little-known pamphlets, booklets, and articles. It is so little known that when I asked the librarians at the front desk about the Colección, they were unaware of its existence. Similarly, the Colección Basave, of the Biblioteca de México, located in the Ciudadela, also in Mexico City, was crucial to this project. The librarians of both institutions, and many others in Mexico, the United States, and Europe, found obscure written materials and put them in my hands, and I am profoundly grateful for their assistance. The other great sources of materials for this book were the second-hand booksellers on Calle Donceles at Calle Brazil in Mexico City. There I found numerous pamphlets and books that I failed to discover anywhere else. Finally, I inherited a marvelous collection of books on the Mexican revolution that was built by Charles C. Cumberland and David C. Bailey and which proved to be a crucial, not to mention very convenient, source for research.

The National Endowment for the Humanities gave me the opportunity in 1988 to begin my research in the Benson Latin American Collection at the University of Texas at Austin. In 1989–90, as visiting professor at the University of Groningen, in the Netherlands, several libraries in the Netherlands and the United Kingdom helped me to continue this project from afar. Central Michigan University awarded me a Research Professorship for the fall semester 1990, which took me to the libraries and archives of Mexico City. I returned during several summers as well as during my sabbatical leave in the winter semester of 1993. I am very grateful for this institutional support.

Conference presentations for the American Historical Association, the Latin American Studies Association, the International Congress of United States and Mexican Historians, and the Mexican Studies Center of the University of Groningen encouraged me to put some ideas together and begin writing. In 1992 anonymous readers for *Mexican Studies/Estudios Mexicanos* raised such insightful questions about a paper I submitted for publication that I reformulated my entire approach to this project. The paper was never resubmitted because it grew into this book. An earlier version of Chapter One appeared as "The Past in the Mexican Revolution," in Hub. Hermans, Dick Papousek, and Catherine Raffi-Béroud, eds., *Concierto Mexicano 1910– 1940: Repercusión e Interpretaciones* (Groningen: Centro de Estudios Mexicanos, 1997). An earlier version of Chapter Six appeared as "La Revolución hecha monumento: El Monumento de la Revolución," in *Historia y Grafía* 3:6 (1996). Along the way I have received advice and assistance in this project from Bill Beezley, Matt Esposito, Javier Garciadiego Dantan, Elaine Lacy, David Lorey, Clemente Martínez, Norma Mereles de Ogarrio, Henry C. Schmidt, Barbara Tannenbaum, and Paul Vanderwood. David LaFrance alerted me to the Colección Instituto Nacional de Estudios Históricos de la Revolución Mexicana in the Archivo General de la Nación de México. Daniela Spenser and I discussed the 1920s during many afternoons at the Hemeroteca Nacional at UNAM. Mark Wasserman read and critiqued an earlier version of this book. I am especially indebted to Samuel Brunk, who read two successive drafts of this book and offered valuable suggestions.

I first started reading the Revolution in a colloquium on the recent historiography of the Mexican revolution taught by David Bailey. My understanding of Mexican history begins there. In more recent times, and during this enterprise especially, I have learned from the marvelous histories written by Bill Beezley, David Brading, Enrique Florescano, Adolfo Gilly, Charles Hale, Linda Hall, John Hart, Friedrich Katz, Alan Knight, Enrique Krauze, Guillermo Palacios, Doug Richmond, Ramon Eduardo Ruiz, Mary Kay Vaughan, and Mark Wasserman. My understanding of cultural politics and collective memory has been influenced by the work of Benedict Anderson, Murray Edelman, Maurice Halbwachs, E. J. Hobsbawm, Patrick H. Hutton, and Edmundo O'Gorman. Influence, assistance, and friendship, of course, imply not even a little responsibility. Finally, Sharon House has accompanied me on this journey into the Mexican revolution and to Mexico itself many times, making it all worthwhile and wonderfully memorable.

20 de Noviembre de 1998

La Revolución

The Pantheon of National Heroes

These historical figures are mentioned throughout the book. This list does not include all national heroes, only those that have the most resonance in Mexican patriotic discourse.

Cuauhtémoc (1502?–1525)

Cuauhtémoc was the nephew of Moctezuma II and the last Aztec king and ruler of Tenochtitlán. He tenaciously defended his people and city against the Spanish conquistadors of Hernán Cortés in the summer of 1521. In August of that year he was captured and later tortured but would not reveal the location of the "lost" Aztec treasure. Cortés took Cuauhtémoc on his expedition to Honduras in 1524–25 but, out of fear of rebellion, the Spaniards tried and convicted the former ruler of treason and hanged him from a tree. Cuauhtémoc, not Cortés, triumphed in death and history as an important symbol of Mexican nationalism. A monument to his honor was raised in Mexico City's Paseo de la Reforma in 1887.

Miguel Hidalgo y Costilla (1753–1811)

The "Father of the Patria," Miguel Hidalgo, a Catholic priest, was one of a group of Creole conspirators in the Bajío region. The conspirators plotted against the Spaniards, who in 1808 had overthrown Viceroy José de Iturrigaray because of his support for Creole autonomy. When the conspiracy was discovered prematurely, Hidalgo called, from his parish church in the town of Dolores, for a popular revolt to be carried out on September 16, 1810. Hidalgo's revolt mobilized tens of thousands of Indians and mestizos and seized the great cities of the Bajío. His advance arrived on the outskirts of Mexico City in October and, despite a costly victory against a royalist army, Hidalgo abandoned his plan to occupy the city. From this point, the popular army suffered defeats by the royalist forces. Hidalgo and other insurgent leaders retreated north and were captured in Coahuila. They were tried in Chihuahua and executed by firing squad in July 1811. The heads of Hidalgo and his commanders were displayed on the four corners of the *alhóndiga* (the city granary) of Guanajuato for the next ten years. The town of his parish was renamed Dolores Hidalgo in his honor and the state of Hidalgo was created in 1869.

José María Morelos y Pavón (1765–1815)

The "Servant of the Nation," Morelos was commissioned by Hidalgo to take the revolt to the south. In November 1810, Morelos ordered the end of slavery and the caste system. Upon the execution of Hidalgo, the southern insurgents continued the struggle. Morelos convened the Supreme National American Congress in Chilpancingo in 1813 and that body named him *generalíssimo* in charge of the executive power. When the Congress moved to Apatzingán in 1814, it proclaimed a constitution. Morelos was captured in 1815, taken to Mexico City for trial, and executed. In 1823 he was declared *Benemérito de la Patria* and his native city was renamed Morelia in his honor in 1828. The state of Morelos was established in 1869.

Benito Juárez (1806–1872)

Juárez, a Zapotec Indian from the state of Oaxaca, led the liberals in the Reform, the revolution of the late 1850s that wrote a new constitution, eliminated the judicial privileges of the Catholic church, separated church and state, and expropriated the property of the Church. He became president in 1858 and led the liberal forces in the War of the Reform (1859–61) against conservatives opposed to the anticlerical measures. In 1861 he was elected president but soon faced the intervention of French forces, who invaded Mexico in 1862 and imposed the Austrian archduke Maximilian von Habsburg as emperor in 1864. Juárez led the Republican forces during the War of the French Intervention (1862–67), which eventually led to victory and the execution of Maximilian. Juárez was reelected president in 1867 and again in 1871. He died in 1872 and was transformed into the premier symbol of nationalism. He was proclaimed *Benemérito de la Nación*. His monument, the Hemiciclo de Benito Juárez, was inaugurated in the Alameda Park in Mexico City during the centenary fiestas of 1910.

Los Niños Héroes (d. 1847)

These "child heroes" were six cadets of the national military academy who were killed during the assault by the United States army upon Chapultepec Castle in Mexico City on September 13, 1847, during the Mexican–American War. The six ranged in age from 13 to 19 years old. One of the cadets, Fernando Montes de Oca, was found after the battle wrapped in a Mexican flag; he apparently had jumped to his death to avoid capture. There are two monuments to los Niños Héroes in Chapultepec Park, where they are honored by an official ceremony every year on the thirteenth of September.

Ricardo Flores Magón (1874–1922)

The "Precursor of the Revolution," was, like Juárez, a native of Oaxaca. Flores Magón began the newspaper *Regeneración* in 1900 to oppose the dictatorial regime of Porfirio Díaz. He was arrested in 1901 and the newspaper was suppressed. In 1904 he and his brother Enrique settled in San Antonio, Texas, and continued to publish *Regeneración* in the face of local harassment. They settled in St. Louis in 1905–06 but persecution there led them to move to Los Angeles, where they began a new publication called *Revolución*. Ricardo Flores Magón was arrested in 1907, tried in 1909, and imprisoned until August 1910. Due to the intolerance in the United States during the First World War and his anarcho-communist ideology, Ricardo Flores Magón was arrested for sedition in 1918 and sentenced to twenty-one years in prison. He died in Leavenworth penitentiary in 1922 and his body was returned to Mexico. Ricardo Flores Magón and the other Magonistas became known during the Mexican revolution as "the Precursors," the intellectual authors of the movement.

Francisco Indalecio Madero (1873–1913)

The "Apostle of Democracy" was the son of one of Mexico's wealthiest families. Madero was born in Parras, Coahuila, and he studied business at a college near Baltimore, Maryland, at the Liceo de Versailles in Paris, and at the University of California at Berkeley. Upon his return to Mexico he administered a family business and became a spiritualist. A landowner with a social conscience, he was involved in local politics beginning in 1904 and became a true believer in democracy. He entered national politics in 1908 with the publication of *The Presidential Succession of 1910*, which diagnosed Mexico's problems and offered democratic practices and political liberty as the remedy. In 1909 he organized the Anti-reelection Center and became a candidate for president in the election of 1910.

Madero's campaign sparked considerable support around the country, but he was arrested in June 1910 and remained in jail during the July election in which Díaz was "reelected." He escaped from jail in October and fled to San Antonio, Texas, where he issued the Plan of San Luis Potosí, the city of his imprisonment. The plan called for a revolution to begin on November 20, 1910. The Madero revolt picked up support in 1911, particularly in Chihuahua in the north and Morelos in the south. When Maderista forces in May 1911 took Ciudad Juárez, on the U.S.–Mexican border, the dictator resigned and left the country.

After a conservative interregnum, Madero was elected president in November 1911 in the most free election in Mexican history. His administration was plagued by a highly critical press and numerous revolts. The president, nevertheless, true to his word, governed as a democrat. In early 1913 a revolt in Mexico City became the pretext for a coup d'etat by a supposedly loyal general, Victoriano Huerta. Madero and his vice-president, José María Pino Suárez, were forced to resign their offices and were murdered on the night of February 22, 1913. With his death, the Apostle of Democracy was transformed into the greatest martyr of the revolution.

AQUILES SERDÁN (1876–1910)

Termed the "Martyr of the Revolution," Aquiles Serdán was killed by the army of the Porfiriato in 1910. The Serdán brothers, Aquiles and Máximo, were the sons of Manuel Serdán, an anarchist who participated in several revolts and who disappeared without a trace. On November 18, 1910, two days before the official launch of the Madero revolt, an informant told the Puebla city police of Aquiles Serdán's intention to initiate the revolt. Five hundred soldiers and police surrounded the Serdán house and a bloody battle ensued. The brothers' sister Carmen escaped before the fighting began and became a noted revolutionary. The state government raised a monument to their honor in the city of Puebla in 1916, and on the fiftieth anniversary of the revolution in 1960 the Serdán house was converted into a regional museum of the Revolution.

EMILIANO ZAPATA (1879–1919)

The "Apostle of Agrarianism," Zapata first defended the pueblo's land by lawsuit and petition while serving as municipal president of his village, Anenecuilco, Morelos. In March 1911 he joined the Madero revolt and organized a guerrilla band that captured the city of Cuautla in May. Zapata became disenchanted with Madero and revolted in November 1911 on behalf of the Plan of Ayala, which called for the redistribution of land, the rule of law, and electoral democracy. Following Madero's downfall, the Zapatistas continued the struggle against the Huerta regime. When Huerta was defeated in the summer of 1914, Zapata took control of Morelos and instituted a thorough land reform.

When civil war broke out between Venustiano Carranza and Francisco Villa, Zapata made an alliance with Villa. In the spring of 1916, Carrancista troops invaded Morelos and the Zapatistas were forced to wage a guerrilla war until 1920. In April 1919 the Carrancistas devised a scheme to lure Zapata to his death. In death, Zapata became a powerful symbol of the agrarian revolution and was appropriated by the postrevolutionary state in the 1920s to bolster its legitimacy.

VENUSTIANO CARRANZA (1859–1920)

Before becoming the "First Chief" of the Constitutionalist movement, Carranza was a successful hacendado from Coahuila. Carranza entered politics in the 1890s. When President Díaz supported another candidate for governor of Coahuila in 1909, however, he joined with Madero. He served as Madero's minister of war and after the triumph finally became governor of his state. When Madero was overthrown and murdered in February 1913, Carranza made history. Following the example of Juárez in 1858, Carranza, at the age of 53 the "old man" of the revolution, rebelled in the name of the Plan of Guadalupe and called for the restoration of constitutional government. He gave himself the title of "First Chief of the Constitutionalist Army" and recruited supporters. From early 1913 until the summer of 1914, Carranza coordinated the armed struggle against the government of General Huerta. He opposed the United States intervention and occupation of the port of Veracruz in the spring of 1914 despite its anti-Huerta objective to deprive the regime of German armaments.

In the fall of 1914 revolutionary generals organized the Convention of Aguascalientes, which quickly disavowed Carranza's leadership. The split between Villa and Carranza, however, forced Obregón, Carranza's most powerful general, to side with the latter. Again, following the example of Juárez, Carranza retreated to Veracruz (now free of U.S. troops) where he proclaimed the "Additions to the Plan of Guadalupe," the laws of the new reform, providing for land reform, civil marriage, municipal autonomy, and the independence of the judiciary. In the spring of 1915, General Obregón defeated Villa in a series of battles. In late 1916, Carranza convened a constitutional convention in Querétaro. The delegates exceeded his modest reforms and wrote the Constitution of 1917, which included many of the social and economic reforms for which the revolutionaries had fought. The new constitution also established rules of politics and Carranza was elected constitutional president of Mexico in May for the term 1917–1920.

As president Carranza turned more cautious and conservative, refusing to implement in any serious manner the new constitutional reforms regarding land, labor, the Church, and foreign economic holdings. In 1920, near the end of his term, he attempted to impose as his successor the ambassador to the United States, Ignacio Bonillas. A rebellion by the state of Sonora on behalf of Álvaro Obregón developed rapidly in the spring, obtaining support from most of the army. Again Carranza retreated toward Veracruz, but he was stopped in transit. Carranza and his party headed north on horseback. On the night of May 20–21 their camp was discovered and attacked by Obregonistas. The First Chief died in the confusion. His body was returned to Mexico City and buried in the Dolores cemetery. In 1942 — on the twenty-fifth anniversary of the promulgation of the Constitution of 1917—a copper urn containing his ashes was deposited in a crypt within the Monument to the Revolution.

Francisco "Pancho" Villa (1878–1923)

The "Strong Arm of the Revolution" was born Doroteo Arango in the state of Durango, changing his name to Villa to escape the law. A muleteer and bandit, in 1910 he joined the Madero revolt in Chihuahua. In 1912 he fought the anti-Madero revolt of his former chief, Pascual Orozco. In 1913 he raised a military force to fight the Huerta regime and became one of the most important commanders in the Constitutionalist army. His División del Norte captured Torreón and Zacatecas and paved the way for Huerta's defeat. A growing split between the First Chief and Villa became evident by the spring of 1914 and became definitive in the fall of that year. When Carranza abandoned Mexico City for Veracruz in late 1914, the triumphant forces of Villa and Zapata occupied the city. The two popular caudillos posed for a famous picture in the National Palace, with Villa sitting in the presidential chair. Villa's power would never be greater.

In the spring of 1915 the armies of Villa and Obregón met in a series of battles that determined the fate of Mexico. Defeated but not destroyed, Villa withdrew to Chihuahua and at the end of 1915 turned his wrath against the forces of General Plutarco Elías Calles in Sonora. Again, Villa was defeated and reduced to a guerrilla. When the United States government recognized Carranza in October 1915, Villa felt betrayed and retaliated with a raid on the New Mexican town of Columbus in March 1916. This outrage led to the "Punitive Expedition," an American intervention led by General John J. Pershing to capture, or at least disperse the forces of, the "bandit." Villa eluded Pershing and the forces of Carranza for the next few years, while still demonstrating his sting. With the downfall of Carranza in 1920, Interim President Adolfo de la Huerta negotiated the retirement of Villa: he and his men laid down their arms and the government awarded them a year's wages and the hacienda of Canutillo. Three years later, on July 20, 1923, Villa was killed while driving through the town of Parral. Some blamed Obregón and Calles, others blamed a private grudge. After three years in the grave, Villa's skull was stolen by grave robbers. Fifty years later, in 1976, the remains of Pancho Villa were deposited within the Monument to the Revolution.

Felipe Carrillo Puerto (1872–1924)

The "Saint of the Proletariat," this future governor of the state of Yucatán was born in the town of Motul. He served as an agronomist with the Zapatistas in Morelos in 1915 and returned to Yucatán that same year when General Salvador Alvarado took control of the state on behalf of the Constitutionalist movement. Under Alvarado's protection, Carrillo Puerto created the Leagues of Resistance, armed agrarian organizations composed of tens of thousands of Indian peasant farmers. He also established the Socialist

Party of the Southeast. When Alvarado left Yucatán in 1918, President Carranza persecuted the socialist party, in 1919 driving Carrillo Puerto into exile for having endorsed Álvaro Obregón's candidacy for the presidency.

Carrillo Puerto returned to Yucatán after Carranza was overthrown, worked to rebuild his leagues and the socialist party during the term of a caretaker socialist government in 1920–22, and was elected governor in his own right in 1922. When the de la Huerta rebellion erupted in late 1923, Governor Carrillo Puerto was captured; he was executed in the state capital on January 3, 1924. The state of Yucatán erected a monument to his honor in January 1926 in Mérida: an inscription on it reads, "His Blood Will Make the People Fruitful."

ÁLVARO OBREGÓN SALIDO (1880–1928)

The "Caudillo of the Revolution," Obregón, a native of the state of Sonora, was a modestly successful farmer during the Porfiriato. He did not take part in the Maderista revolt of 1910–11, an omission he always regretted. In 1912 he fought against the anti-Madero rebellion of Pascual Orozco and in 1913 he joined the Constitutionalist movement led by Venustiano Carranza. He soon became one of the three leading commanders of the Constitutionalist army (as general of the army of the northwest) and was the official who accepted the surrender of the federal army in 1914. When Carranza and Villa split in the fall of 1914, Obregón remained loyal to the First Chief. During a series of battles in the Bajío in the spring of 1915, Obregón decisively defeated Villa, although in the course of one engagement he was wounded by an artillery shell and lost his right arm.

Obregón played an important role in support of the radical delegates during the constitutional convention of 1917. In 1919–20 he became a candidate for president, and when it became clear that Carranza intended to impose his own candidate upon the country, Obregón and his fellow Sonorans Adolfo de la Huerta and Plutarco Elías Calles launched a revolt that overthrew Carranza and led to the First Chief's death. Obregón was elected president in 1920 (serving 1920–1924), and his imposition of Calles as his successor led to the unsuccessful de la Huerta rebellion in 1923–24. Obregón turned over power to Calles in 1924 and engineered a reform of the electoral laws that would permit non-consecutive reelection. He was reelected president in 1928 and shortly thereafter was assassinated by a Catholic fanatic.

Chronology of Events, 1810–1910

1810	This year marks the beginning of the struggle for independence led by Father Miguel Hidalgo.	The Kingdom of New Spain has a population of some six million people.
1811	Hidalgo's revolt is crushed and he is executed.	Alexander Von Humbolt's *Map of New Spain* is published in France.
1821–1822	Independence is attained in 1821 by Generals Agustín de Iturbide and Vicente Guerrero.	The United States grants diplomatic recognition to Mexico in 1822.
1823	The Mexican Republic is established.	The tricolor national flag, with an eagle perched on a nopal cactus, is authorized.
1831	Vicente Guerrero is tried, convicted of treason, and executed.	A national museum is established from the Conservatorio de Antiguedades.
1849	Gold is discovered in California, territory lost in the war with the United States in 1847–48.	A national library is founded.
1854–1855	With the Ayutla revolt of 1855, Santa Anna is ousted from power.	A national anthem is approved by the Congress in 1854.

1856–1861	In the period of the Reform and the War of the Reform between Liberals and Conservatives, the Liberal Party and Mexico itself are led by Benito Juárez.	The first national postage stamp, with an engraved image of Father Hidalgo, is issued.
1857	The liberal federal Constitution of 1857 gives the nation its first bill of rights.	There are nearly eight million Mexicans according to the census.
1862–1867	Louis Napoleon Bonaparte sends the French army to the New World, imposing the Austrian archduke Ferdinand Maximilian of Hapsburg as emperor of Mexico.	A monument is dedicated to Morelos in 1865 in the Plazuela de Guardiola in Mexico City.
1862	On the fifth of May Republican forces repel a French assault on the city of Puebla. This victory later becomes a national holiday but at the time only delays the French occupation of Mexico by one year.	The Art Academy of San Carlos, founded in 1785, is renamed by Maximilian the Imperial Academy.
1867	President Benito Juárez returns to Mexico City and is reelected to a third term.	Gabino Barreda's Independence Day oration interprets Mexican history as a struggle between a negative spirit and a positivist spirit embodied by the liberal republican forces.
1872	President Juárez dies and Sebastián Lerdo de Tejada becomes acting president.	

1876–1911	Termed the Porfiriato, the age of Porfirio Díaz sees the general elected to Mexico's highest office seven times.	During the Porfiriato, Mexico builds its railroad system, installs its telegraph and telephone systems, and solves the drainage problems of Mexico City.
1887	Mexico's mining industry is revived during the 1880s as a result of a new mining code, foreign investment, and modern machinery.	Construction of a monument to Cuauhtémoc, located in the Paseo de la Reforma in Mexico City, is initiated.
1900	The Flores Magón brothers begin publication of *Regeneración*, a Mexico City weekly critical of Porfirismo.	Justo Sierra publishes the multivolume national history entitled, *México: Her Social Evolution*.
1904	The Mexican Liberal Party is formed by Ricardo Flores Magón.	Mexico's first genuinely modern novel, *Santa* by Federico Gamboa, is published in 1902.
1906	Mexican workers at the Cananea Copper Company go on strike and are violently suppressed. The following year workers at the Rio Blanco textile mills also go on strike and are gunned down by federal troops.	To mark the centennial of the birth of Benito Juárez, construction begins on a great monument in his honor in Mexico City, the Hemiciclo de Juárez on Avenida Juárez.
1909–1910	Francisco I. Madero publishes in 1910 *The Presidential Succession*, which calls for a peaceful end of presidential dictatorship.	In 1909, Andrés Molina Enríquez publishes *The Great National Problems*, a critical analysis of Mexico's agrarian crisis.

1910   Porfirio Díaz is reelected to the presidency and Madero's anti-reelectionist campaign is stopped by his arrest in the spring. When he is released, Madero calls for a national uprising for November 20, 1910.

In September, the Porfirian regime devotes great resources to celebrate the centennial of Independence, which includes the unveiling of the Monument to Independence on the Paseo de la Reforma.

INTRODUCTION

The Revolution with a Capital Letter

WE MEXICANS MAKE a distinction, one of Mexico's most well-known political leaders, Moisés Sáenz, explained in 1929, "between the Revolution with a capital and revolutions with a small letter."[1] The Revolution with a capital letter, he intended to convey, was commendable and justified, almighty and all-encompassing. A chorus of voices agreed. During the preceding two decades scribblers, journalists, politicians, intellectuals, propagandists, and other insurgent spokesmen and women throughout Mexico, the so-called *voceros de la Revolución*, had invented and constructed the Revolution with a capital letter in their pamphlets, broadsides, proclamations, histories, articles, and editorials. During the two decades following Sáenz's 1929 statement, the Mexican government learned how to exhibit, disseminate, and perform the Revolution with a capital through festivals, monuments, and official history and thus to educate and inspire its citizens.[2] Mexicans invested a lot of meaning in their Revolution with a capital letter during this century and that process of investment is the subject of this book.

THE WORLD HAS JUMBLED ITS CATALOG

"These are times of chaos; opinions are a scramble, parties a jumble; the language of new ideas has not been created. . . . It is the problem of this time to classify things and men. . . . The world has jumbled its catalog." So wrote Lamartine in another revolutionary age.[3] The Mexican troubles of the second decade of the twentieth century were similarly complex, confusing, and ambiguous. Following events from the White House, President Woodrow Wilson complained, "I was very much confused because the narratives did not tally."[4] In 1916, Luis Cabrera admitted that the dominant impression regarding the "Mexican situation," not only abroad but in Mexico itself, "is of absolute chaos. The causes each Government, each caudillo, each conspirator, each politician, or each writer give as the reasons for the

Mexican Revolution, are as numerous as they are diverse, some are immediate, others are remote, but it is almost impossible to understand."[5] The tempest of events was accompanied by a torrent of words.[6] These words mostly tried to make sense of the events and give them order, direction, and meaning, to reorder the catalogue. This ordering of the recent past was necessary, because, as Hans Kellner writes, "historical events do not represent themselves, they are represented, they do not speak, they are spoken for."[7]

Contemporaries told stories, drew comparisons, and made arguments about recent events in particular ways to justify their actions, to condemn their enemies, to win converts, and to do much more. Their talking, singing, drawing, painting, and writing invented *la Revolución*: a name transformed into what appeared to be a natural and self-evident part of reality and history. This talking and writing was also part of an older, larger, and greater project of *forjando patria*, forging a nation, inventing a country, imagining a community across time and space called Mexico. *La Revolución* became part of the master narrative—the "stream of tradition" as Isaiah Berlin calls it—that created, shaped, and is the nation of Mexico.[8]

What is a nation? It is a large-scale solidarity, Ernest Renan said in 1882. A century later the term was updated by Benedict Anderson to "an imagined community." According to Renan and Anderson, it is not ethnicity, religion, material interest, language, military necessity, or geography that comprise the fundamental and indispensable forces creating and maintaining that solidarity. The key is memory, myth, and history, organized remembering and deliberate forgetting. For Renan it is "a rich legacy of memories . . . the desire to live together, the will to perpetuate the value of the heritage that one has received in an undivided form."[9] For Anderson it is "the expression of an historical tradition of serial continuity."[10] When we say "national identity," Jean Meyer writes, "we are also saying 'history.'"[11] And even then the nation is still only a "problematic, protean and artificial construct."[12]

A basic "story line," the master narrative, "is culturally constructed and provides the group members with a general notion of their shared past." It contributes to the formation of a nation by "portraying it as a unified group moving through history."[13] Poets, journalists, teachers, politicians, and writers are often more influential in composing the master narrative than are professional historians. The master narrative is collective memory, national mythology, official and unofficial, formal and folk history all rolled into one, promoting national fraternity and solidarity among citizens.[14]

For nearly two centuries Mexicans have been preoccupied by the transcendent struggle to define and construct that solidarity. No one has ever doubted its necessity. Regarding Mexico's perilous national cohesion, Lord Acton wrote in 1862:

> The vanity and peril of national claims founded on no political tradition, but on race alone, appear in Mexico. There the races are divided by blood, without being grouped together in different regions. It is, therefore, neither possible to unite them nor to convert them into the elements of an organized State. They are fluid, shapeless, and unconnected, and cannot be precipitated, or formed into the basis of political institutions.[15]

Mexico, in fact, did found its national claim on a political tradition, a master narrative. We must first look to national history in order to better understand the invention, construction, and significance of *la Revolución*.

NARRATING THE NATION

The first national historians of the nineteenth century looked for the origins and nature of Mexico in the contrasting interpretations of the sixteenth-century conquerors, chroniclers, and missionaries. Traditionalist hispanophile conservatives were influenced by the original imperial school of history. Hernán Cortés, in his letters to Emperor Charles V, and the chronicles by Gonzalo Fernández de Oviedo, Francisco López de Gómara, Bernal Díaz de Castillo, and Gonzalo Jiménez de Quesada, justified and glorified the military conquest of the Aztec empire. The Spanish chroniclers emphasized individual heroism but displayed a messianic sense of history. They generally denigrated native culture, characterized it as brutal and savage, and particularly condemned its idolatrous and "satanic" nature. Nineteenth-century conservatives accordingly interpreted the conquest as the birth of the Mexican nation, Cortés as its founding father, and the apparition of the Virgin Mary, as the Virgin of Guadalupe (only ten years following the conquest), as its christening.[16]

Rationalist hispanophobe liberals imagined a very different Mexico, one that was derived from very different and more complicated traditions. Their condemnation and rejection of the conquest was based on the chronicles and histories of Bartolomé de las Casas, Jerónimo de Mendieta, and Agustín Dávila Padilla. Their appreciation, even glorification, of the ancient Mexicans was based on the early Franciscan ethnologies of Toribio de Benavente (Motolinia) and Bernardo de Sahagún and the later elaborations of Carlos de Sigüenza y Gongora and Francisco Xavier Clavijero. A sophisticated anti-Spanish Creole patriotism was forged in the seventeenth and eighteenth centuries, and it interpreted the conquest as the beginning not of the nation but of hundreds of years of colonial captivity and exploitation tempered by valiant evangelization. The Mexican nation from this perspective arose from an ancient indigenous past, was brought to the Christian faith originally by the apostle St. Thomas and later by saintly missionaries, and was blessed by the Virgin of Guadalupe. This providential nation, the new Jerusalem in Anahuac, was awakened to freedom by Father Miguel Hidalgo's *Grito de Dolores*—his declaration of independence and call for revolution—in 1810 and shepherded to independence by Agustín de Iturbide in 1821.[17]

National historical writing began with the revolution for independence of 1810–11, which came to be known as the Insurgency. Fray José Servando Teresa de Mier (*La Historia de la Revolución de Nueva España antiguamente Anahuac*, 1813) and Carlos María de Bustamante (*Cuadro histórico de la revolución de la America mexicana*, 1823–32) provided historical justification for the Insurgency and the rebirth of the Mexican nation. In exalting the last Aztec emperor Cuauhtémoc and the Insurgency's leaders Hidalgo and José María Morelos, they tried to give the infant country the prepackaged heritage found in Creole patriotism. Liberal ideologues and part-time historians, José María Luis Mora (*México y su revoluciones*, 1836) and Lorenzo de Zavala (*Ensayo histórico de las revoluciones de México*, 1831) could not accept the fundamental premise of Creole patriotism, that is, Mexico's providential history. Their anti-Spanish interpretation emphasized condemnation of the Church—which had itself condemned the Insurgency—as part and parcel of three centuries of Spanish colonialism. Thereafter, anticlericalism would be the touchstone of liberal ideology and historiography.[18]

During the first decades following national independence no one faction or ideology dominated politics and the state. The historical vision of Mexico advanced by an emerging liberal tradition was contested by an emerging conservative one as represented by Lucas Alamán (*Disertaciones sobre la historia de la República mejicana*, 1844–49, and *Historia de Méjico*, 1849–52). Alamán argued that the Church was Spain's premier gift to Mexico and the core of Mexican nationality. The liberator was not Hidalgo, the excommunicated rebel priest who was defeated and executed in 1811, but the former royalist soldier Agustín de Iturbide, who achieved national independence with a guarantee to maintain the Catholic religion.[19]

The first great non-Mexican contribution to Mexican historiography, William H. Prescott's romantic epic, *The History of the Conquest of Mexico* (1843), affirmed the conservative tradition even though it came from the pen of a New England Protestant. (This was no coincidence, since the Yankee historian was favored by the collegial advice and assistance of Alamán and Joaquín Garcia Icazbalceta.) Prescott's disdain for the "barbaric" Indians concurred with the conservative vision of the nation founded by Hernán Cortés, the Conquistador.[20]

These two opposing, nearly contradictory visions of the Mexican past, present, and desired future inspired almost perpetual political conflict. The liberal revolution in the 1850s called the Reform and the subsequent liberal victories in the War of the Reform (1859–61), as well as the French Intervention in the 1860s, roundly defeated and thoroughly discredited the conservative cause in Mexico. Liberals officially proclaimed their cause to be the cause of the nation, their heroes to be Mexico's heroes, their enemies Mexico's enemies, and their interpretation of national history to be *the* history of Mexico. This vision was reinforced in the 1860s and 1870s by the essays and orations of Ignacio Ramírez and Ignacio Manuel Altamirano, which adopted the indigenism of Creole patriotism (and the Black Legend of Bartolomé de las Casas for good measure), but which replaced its providential view of history with a quasihistoricist evolutionary one and its mystical Catholicism with radical anti-clerical hispanophobia. Naturally, they glorified the Insurgency and its sequel, the Reform. Mexico at last possessed a master narrative that found its expression and glorification in official histories, school textbooks, commemorative monuments, and patriotic orations.[21]

During the Restored Republic (1867–76), the first period of relative tranquillity after the Reform, at all levels of instruction national history acquired a significance never before seen. New manuals of history and school texts appeared that possessed one fundamental purpose: "to create the myths that sustained nationality and the heroes that it symbolized; and above all to put forward an analysis conforming to the dominant political ideology."[22]

Conservative historians in the age of liberal ascendancy did not disappear but performed other duties—preserving historical documents and manuscripts and publishing impressive documentary collections. Manuel Orozco y Berra, director of the national archives and the national museum, Joaquín García Icazbalceta, Francisco Pimentel, Francisco del Paso y Troncoso, and Carlos Pereyra published thick volumes of colonial documents and brought out new editions of classic colonial ethnologies and chronicles. José Fernandez Ramírez, a liberal, spent a lifetime collecting historical documents and books and became perhaps the most respected historian of his time. These men were talented scholars, not dabblers in history. Although they contributed little directly to the master narrative, they were giants of colonial historiography. Twentieth-century historians have come to depend on their scholarship.

Mexico's first official history, the five-volume *México a través de los siglos* (1887–89), was the most ambitious and successful national history of the nineteenth century. Its many reprints can be found yet today in most bookstores and in many homes. Vicente Riva Palacio and three prominent liberal intellectuals integrated what had been different, neglected, and often opposed pasts into one conciliatory national history. They structured national history into five epochs, one per volume: the ancient Mexican civilizations, colonial New Spain, the Insurgency, independent Mexico, and the Reform. A little more than a decade later, Justo Sierra and the leading lights of the next generation of liberals produced a similar monumental official history, *México, su evolución social* (1900–02). Sierra's history, unlike its predecessor organized thematically, was politically sycophantic toward the current regime of General Porfirio Díaz, hero of the war against the French, seeing it as the triumphant culmination of a long struggle against the dark forces of colonialism, clericalism, and conservatism. It was also self-consciously scientific in its social Darwinist conception of Mexico as an organism that had evolved from both Indian and Spanish roots to create a new mestizo people and nation. Together these bibliographic monuments created what Edmundo O'Gorman has termed the liberal synthesis in Mexican historiography. The liberal synthesis, together with a reverence for national heroes and celebration of patriotic holidays, in turn, was the core of what Justo Sierra called "the Religion of the Patria."[23]

The liberal synthesis survived well into the twentieth century. Generations of Mexican schoolchildren learned Mexican history from the multiple editions of Justo Sierra's textbooks (*Catecismo de Historia Patria*, 1894; *Veinticuatro cuadros de historia patria*, 1907; and *Elementos de Historia Patria*, 1894, 1904, 1916, and 1922, in use until 1958). Félix F. Palavicini after the Second World War attempted to update the liberal synthesis in the style of Vicente Riva Palacio and Justo Sierra with his multiauthor and multivolume *México, Historia de su evolución constructiva* (1945). The works of Fernando Iturribarria, Jesús Silva Herzog, and particularly Jesús Reyes Heroles (*El liberalismo mexicano*, 1957–61) argued again that the liberal cause more broadly redefined was and is the cause of Mexico. "Liberalism," Iturribarria wrote, "that is, social democracy has triumphed at last, with the program of the Mexican Revolution."

The turmoil of the second and third decades of the twentieth century interrupted the master narrative at this point. Events needed explaining and naturally observers interpreted them on their own terms and in relation to the master narrative, the liberal synthesis.

REMEMBERING THE REVOLUTION

La Revolución was a product of collective memory, mythmaking, and history writing. Maurice Halbwachs, the first theorist of collective memory, argued that while it is individuals who remember, social groups determine what is memorable and how it will be remembered.[24] Collective memory, then, is the name generally given to "what is remembered by the dominant civic culture."[25] But collective memory, like individual memory, is never a faithful retrieval or reclamation of the past. It does not just happen. As Leon Wieseltier explains, "the memory of an event is an interpretation of an event."[26]

La Revolución, then, was remembered by revolutionary *voceros* and their heirs, often in ideal and mythic ways.[27] "Myth" is defined in modern positivist thought as fictitious or unreliable history, and thus those who came up with the term "myth of the Mexican Revolution" wanted to discredit part or all of *la Revolución*. But "a myth is not an erroneous picture of the world," Stephen Ausband explains, "it is just a picture." William McNeil maintains that truth resides in myth, albeit a simplified and idealized truth and one that often helps to make the complex world intelligible, meaningful, and reassuring.[28] Mythmaking in Mexico, like remembering, involved the reconstruction of the past in the light of the present, and particularly in light of the political necessities of the present. "As do individuals, nations feed on myths, and political systems that come into being through revolution—as happened in America, in France, in Russia—are especially dependent on the creation and maintenance of myths to bolster their legitimacy."[29]

La Revolución was also fashioned by would-be, mostly amateur, historians. Halbwachs made an important distinction between collective memory, which he viewed as "merely" a social construct, and written history, which he considered to be objective knowledge. This distinction today we know is unfounded: "both memory and history look like heavily constructed narratives."[30] Carl Becker long ago characterized "history as the artificial extension of social memory." Although it was formerly considered to be impure, François Hartog writes that "memory is becoming part of the stuff of history: there is now a history of memory." The early history of revolutionary history writing in Mexico supports Philippe Ariès's contention that history emerges out of collective memory and is barely distinguishable from myth.[31]

La Revolución, however, was not remembered, mythologized, and rendered as history the same way by everyone in the early days. The revolutionary mobilization of the 1910s produced several armed factions and political movements that were often in conflict with one another. Given the complexity of any society, there is rarely one collective memory of an event or era; revolutionary Mexico certainly saw several different and competing constructions of its recent past. The past, as well as power, is contested in politics, war, and revolution. In the course of any struggle, the more powerful favor certain memories and myths over others and seek to create an official (and in aspiration dominant or national) memory in order to legitimize existing political authority. The development of an official memory, however, generally does not crowd out or incorporate all other collective memories. Those that resist and withstand the official version, called counter-memories here, may be marginalized or may persist to challenge and pressure the dominant construction.[32] The criteria of success, of course, are not those of truth: "dominant representations may be those that are most ideological, most obviously conforming to the flattened stereotypes of myth."[33]

La Revolución emerged as successive official memories in a process not unlike geologic formation: an uneven sedimentation of memory, myth, and history. It was named, historicized, and reified quite early on. As the postrevolutionary state tried to consolidate power and authority in the 1920s, however, the existence of different, partisan revolutionary collective memories and myths—codified in time into competing revolutionary traditions, each with their own heroes and villains, sacred and bitter anniversaries, myths and symbols—retarded the process. Wounds of memory did not create but rather exacerbated more serious and immediate power struggles. During the 1920s, *la Revolución* was further made permanent and ongoing and all (or nearly all) factions past and present were unified in a Revolutionary Family. Onto this basic construction leaders and regimes could hang their special attributes, from democracy to nationalism, anticlericalism to socialism.

Since to govern is ultimately to make believe ("It is therefore on opinion only that government is founded," wrote David Hume[34]), the postrevolutionary Mexican state sought and built political consensus sacralized by a civil religion to underwrite the new status quo.[35] Healing the wounds of memory was part of the state rebuilding process that in Mexico was called the institutionalization of the revolution. Forging one official, dominant yet fraternal Revolutionary Tradition would help revolutionaries accomplish the goals that tradition is designed to accomplish: to disseminate *la Revolución* in the present and transmit *la Revolución* to succeeding generations, in the process to inculcate beliefs, legitimize institutions, and promote social cohesion. The Revolutionary Tradition, however, was intended first and foremost to reinforce elite and thus national political unity, to establish a solid historical foundation upon which to unify all revolutionary factions past and present.[36]

If, as Michael Walzer writes, "the union of men can only be symbolized," the Revolutionary Tradition—the public face of *la Revolución*—was crucial to forging harmony within the Revolutionary Family and the memory-nation.[37]

NATION AND REVOLUTION ARE ONE

What made *la Revolución* so affective and effective, powerful and enduring was its seamless integration into Mexico's "religion of the patria." In postrevolutionary Mexico, very much like the French Third Republic described by Pierra Nora, "history, memory, and the nation enjoyed an unusually intimate communion."[38] It is difficult to tell where the older liberal synthesis ends and *la Revolución* begins. "Nation and revolution are indissolubly one," John Gunther recognized in 1940.[39] This is in large part because, as Samuel Inman had written two years earlier, "the Revolution has become a religion."[40] That religion, the religion of the patria, was the reverence of Mexico's struggle for nationhood in three successive revolutions.[41]

In the updated master narrative, the regime of Porfirio Díaz was transformed from the apotheosis of liberal evolution to yet another dark period of reactionary ascendancy similar to the centuries of Spanish colonialism, the decades of conservative misrule after 1821, and the few years of the French-imposed reign of Maximilian in the 1860s. *La Revolución*, naturally, took its former exalted place. It became the third revolution after the Insurgency and the Reform that created and shaped the nation. It became the apotheosis of liberal evolution and popular revolution: national history led inexorably to this glorious age. *La Revolución*, however, did not bring an end to history. Its reforms remain unfinished, its objectives not yet met. The Reaction within Mexico and imperialism without, although defeated, are not extinguished. The struggle, therefore, will continue, *La Revolución* must continue. And the nation shall continue to progress and unite.[42]

How did this happen? We return to the issue that opened this introduction: Mexicans invested a lot of meaning in their Revolution with a capital letter. Part One of this book narrates the construction of *la Revolución* in memory, myth, and history from 1911 to 1928 in three chapters. How *la Revolución* first took shape is considered. The development of different and often opposing revolutionary traditions in the 1910s and the early efforts taken in the 1920s to forge one unified and unifying narrative of the Revolution is then addressed. The assassination in 1928 of Mexico's strong man, Álvaro Obregón, marks the acceleration of the "institutionalization of the revolution," a process of political consolidation and unification that included the formation and dissemination of a Revolutionary Tradition.

Part Two analyzes the Revolutionary Tradition in three different incarnations or performances: as an annual festival, a commemorative monument, and official history. These incarnations represent different forms of organized remembering and different ways to represent and broadcast the past, to make it relevant and alive in the present. Chapter Four looks at the history of national festivals and the rise of Mexico's official Revolution Day, the twentieth of November. Chapter Five studies the history of revolutionary monuments and the construction of the greatest of them all, the Monument to the Revolution. Chapter Six considers the appearance of revolutionary historiography and the development of official histories of the revolution. The Conclusion analyzes how in recent decades various political groups and governments have both affirmed and subverted the Revolutionary Tradition and, therefore, *La Revolución* itself.

The Mexican political system during most of the twentieth century has based its legitimacy largely on *la Revolución*. The state and the dominant party, accordingly, are the culmination and continuation of the Mexican revolution. *La Revolución* is identified with the most sacred values and the highest principles of the Republic, as well as the greatest needs and aspirations of its people.[43] The revolutionary origins of the political system and that system's faithful adherence to *la Revolución* have justified the existence of the system, the hegemony of the official party, and the authority of the successive regimes that take power every six years. This pattern for support is changing, however. The system has deviated from its founding principles as Mexican civil society has changed and awakened. Opponents of the government have embraced *la Revolución* and are making it their own. The Revolutionary Tradition will surely survive the downfall of the postrevolutionary political system just as the older Liberal Tradition survived the downfall of the Porfirian political system. Long will Mexicans proclaim, *¡Viva La Revolución!*

⟨ℰ⟩⟩⟩~ *Chronology of Events, 1911–1928*

1911	Madero's rebellion forces Díaz to resign and leave the country in exile in May.	Construction of a new national theater is suspended, not to be resumed and completed until the 1930s.
1911– 1913	The presidency of Madero	
1911	The proclamation of the Plan de Ayala, justifying rebellion against the Madero government, is signed by Emiliano Zapata in Morelos.	Interim President Francisco León de la Barra inaugurates a monument to Morelos in the Ciudadela, Mexico City.
1912	The rebellion of Pascual Orozco against the Madero government in Chihuahua	Governors Abraham González in Chihuahua and Venustiano Carranza in Coahuila restrict the sale of alcoholic beverages and regulate prostitution, pro-
1913	The Madero government is toppled by a conservative coup and the president and vice-president are murdered. General Victoriano Huerta becomes president.	hibit gambling, open new schools, raise teachers' pay, begin adult literacy classes, and maintain the Porfirian curriculum of civic liberalism.
1913	The proclamation of the Plan de Guadalupe, justifying rebellion against the Huerta government, is publicized by Venustiano Carranza, the Maderista governor of Coahuila.	Carranza's Plan de Guadalupe seeks legitimation in national history by calling for the restoration of the Constitution of 1857.

1913–
1914	Civil war rages between the Huerta government and the Constitutionalist movement, led by First Chief Carranza.	The Huerta regime increases spending for education and studies the problem of land distribution. Minor projects are initiated to improve the lives of Indians. In retrospect, the historian Michael Meyer argues, the regime was no counter-revolution, in that it did not seek to reestablish a Porfirian status quo.
1914	The Constitutionalist movement defeats the federal army by the summer, but distrust between Carranza and one of his generals, Francisco Villa, threatens the unity of the victorious coalition.	
1914	The Aguascalientes convention in the fall of the year attempts to prevent conflict between Carranza and Villa. It fails, and Villa and Zapata form a loose alliance against Carranza.	When Zapatista forces enter Mexico City in late 1914 they remove the street signs along Avenida Madero; Francisco Villa has them restored.
1914	Carranza makes a tactical retreat to Veracruz in November and the forces of Villa and Zapata occupy Mexico City.	In retreating, Carranza follows the example of Benito Juárez, who had moved his government to Veracruz in 1859 during the War of the Reform.
1915	"The War of the Winners" is a civil war between Carranza's forces and those of Villa and Zapata. In a series of decisive battles in the spring of 1915,	In this year, Mariano Azuela publishes *Los de abajo*, the classic novel of the Mexican revolution. The story follows the career of a revolutionary,

Carranza's best general, Álvaro Obregón, decisively defeats Villa.

Demetrio Macías, who is caught up, without understanding why, in what appears to be an endless conflict.

1916–1917 From November to February supporters of Carranza meet in convention in Querétaro and write a new "revolutionary" charter, the Constitution of 1917.

Carranza places the national iconic image, the eagle clutching a serpent on a nopal cactus, on national coins for the first time.

1917–1920 In May 1917, Carranza is elected constitutional president.

The first revolutionary monument, to the Serdán brothers, is unveiled in the city of Puebla in 1916. The Historical Museum of Churubusco, in the southern district of Mexico City, commemorating the war with the United States, is inaugurated in 1919.

1919 Emiliano Zapata is lured into a trap by one of Carranza's officers and murdered in April 1919.

1920 The Plan of Agua Prieta is proclaimed, justifying rebellion against Carranza.

1920 The interim government of Adolfo de la Huerta negotiates a peace agreement with Villa and the leaders of the Zapatista movement.

1920–1924 The election and presidency of Álvaro Obregón

In 1921 the Obregón regime puts on a commemorative extravaganza to rival Díaz's centennial celebration of Independence. This second festival, marking the achievement of Independence, has a more populist character than did the 1910 celebrations.

1922	The remains of Ricardo Flores Magón are returned to Mexico from the United States and honored by a state funeral.	The great renaissance of Mexican art, the muralist movement, begins when Education Secretary José Vasconcelos invites artists to paint Mexican subjects on the walls of a new education department building, an agricultural school in Chapingo, and the National Palace, among other sites.
1923–1924	The rebellion of de la Huerta against Obregón is defeated; Felipe Carrillo Puerto, socialist governor of Yucatán, is murdered in the revolt.	
1923	In the summer of 1923, Francisco Villa is assassinated in Parral, Chihuahua.	In 1924 there are about one thousand federal rural schools in operation.
1924	By the end of Obregón's term some 3 million acres have been redistributed to 624 villages. The number of villagers receiving land is calculated at 140,000.	At the beginning of the Calles presidency, the muralists José Clemente Orozco and David Alfaro Siqueiros are fired by the Ministry of Education.
1924–1928	This period sees the election and presidency of Plutarco Elías Calles, Obregón's hand-picked candidate and fellow Sonoran.	In 1925, Madero becomes the first revolutionary hero to have his name inscribed on the wall of the national congress.
1926–1929	In the Cristero rebellion, conflict between the national government and the hierarchy of the Catholic church provokes massive peasant rebellion in	Muralist Diego Rivera adapts to the Calles regime and paints the chapel at the agricultural school at Chapingo. Upon finishing these murals, he visits

west-central Mexico. In the struggle, 65,000 to 80,000 Mexicans are killed.

Moscow by invitation of the Soviet Union, for the tenth anniversary of the Russian Revolution.

1927 Supporters of Obregón pass a law permitting the former president to seek another term. This violation of the principle of "No Reelection" sparks the rebellion of Generals Francisco Serrano and Arnulfo Gómez, which is crushed in two months.

In 1928, Martín Luis Guzmán writes *El águila y la serpiente* (The Eagle and the serpent), a documentary novel about the revolution in the north. In 1929 he publishes *La sombra del caudillo* (The Shadow of the caudillo), a novelistic treatment of post-revolutionary politics.

1928 Álvaro Obregón is elected president for the term 1928– 34. On July 17, José de León Toral, a fanatic Catholic, shoots Obregón in the head five times, killing the Caudillo of the Revolution.

A *corrido* verse on the death of Obregón reads: "And so ends his life / the one-armed hero of León / for sustaining his ideals / in honor of the Nation."

Part One
CONSTRUCTION

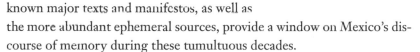

What follows is the history of
la Revolución as invented and
constructed by the *voceros de la
Revolución*, who produced revolutionary speeches, manifestos, and other writings in the
Mexico of the 1910s and 1920s.
Nearly every scrap of public political language in the period included some representation of the
recent past. All of these writings, the well-
known major texts and manifestos, as well as
the more abundant ephemeral sources, provide a window on Mexico's discourse of memory during these tumultuous decades.

There were several famous and many more nearly anonymous *voceros de
la Revolución*. Gaspar Bolaños of Jalisco is a good example of the latter. He
began his revolutionary propaganda career in 1910 in Guadalajara with
newspaper articles in favor of Madero. This activity earned him an invitation to join the League of Friends of the Country, a civic organization that
sponsored patriotic events. As a member, he spoke on the occasion of the
official renaming of Calle Bernardo Reyes to Avenida Francisco Madero
in 1914. When the Constitutionalist forces of General Manuel Diéguez
took Guadalajara that same year, Bolaños joined the staff of the official
newspaper, *El Reformador*, writing articles and editorials. The Constitutionalist government also appointed Bolaños history professor at the state
teachers college. He was proud to declare in 1916:

> It was precisely in the liberal press, which published my articles, that
> I performed my important antireactionary and anticlerical work, to
> the point that the Constitutionalist government of Jalisco was proud

to declare that those good liberal writers have opened the road to the Revolution in that state. That worthy writing that I did in Guadalajara provoked many attacks in the press and even physical threats by religious and political fanatics.[1]

Bolaños and the other *voceros* in Guadalajara, El Paso, Puebla, and Veracruz, in Mexico City, New York, Havana, Paris, and many more cities within and without Mexico, saw themselves as interpreting Mexican reality, simply making sense of events. In so doing, however, they were constructing something that did not exist before, something that acquired a remarkably consistent and durable shape, something they named *la Revolución*.[2]

This revolutionary construction in Mexico, compared to other, later twentieth-century revolutionary (and fascist) societies, was singular. In the Soviet Union, China, and Cuba, as well as fascist Italy and Germany, the state created an authorized monolithic collective memory, a revolutionary myth and official history tied to a "cult of personality." Perhaps because the Mexican revolution came early and first, because of the weakness and disintegration of the state in the 1910s, and because of the divisiveness among revolutionaries, in Mexico memory, myth, and history were elaborated not by the state but by diverse individuals sympathetic to the promise of revolutionary transformation. The state that was reconstructed after the revolution did not need to invent *la Revolución*: the *voceros de la Revolución* were already on the job. The pronouncements of the state, therefore, are less significant than are the plethora of writings by the revolution's scribblers.

Public expressions of history are ubiquitous forms of evidence. They are also reliably contemporaneous. Given the recent development of oral history in Mexican studies, the interviews conducted by historians tell us what people remembered many decades after the historical episodes themselves (and, significantly, decades after the construction of *la Revolución*). The value of these personal expressions of memory has been compromised by time itself. Embedded in contemporary public expressions one finds a more pristine sense of collective remembrance, as well as traces and clues regarding the process of the construction of collective memory, public myth, and official history. "No single enunciation can itself constitute evidence for an argument about political language," argues Dror Wahrman, "it is only persistent repetition which turns a disembodied utterance about politics into a resonant utterance which in itself forms a meaningful part of the political process."[3]

This book examines Mexico's literate middle-to-high culture and the construction of a national, and ultimately dominant, collective memory, public myth, and official history. The many authors of the evidence presented here were mostly middle-class urbanites. Many hailed from Mexico City, although during the violent decade of 1910–20 more than a few wrote and published their works in provincial cities and outside of Mexico altogether. Although voices from the provinces are heard here, the focus is not provincial and so no claim can be made regarding the provincial (even less the local) variations and contradictions that certainly existed.[4] The voices of village Mexico, the people who told and sang their stories instead of writing them, are sometimes listened to here but, again, they are not given center stage. Provincial and folk memory are important subjects that deserve their own historians. It is my hope that these future historians will find this book something of a stepping-stone, helpful in their endeavors to take this subject further, better to understand it.

The narration that follows in the first three chapters examines the events of the 1910s and 1920s as contemporaries viewed and interpreted them. We must remember that they did not possess our privileged hindsight. Many Mexicans would echo Joseph de Maistre, who looked at his French homeland in 1794 and admitted that "for a long time we did not understand the revolution we are witnessing." To prepare the reader for the confusion of contemporaneous perspective, an overview of the events of the period is presented first.

Publication of the Plan of San Luis Potosí, a call by Francisco I. Madero for rebellion in November 1910, began a chain of events that led to the downfall of the regime of Porfirio Díaz six months later. Six years earlier, an opposition party, the Partido Liberal Mexicano (Mexican Liberal Party, PLM) led by Ricardo Flores Magón, had formed and initiated serious criticism of the Díaz regime, but it played only a small part in the 1910 national rebellion. The Magonistas, as well as many Maderistas, were critical of the negotiated settlement of the rebellion, the Treaty of Ciudad Juárez, which obtained Don Porfirio's resignation and exile but maintained the federal army, national congress, supreme court, and most state governors from the previous era. The treaty also established an interim presidency, given to Francisco León de la Barra, the Díaz regime's ambassador to Washington, which would govern the country until a national election in November 1911.

The Madero government brought into office by the 1911 election faced several rebellions by old enemies as well as former supporters (such as Emiliano Zapata and his followers in the state of Morelos and Pascual Orozco in Chihuahua), and in February 1913 the president was murdered and the government finally overthrown by one of Madero's generals, Victoriano Huerta. This coup provoked a new rebellion led by the Maderista governor of Coahuila, Venustiano Carranza. During a hard-fought campaign, Carranza's Constitutionalist movement descended on central Mexico from the northern tier of states, by the summer of 1914 forcing Huerta into exile. Following the example of the French Revolution, that October the revolutionary factions met in convention in the city of Aguascalientes to define the revolution, chart the needed reforms, and unify the fractious caudillos.

The victorious Constitutionalists splintered in the fall of 1914 and a new civil war erupted. Carranza's faction warred with Francisco Villa's army from Chihuahua and Zapata's guerrilla forces. Due to Carranza's talent for politics and the military ability of General Álvaro Obregón, who had learned a thing or two from the battles raging in Europe at the time, Carranza's forces were victorious by the spring of 1915. Carranza established a national government, sponsored a new constitution, and was elected president in 1917. The respected and successful First Chief of the Constitutionalist movement was less politically adept as president. His proconsul in Morelos managed to lure Zapata into a trap and had him killed in 1919. When in 1920 Carranza tried to impose a handpicked successor to carry on his rule, he was overthrown and murdered by a rebellion headed by Obregón, Plutarco Elías Calles, and the governor of Sonora, Adolfo de la Huerta.

With this victory, the Sonorans took charge of Mexico. Elected president the same year as Carranza's fall, Obregón served a four-year term and in 1924, after a bloody military uprising, imposed his own hand-picked successor, Calles. Francisco Villa, who had retired in 1920 to a government-granted hacienda, was assassinated in Parral, Chihuahua, in 1923. Villa's supporters blamed Obregón and Calles for his death, and they were most likely right. Nonetheless, Calles served a four-year term as president and prepared the way for the reelection of Obregón in 1928. During the Calles presidency, the regime began to enforce harsh constitutional provisions concerning the Catholic church, and this persecution provoked Cristero rebels in west-central Mexico to sustain a massive, three-year insurrection against the national government. The Obregón and Calles regimes began to address the land-tenure problem that had motivated many revolutionary villagers and intellectuals during the teens, and which had been practically ignored by President Carranza. The Sonorans also began to build the institutions needed to promote economic growth and development, invested in education in the cities and isolated rural villages, and tolerated more radical provincial regimes, often termed "socialist," which implemented significant land and labor reforms.

In 1927 the supporters of Obregón in Congress rewrote the electoral laws to permit non-consecutive reelection and thus to allow another term for Obregón, the Caudillo of the Revolution. Once again the presidential election season was marred by a military rebellion. As in 1923–24, the rebellion was crushed and purges followed. Obregón's campaign in 1928 was a triumphal march across the country and culminated in his election to a six-year term. "I have proved that the presidential palace is not necessarily the ante chamber of the cemetery," Obregón told Calles.[5] He spoke too soon. On July 17, at a banquet in his honor, the caudillo was assassinated by a young man who supported the Cristero movement and believed he acted on behalf of God. Madero, Zapata, Carranza, Villa, and now Obregón had met violent deaths and the revolutionaries were as divided as ever.

1   1911–1913

"Every event's name is itself an interpretation."[1]

MEXICAN REVOLUTIONARIES carried on an uninterrupted discourse of memory during the 1910s and 1920s. From the beginning of the revolutionary movement, these *voceros de la Revolución,* a rather thin but widely scattered stratum of insurgent literati, wrote about recent events as a singular historical phenomenon. They agreed on many aspects of contemporary history and, as a result, constructed *la Revolución Mexicana* as an imagined force and invented tradition in Mexican history and political life. Political factionalism, however, produced a number of fundamental disagreements about the past. Different revolutionary movements created distinct revolutionary traditions within *la Revolución,* and these competing and often hostile revolutionary traditions characterized Mexico's new political culture. Still, imaginings of fraternity in the 1920s, in the form of a "revolutionary family," accompanied the process of political consolidation.

Edmundo O'Gorman began his classic "inquiry into the historical nature of the New World and the meaning of its history" with this unusual challenge: "The most important problem concerning the history of America is the need of giving a satisfactory explanation of the way in which America appeared as such on the historical scene." For O'Gorman, the way in which America "appeared as such" involved a process of invention more than discovery. America did not emerge "full-blown as the result of the chance discovery" but "developed from a complex, living process of exploration and interpretation." O'Gorman's fundamental point is that the meaning of important and complex events is never self-evident; they are and have to be imagined, invented, and constructed, "within the framework of the image of reality valid at a particular moment."[2] This approach can usefully be followed with regard to the events that enveloped Mexico during the second decade of this century. What follows here is a new kind of history of the Mexican revolution, an account of the way in which *la Revolución* appeared and developed as such on the historical scene and came into historical being.[3]

Madero, his followers, and the revolutionary critics invented the first, enduring representations of the Mexican revolution in the discourse of memory that began upon their triumph in the spring of 1911. Their accounts of the rise of political opposition and the insurrection against President Díaz did not mirror a reality exactly but created one, *la Revolución*, by organizing meaningful perceptions abstracted from a complex experience.[4] This is not to say that Maderistas and other revolutionaries produced an image of the past that was wholly untrue or even greatly distorted. The events surrounding and following the 1910 rebellion were sufficiently complicated and ambivalent to admit a variety of interpretations and a diversity of meanings. Novelists throughout the decade, Mariano Azuela best of all in *Los de abajo*, presented images of chaos and unexplained or unexplainable events. "You ask me why I am still a rebel?" one of Azuela's characters asks. "Well, the revolution is like a hurricane: if you're in it, you're not a man . . . you're a leaf, a dead leaf, blown by the wind."[5] Politicians, however, have to find meaning and invent it. The invention of *la Revolución* by Maderistas and their rivals entailed the mythic reconfiguration of the immediate past.[6]

Mexico's past is littered with numerous revolutions, yet all Mexicans know that *la Revolución* refers to the one that began in 1910. They know that this particular set of events was one of the great revolutions of world history, a revolution that significantly transformed Mexico for the better. This term has long been taken for granted, viewed as a transparent tag, an obvious description of the objective reality of a portion of the Mexican past. It has, in fact, always been more evocative and emotive than descriptive. "It almost seems that the word 'revolution' itself," writes Reinhart Koselleck, "possesses such revolutionary power." In Mexico, especially, it became the "magic word."[7]

It was not always so in Mexico. During much of the nineteenth century, "revolution" referred to both grand and petty political and social upheavals that could just as likely bring forth pernicious results as beneficial ones. The French Revolution had more detractors in early Republican Mexico than sympathizers, and the insurrection led by Father Hidalgo in 1810, being closer in time and space, was even more controversial.[8] We would expect the conservative thinker Lucas Alamán to portray 1810 as the "vandalistic revolution," but early liberals such as Servando Teresa de Mier (1765–1827), Lorenzo de Zavala (1788–1836), and José María Luis Mora

(1794–1850) were also quite immune from any romantic attachment to revolutionary change. The revolution of 1810 was necessary for achieving independence, noted Mora in a famous passage, but it was also "pernicious and destructive of the nation."[9] Only Carlos María de Bustamante (1774–1848), writes Enrique Krauze, "had seen Hidalgo's war with the eyes of a Mexican Michelet: the enlightened priest leading a people thirsty for liberty, prosperity, and justice."[10]

Most of the time, Mexicans in the nineteenth century used the terms "revolution" and "pronouncement" (*pronunciamiento*) interchangeably to refer to revolts against an incumbent government.[11] "Revolutionaries" were simply rebels and insurrectionaries, a status that came to an end if the revolt succeeded and its leaders took over the government.[12] An aphorism from the early Republican era captures one of the trivial causes of many insignificant revolts: "When salaries are paid, revolutions fade."[13] A particularly efficient revolt against Antonio López de Santa Anna in 1839 became known as the "three-hour revolution."[14] Most revolutions of independent Mexico, lamented Ignacio L. Vallarta in 1855, could be summed up as "simply the pursuit of political power."[15] The concept of revolution in Mexico before mid-century was impoverished compared to our twentieth-century usage, its meaning quite narrow and ideologically neutral. This limitation began to change, however, with the 1855 "Revolution of Ayutla."

That political movement brought to prominence and power a new generation of liberals who viewed both the French Revolution and the Insurgency of 1810–11 far more favorably than had their predecessors. From the viewpoint of the liberals of the Reform, writes David A. Brading, "if the liberal patria was founded during the Insurgency, it was inspired by the ideal and the example of the French revolution."[16] The liberal press proclaimed in 1856 that "Mexico is experiencing its '89."[17] There were abundant references, positive and negative, comparative and prescriptive, to 1789 during the debates in the Constitutional Congress of 1856–57.[18] Benito Juárez remarked in 1859 that he was "of one mind with the [French] revolutionaries of '93, whose humanitarian ideas we now have the honor to be implanting in Mexico."[19] Throughout Mexico in this period political associations appeared that were patterned after and functioned "point by point" along the lines of revolutionary French clubs.[20]

An even more important precedent and parallel, however, was that of 1810. "The revolution of Hidalgo was the revolution par excellence,"

Guillermo Prieto proclaimed in 1855. "The revolution of Álvarez is the same revolution as Hidalgo, it is the same struggle of the people against their tyrants."[21] Ignacio Ramirez (1818–79), Ignacio Manuel Altamirano (1834–93), and Ignacio L. Vallarta (1830–93) similarly viewed the insurgency of 1810 as the rebirth of Mexico and the beginning of a glorious Mexican revolutionary tradition continued in their time. In the fiftieth anniversary commemoration of 1810 in Veracruz, Ignacio Mariscal placed the Reform alongside the Insurgency as well as the French and American revolutions. Mexicans began to make distinctions regarding revolutions and to endow the concept with new meanings and significance.[22]

During the Porfirian era, among Mexican intellectuals the concept and precedent of revolution became more and more respectable. This was in part due to the creation of the conservative Third Republic in France and its invention of a rather bland and noncontroversial version of the country's revolutionary tradition.[23] In 1881, one year after July 14 became an official festival of the French Republic, the date was celebrated as a holiday for the first time in Mexico City. Thereafter, the day was commemorated regularly in Mexico City and Puebla and often celebrated as if it were a patriotic fiesta.[24] "We are the children directly of that revolution of 1789," Altamirano exclaimed in his toast to the newly arrived French ambassador, "and our ideas are those proclaimed in the Constituent Assembly."[25] In the town of Tetela de Ocampo in Puebla—hardly a cosmopolitan center— in 1888, Guy Thomson has found, funeral orations reflected "a reverence for the principles of the French Revolution."[26]

Altamirano was one of the last spokesmen of the Reform generation and his radicalism was not passed on to the new liberal intellectual establishment that came to accept and defend the order and progress of Porfirio Díaz's Mexico. The members of the new generation criticized the Jacobinism of the "liberals of the old school" and were hardly enthusiasts of revolutions past or present. Mexico's most serious student of the French Revolution, Justo Sierra, affirmed its noble principles but also condemned its excesses and its degeneration into dictatorship. Sierra viewed that revolution, nevertheless, as a great development in modern history, "the beginning of an epoch for the civilized peoples." He defined revolution as the violent acceleration of a nation's evolution and noted at the beginning of the new century that there had been only two revolutions in independent Mexico's past: the Insurgency and the Reform. "In the perspective of history," Sierra wrote, "the two revolutions are successive phases of a single social movement: the first being emancipation from Spain, the second, emancipation from the colonial system."[27] The Porfiriato's greatest intellectual ratified the notion, invented during the Reform, of Mexico's revolutionary origins and continuing tradition. The Porfirians, like the Radical Socialists of the Third Republic ("red on the outside, white inside"), annexed the liberal tradition and concentrated on its symbolic institutionalization in commemorative festivals and monuments.[28]

Emilio Rabasa, in his 1887 novel *La Bola*, condemned revolt and idealized revolution. It is clear that Rabasa had in mind the difference between the great revolutions of world history and the numerous petty pronouncements (*bola*) that plagued nineteenth-century Mexico.[29] "Revolution unfolds around an idea, moves nations, modifies institutions and needs citizens," Rabasa wrote; "*la bola* does not require principles, nor does it ever have them; it is born and dies in an impoverished material and moral state, and needs ignoramuses." In a word, he continued, revolution "is the daughter of progress of the world, and an inescapable law of humanity." *La bola*, the brawl, on the other hand, "is the daughter of ignorance and the inevitable punishment of backward peoples."[30]

By the end of the Porfiriato the term "revolution" was a richer and more complex word, carrying more nuanced meaning and more historical resonance. It was not, however, a completely new term; many Mexicans still used the term in its earlier, narrower, and plural sense. During the armed struggle, Maderistas often used the terms "revolution" and "insurrection" (and "revolutionary movement" and "insurrectional movement") interchangeably. Madero himself later took pains to emphasize that the Revolution of 1910 was unlike "the majority of Mexican revolutions," since it did not "proclaim principles to deceive the people" or "distribute the nation as spoils of war."[31] Indeed, for some time to come journalists and politicians would refer to specific revolts as "revolutions."

However, even in 1910 and 1911 the use of the term to refer to the rebellion against Porfirio Díaz had begun to take on the characteristics of a Pavlovian cue. José María Pino Suárez, soon to become Madero's vice-president, quoted Marx to the people of Yucatán in April 1911 and left nothing to the imagination: "Revolution is progress."[32] With the resignation of Díaz in May 1911, his toppled regime and epoch was immediately denominated the "ancien régime" in an obvious reference to 1789. In the summer of 1911, Luis Cabrera proclaimed that "the revolution is revolution," meaning a genuine social revolution and not a mere change of government.[33] Every name is a metaphor, argues Ernst Cassirer[34]: among the educated in Mexico the term "revolution" increasingly conjured up the heroic years of 1789, 1810, and 1855, rather than "the uncounted political movements of a farcical-tragic manner that have a scourge of the Republic."[35]

Between 1911 and 1913, however, as Maderistas and other revolutionaries participated in a discourse of memory intended to help guide them in shaping ongoing events, two significant enhancements were made to the term "revolution" as it applied to 1910 and later. First, *la Revolución* was historicized: it was portrayed as the third stage of an ongoing revolutionary tradition that began with the Insurgency of 1810 and continued with the Reform of the mid-to-late 1850s. The Revolution of 1910 was placed in a reassuring nationalistic and patriotic context. In this way Maderistas were able to call upon venerated national heroes to justify their leadership and policies; in effect, they presented the Maderista cause as identical with the cause of Mexico. Second, *la Revolución* was reified: it was presented as an autonomous force of nature or history destined to transform Mexico regardless of Madero's mistakes and conservatism and despite the machinations of "reactionaries" pitted against it. In this way, revolutionaries disenchanted with or opposed to Madero justified their actions and rallied their supporters. These enhancements transformed an evocative but multiversant concept into a myth.

Maderista discourse of memory sought to justify the rebellion and the authority of the new government largely by means of historical representation. Their efforts required the characterization of Díaz and his regime as outside and against the liberal revolutionary tradition and the identification of Madero's rebellion with that same tradition and therefore with the patria itself. In this respect, the Maderistas were following a well-worn path: "the past has always been the handmaid of authority," as J. H. Plumb put it.[36]

"To pass judgment on the practices of the old regime," Paul Connerton explains, "is the constitutive act of the new order."[37] Maderistas did this first of all with a designation. In an obvious reference to the French Revolution, the Díaz government was reconstructed as the old regime, the "ancien régime" (*el Antiguo Régimen*), or just as frequently, "the Dictatorship" (*la Dictadura*), discredited by its very name. The *Antiguo Régimen* was the antithesis of *la Revolución:* feudal elites defeated by a mass popular movement of political and economic liberation, a despotic dictatorship replaced by a genuinely democratic government, the interests of a few superseded by the well-being of all. The *Antiguo Régimen* was also compared unfavorably to its predecessor. Díaz, Luis Cabrera charged, betrayed "the principles of liberty and equality that had conquered in 1857."[38]

As Maderistas consigned the Díaz regime to a kind of national historical purgatory, they placed the Revolution of 1910 in distinguished company. They were nearly unanimous in comparing and conjoining *la Revolución* with Mexico's two great revolutions of the past century, that of Independence (1810–21) and the Reform (1855–60). In one of the first and most popular histories of the events of 1910–11, its authors noted that "for the third time in the history of Mexico, the cause of the many achieved a sensational and complete triumph over the cause of the few."[39] In another, the authors noted that "our history has registered but three revolutions—Independence, the Reform, [and] that which emancipated us from Díaz."[40] Professor Braulio Hernández compared Madero favorably with the apostle of Mexico's first revolution, Hidalgo, while Rogelio Fernández Güell viewed Madero as "the modern Juárez."[41]

Francisco Madero himself devoted much of his speech commemorating the second anniversary of the "sacrifice" of Aquiles Serdán, the first martyr of *la Revolución* (see the Pantheon of National Heroes in this volume), to the place in history of the Revolution of 1910. He began by noting that the events of 1910 had not been properly understood. Some apparently believed, Madero noted in reference to Pascual Orozco—a Maderista who had turned against Madero—that this revolution, like most revolutions in Mexico, was really about the division of the spoils. It was, and in time would be recognized as, "the third revolution of principle that has occurred in the Republic, one that complements the other two." The first revolution, which was incited by Hidalgo, removed the "Spanish yoke," but the same privileged classes that had dominated the people during the Spanish period returned to seize power. The second revolution, "the glorious revolution of Ayutla," which began the Reform, Madero continued, returned to the people their rights and placed the "rights of man" in the Constitution of 1857. That triumph, however, was snatched away by a dictator and the people again became the victim of the same privileged classes that had always ruled.

"The third revolution that has proclaimed principles has now come," Madero declared. These principles, "Effective Suffrage and No Reelection," have become firmly established in the national conscience. If the people are satisfied with the Revolution of 1910, he noted, if they are happy and understand the great achievement they have attained, if they appreciate the "beautiful liberty that now is their patrimony," then "this revolution will be the one that has returned forever the peoples' rights."[42]

To Madero, the Revolution of 1910 was a genuine and radical one, but he did not understand or accept the concept of a social revolution. In an address given in Veracruz in September 1911, Madero emphasized that social and economic progress "cannot be brought about by a revolution, nor by laws, nor by decrees."[43] The "socialist appeal" of despoiling private property was beyond Madero's contemplation.[44] Not unlike his Porfirian teachers, Madero believed that progress is a product of the labor of all social classes, and thus instantiated in a slow, peaceful evolution.

After May 1911, Madero spoke of "the revolution" as an event of the past, something closed and concluded.[45] A number of Maderistas, but especially those revolutionaries critical of Madero's conservatism, developed a much broader, transcendent conception of *la Revolución. México Nuevo*, the newspaper of more radical Maderistas, viewed the insurrection as only one stage of *la Revolución*. According to the paper's editor, Roque Estrada, *la Revolución* was composed of four stages: Elaboration, Concentration, Destruction, and Reconstruction. The last stage, Reconstruction, defined as "the work of government, seeking to implement the sensible promises of the insurrectionaries," was ongoing, and therefore *la Revolución* was ongoing.[46] On the other hand, Luis Cabrera, another of Madero's prominent revolutionary critics, argued that "*la Revolución* properly called, that is to say, the destructive period, has not yet ended." When the ancien régime is completely demolished, noted Cabrera, *la Revolución* would then begin the task of reconstruction.[47] For T. F. Serrano, such distinctions were unimportant: "*La Revolución* continues its march, slow but sure, devastating and imposing."[48]

These statements indicate more than simply the idea of a transcendent or continuing revolution. Some revolutionaries at this early point began to reify *la Revolución*. Reification, according to Peter L. Berger and Thomas Luckmann, "is the apprehension of human phenomena as if they were things, that is, in non-human or possibly supra-human terms."[49] The reified revolution was concrete, independent, and autonomous, something outside, above, and nearly beyond human agency (rather than simply a concept, a particular way of analyzing events). It gained a solidity in print that it never had in reality. Roles as well as revolution were reified: revolutionaries did not make *la Revolución*, rather *la Revolución* acted through revolutionaries. The reification of roles produces a world "in which human actions do not express human meanings but rather represent, in priestly fashion, various super-human abstractions they are supposed to embody."[50]

The very fact of naming certain events *la Revolución* involved "thingification," the invention of an experienced object, which by itself granted it a certain autonomy and independence.[51] One of the first and best examples of Maderista reification of *la Revolución* and the roles of revolutionaries is found in the pages of *México Nuevo:* "It is not individuals in arms who have made and are making *la Revolución:* it is *la Revolución* that is making individuals in arms." *La Revolución,* furthermore, "is not a man or a group of men. . . . It is the national spirit in action! It is the inexorable social dynamic!"[52] For Rafael Martínez, writing in 1911, "*la Revolución* was a martyr in Aquiles and Máximo Serdán; capable and just in González, Moya, and Guillermo Baca, and apostolic, noble, and liberating in he who was its caudillo."[53]

Revolutionaries not only reified *la Revolución* but also its historical nemesis: *la Reacción.* In revolutionary discourse the Reaction survived the fall of the dictatorship in May 1911 and embarked upon counterrevolution. As Cabrera put it: "By mid-July 1911, the struggle between *la Reacción* and *la Revolución* had arrived at the point of open struggle."[54] Revolutionaries reified the roles of counterrevolutionaries as well as revolutionaries. Individuals did not effect counterrevolution, the counterrevolution acted through individuals. This is clearly expressed by Ramón Puente in 1912: "*La Reacción* looked for a Maderista," and it found one in Pascual Orozco. The Reaction then proceeded "to empower Orozco and then lead him against Madero. That was the problem."[55]

Reification of *la Revolución* served several purposes. First and foremost it helped people make sense of complex events. "If social life is to be 'meaningful' to its participants," Burke Thomason writes, "perhaps it must be accepted that these meanings will unavoidably take on a kind of thing-like, unconstructed, merely 'discovered' reality."[56] Second, the reified Revolution justified and legitimized the actions of revolutionaries and the new regime. If *la Revolución* was a force above and beyond human production, inevitable and inexorable, it was destined to be. Revolutionaries, therefore, were on the "side of history," success was guaranteed and opposition was futile.

Those revolutionaries who were dissatisfied with Madero's leadership or opposed it altogether, furthermore, were especially given to reification. They placed their hope in something greater and more radical than Madero: *la Revolución* itself. For Roque Estrada, the ill-advised and unfavorable Treaty of Ciudad Juárez in May 1911 ended the insurrection, "but not *la Revolución.*" A few months later, Cabrera complained of the survival of elements of the ancien régime within the interim government (May–November 1911) of President Francisco León de la Barra. Not all was lost, however, because "*la Revolución* would continue as a living force." For a critical revolutionary congressional deputy in October 1912, although the regime had attempted to smother it, "that revolution is still afoot." In January 1913 the Bloque Liberal Renovador (the Renovators, the radical Maderistas in Congress) informed Madero that "the Revolution goes to its ruin, dragging down the government emanating from it, simply because it has not governed with revolutionists."[57] Their solution: "It is necessary, Señor Presidente, that *la Revolución* govern with revolutionaries."[58]

In one of his many interesting digressions, Alan Knight criticizes the idea of the Revolution "as a clearly defined, consistent entity, as a kind of club, with approved, paid-up members inside, and blackballed cads outside." He is, of course, speaking to his contemporary readers and historian colleagues, trying once and for all to have us understand that what happened in Mexico between 1910 and 1920 was "a complex, collective experience." Knight's warning, written in 1986, demonstrates the staying power of the reification of *la Revolución* begun in 1911–13.[59]

Maderista discourse constituted only part of the deluge of rhetoric flooding Mexico from May 1911 to February 1913.[60] Maderistas were not the only revolutionaries contributing to the discourse of memory. For the anarchist Partido Liberal Mexicano (PLM) of Ricardo Flores Magón, there had been no revolution at all. The PLM disputed "the victory of the followers of the bourgeoisie, that is: Maderistas, Reyistas, Vazquistas, *científicos,* and the many others whose only object is to put a man in the presidency."[61] In their rebel Plan of Tacubaya of October 1911, Emilio Vázquez Gómez, an unhappy former Maderista, and his followers praised the glorious Revolution of 1910 and condemned Madero for subverting it. "We do not fight against *la Revolución*, but for it and we will continue the movement that Madero failed."[62] Similarly, the followers of Emiliano Zapata of Morelos claimed fidelity to the Revolution of 1910 and charged that Madero had not allowed it to follow "its course until the full realization of its principles."[63] *La Revolución* was bigger than Madero and outside his control. "*La Revolución* began, has continued its course, and still exists, because of the 'United Will' of the innumerable popular masses."[64]

Tales are tools, Clifford Geertz tells us; people make sense of their world by telling stories about it.[65] This early revolutionary storytelling, or discourse of memory, named, historicized, and reified *la Revolución*. It became part of an historical trinity, fixed in memory as no less significant than the revolutions of Independence and the Reform and equally liberating. It is in this discourse that the transcendental revolution was constructed. The invented revolution of the Maderistas, however, constituted one of several competing discourses of memory at this time, an incipient, far from dominant, official memory. Its significance lies not in its contemporary influence (which was undoubtedly slight) but in its power with a relatively small number of dedicated revolutionaries who later, under different circumstances, elaborated, refurbished, and disseminated their recollection, conception, and representation of *la Revolución*.

The revolutionaries who criticized Madero for compromising with the powerful elements of the old regime were soon proven right. Madero had disarmed most revolutionary forces and spared the federal army. The institutions of Porfirian Mexico at all levels survived the transition and unmercifully criticized and undermined the new regime. Two of the most noted figures of the Porfirian regime rebelled against Madero: General Bernardo Reyes, the former governor of Nuevo León, rebelled in December 1911, and Félix Díaz, the former dictator's nephew, rebelled in October 1912, but both promptly found themselves in prison in Mexico City. In early February 1913, a federal army general and a group of armed supporters freed Reyes and Díaz. When Reyes tried to take the National Palace, he was killed. The other conspirators regrouped in the city's main military repository, the Ciudadela. At this point President Madero put his faith in the wrong soldier. He named General Victoriano Huerta commander-general of the city, in charge of the defense of the government. For the next ten days, the "tragic ten" as Mexicans call them, the two forces traded artillery fire, although few shells landed anywhere near their supposed targets. General Huerta had made a secret agreement with the conspirators to create sufficient chaos to warrant the overthrow of Madero. Huerta arrested Madero and his vice-president on February 18, forced their resignations, and three days later, in the early hours of February 22, had them murdered. *La Revolución*, apparently dead, was, in fact, being reborn.

2 1913–1920

"Warring authorities mean warring pasts."[1]

MANY SELF-STYLED revolutionary movements appeared in Mexico following the destruction of the Madero government. These groups fought a common enemy in Victoriano Huerta, as well as vying with one another. The next few years witnessed a jumbled parade of "*istas*"—Maderistas, Magonistas, Zapatistas, Constitucionalistas, Convencionistas, Villistas, and Carrancistas, to name only the most prominent. There came to be, in short, competing revolutionary traditions, each sustained by dissonant collective memories. One faction, in time, achieved political and military predominance, became the national government of Mexico, and constructed and disseminated an official memory of *la Revolución*. While the collective memory of the Constitucionalistas–Carrancistas became the official memory, it fell short of becoming the dominant national memory. It was contested by the counter-memories of Villistas, Zapatistas, and Magonistas and was reduced to a counter-memory itself with the Agua Prieta revolt in 1920.

The coup of February 1913 that brought down the Madero government and elevated General Huerta to power provoked the formation of the Constitutionalist movement. This loose association of regional armies and Maderista holdouts, forged and barely coordinated by the governor of the northern state of Coahuila, Venustiano Carranza (its "Primer Jefe"), sought the destruction of "Huertista militarism and reactionary clericalism" and the restoration of constitutional government. By the summer of 1914 the Constitutionalist movement had defeated Huerta and the federal army, and not long thereafter it split into hostile factions that again threw Mexico into civil war. The victory of Carranza and his loyal generals by mid-1915 gave that faction control of Mexico City and the national government, and indeed of most of the country. Carrancista military caudillos and políticos wrote a new "revolutionary" constitution that was promulgated on February 5, 1917. Carranza was constitutionally elected to a four-year term as president a few months later.

The assassination of Madero (and his vice-president Pino Suárez) immediately gave rise to a popular and powerful legend that became a crucial element of *la Revolución*. "Madero the martyr meant more to the soul of Mexico than Madero the apostle."[2] A halo, rumor had it, appeared above the head of the dead president in the morgue.[3] Without planning or leadership, people set up a humble shrine at the site of the murders. The "apostle" became the "martyr," "the immaculate caudillo," the "Mexican Jesus."[4] Isidro Fabela wrote, "Madero was not born to be a president but a symbol."[5] Many revolutionaries forgot their disagreements. Gonzalo de la Parra remarked, "I repented my intemperance for Madero." After the assassination, he continued, "Madero became greater in my eyes and I was dazzled. I saw the halo around his head and I believed in the fanaticism of those who understand martyrs."[6] Like all apostles, Luis Seoane wrote in 1920, "they hated him unto death and glorified him into immortality."[7]

After Constitutionalist armies defeated Huerta and took control of Mexico City, Carranza, Obregón, and other Constitutionalists made pilgrimages to Madero's tomb in the Panteón Francés. Evening ceremonies always followed visits by important callers. Workers organized by factories in "interminable processions" deposited floral wreaths. There Jesús Urueta, "in phrases full of ardor and vehemence, remembered the martyr, the man who sacrificed his life to liberate an oppressed people."[8] When Pancho Villa paid his respects a few months later, the camera captured his tearful face. Villa reburied Madero in an impressive ceremony in the Panteón Español and named a major thoroughfare Avenida Francisco I. Madero.[9] Villista speakers decried the presence of Madero's enemies among the advisors and supporters of Carranza, just as Carrancista speakers had earlier denounced the same with Villa.[10]

Corridos, popular ballads—"a valuable index to popular thought," Ernest Gruening noted[11]—seldom showed great personal devotion to Madero before his death. "But following his dramatic assassination," Merle Simmons notes, "the deep affection which the people felt for Don Pancho came strikingly to the fore." In the *corrido*, "The Death of Madero, Part One," Madero and Pino Suárez were remembered this way:[12]

Los muertos se sienten mucho
cuando son como éste buenos,
nos enseñó Democracia
y jamás le olvidaremos.

The deaths are deeply felt
when they are like these such good men,
who taught us Democracy
and our memory of them will never end.

From its beginning, the Constitutionalists viewed (or at least portrayed) their movement as the continuation of the Revolution of 1910 and the Huerta regime as the reappearance of the ancien régime and the work of the Reaction. Sonoran rebels declared in March 1913, for example, that "we come, ultimately, to fight without letup and with tenacity, against evil and in order to continue the Revolution of 1910."[13] For Lieutenant Colonel David Berlanga, "Huerta was despotism, the restoration of the Porfirian regime. Carranza was democracy, the restoration of the Maderista regime."[14] The character of *la Revolución*, however, was changing. Continuity did not preclude some modification. "This movement," noted Sam Navarro, "is not simply the continuation of 1910. It recognizes as fundamental, not just political problems but the unresolved economic problems, something that everyone recognizes without discussion throughout the Republic."[15] For General Lucio Blanco, similarly, "*la Revolución* is beginning to organize itself in a way to resolve one of the great problems that constitutes, without any doubt, the principal axis of prosperity of our Patria: the equitable redistribution of land."[16]

For Carranza and many of his followers the question of historical continuity was somewhat problematic. Their praise of Madero (particularly Maderismo as movement and government) was nearly always tinged with direct or implied criticism. The Revolution of 1910 was no more than a political revolution that was fatally compromised from the beginning by the Treaty of Ciudad Juárez: "the Revolution of 1910 failed in the peace treaty of Ciudad Juárez."[17] In a 1914 interview, Carranza noted that the revolution he led was "a Social Revolution. Madero's was merely political: the struggle for Effective Suffrage and No Reelection. The needs of the people, you can believe me, are much deeper."[18]

Carrancistas in general were ambivalent about the Maderista past. Madero, "the apostle" and "the martyr," was sacrosanct; Madero and Maderistas as practical revolutionaries and politicians, however, were faulted for their political errors. It is for this reason that Arnaldo Córdova calls Carrancismo the "self-criticism of Maderismo."[19] "There must be trust in those who are today the leaders of *la Revolución*," noted an editorial in *El*

Renovador in 1914, "for they are convinced that the original sin of the Apostle of *la Revolución* was making a deal with the putrid elements of Porfirismo."[20] This attitude was also inspired by Carrancista antagonism toward the Madero family. In the opinion of Francisco Padilla González, the brothers of the martyr conspired against Madero's noble ideals when they later opposed Carranza and became "the most evil of the instruments that conspired against the ingenuous aspirations of our race."[21]

While Carrancistas often distinguished "la Revolución Constitucionalista" from "la Revolución de 1910," they nevertheless viewed both as one transcendent revolution: "*la Revolución* initiated in 1910 by the Apostle Madero, and carried on by the Honorable Constitutional Governor of Coahuila don Venustiano Carranza."[22] Carrancista discourse of memory adopted the invented revolution of the Maderistas and modified certain aspects of it. *La Revolución* remained popular and liberating. It was viewed as the third stage of a longer, ongoing popular struggle begun in 1810, renewed in 1855, and resumed again in 1910 and 1913. While Maderistas viewed the Revolution of 1910 as a genuine revolution, Carrancistas were adamant that the renewed struggle of 1913 onwards constituted "a true social revolution." One supporter called it "the greatest social revolution of our time."[23] While this phrase did not have the same meaning for all Carrancistas, "social revolution" generally signified social, economic, nationalist, and moral reform.

Carrancistas were remembering and reinventing *la Revolución* during a period of great political turmoil that shaped their discourse. The Constitutionalist movement was unified during the struggle against Huerta, but with the defeat of the federal army in the spring and summer of 1914 factionalism shattered the coalition. Distrust and disagreement led to a break between Carranza and General Francisco Villa, caudillo of the División del Norte out of Chihuahua, a rupture that could not be healed by the revolutionary convention that met in Aguascalientes during the fall. Zapatistas, who had fought the Huerta dictatorship but had not joined the Constitutionalist coalition, during the convention formed a loose alliance with Villa against Carranza. The new "war of the winners" was accompanied by a war of words, rhetoric about the past as well as about projected futures.

For the Villistas, *la Revolución* encompassed Madero's insurrection against Díaz and the Constitutionalist struggle against Huerta. Unlike Carrancistas, Villistas viewed themselves first and foremost as faithful Maderistas: "the plan of San Luis," they asserted, "still has followers and repre-sentatives."[24] This attitude both reflected and motivated the drift of a number of "old" Maderistas and several members of the Madero family into the ranks of Villismo in 1913 and 1914.[25] Villistas defined their ene-mies and friends through the lens of Maderismo. T. F. Serrano, for example, charged that "at the side of Carranza one finds the enemies of Maderismo, this is something everyone knows." Zapatismo, on the other hand, he claimed, "is simply a branch of Maderismo."[26] Villistas charged that Obre-gón, as municipal president of Huatabambo, Sonora, had worked against the triumph of Maderismo in 1911 and hindered the careers of several rev-olutionary generals "simply because they were Maderistas, and Obregón never was one. It is the same obsession of Dn. Venustiano [Carranza]."[27]

Villa's opposition to Carranza in 1914 and after was based largely on two supposed infidelities: Carranza betrayed both the revolutionary ideals of a democratic government and the socio-economic reforms needed to assure the improvement of the disinherited classes. Villa demanded from the Mexican people a new sacrifice "so that *la Revolución* can realize its be-loved principles definitively."[28] And he was the man, according to the Vi-llista propaganda machine, destined to achieve them: "the liberator of the masses, and a champion of true democracy."[29]

For the Zapatistas, *la Revolución* encompassed neither Maderismo nor Constitucionalismo. In stark contrast to their Villista allies, Zapatistas por-trayed Maderismo in the harshest manner: "the Maderista government was simply a parody and ridiculous falsification" of the revolution.[30] *La Revolu-ción* was "the popular movement" that began in 1910 against *la Dictadura*, continued against Madero, the author of the "bitter betrayal" of the Treaty of Ciudad Juárez, reoriented in favor of the ideals of "the peasant farmer" with Zapata's 1911 Plan of Ayala, and continued against Huerta and Ca-rranza. Within *la Revolución* was "the agrarian revolution": "the great movement of the South, supported by the entire peasant farmer popula-tion of the Republic."[31] *La Revolución*, however, "ratifies each and every one of the indicated principles of the Plan of Ayala."[32]

Zapata's charge against Carranza was similar to Villa's: Carranza be-trayed *la Revolución*. "Carranza in *la Revolución*," Zapata declared in 1916, "represents lying, treachery, deceit, vicious and scandalous deception. He pretends to be the genuine representative of the Great Masses of the People, and we have seen, he not only tramples on each and every revolutionary principle, but harms with an equal despotism, the most precious rights and the most respectable liberties of man and society."[33]

One episode provoked by a Zapatista at the 1914 Aguascalientes convention revealed the already sacred quality for revolutionaries of Mexico's master narrative. Antonio Díaz Soto y Gama, the vice-chairman of the Zapatista commission, refused to follow his convention colleagues and sign the Mexican national flag. He believed *la Revolución* should completely supersede Mexican history in the manner of the French Revolution. He proclaimed:

> In the last analysis this flag represents nothing more than the triumph of the clerical reaction championed by Iturbide. I, gentlemen, will never sign this banner. We are making a great revolution today to destroy the lies of history, and we are going to expose the lie of history that is in this flag. That which we have been wont to call our independence was no independence for the native race, but for the creoles alone.[34]

As Soto y Gama was speaking, angry members from the floor interrupted with jeers. One observer reported that "the delegates screamed at one another, with left hands pounding their chests, and their right hands on their pistols, for all were mad."[35] This was not the French Revolution: Mexican revolutionaries did not seek to abolish history and begin the nation anew. They saw themselves as part of a revolutionary tradition symbolized by the tricolor red, white, and green flag.

As the revolutionary convention fell under the control of Villa in the fall of 1914, Convencionistas—a temporary hybrid of uncertain allegiance—attempted to synthesize the memories and programs of Maderistas, Constitucionalistas, Villistas, and Zapatistas. Convencionistas put their faith not in military chiefs but in *la Revolución* itself. "Instead of shouting vivas to the caudillos who are still alive and who have not yet been judged by history," noted the keynote speaker at the convention, Antonio Villareal, "we should shout, 'Gentlemen, long live the revolution.'"[36] By mid-1915, a rump convention came under the control of Zapatistas and thereafter (until its dissolution in May 1916) disseminated Zapatista propaganda.[37]

The Magonistas represented less a revolutionary faction than a revolutionary (or anarchist) "voice" after 1912 (a voice heard at Aguascalientes through Soto y Gama of the Zapatista faction).[38] They are considered here in part because their ideas did influence revolutionaries in other factions; Obregón, for instance, was an avid reader of *Regeneración*, the highly influential Magonista newspaper.[39] During the 1910s, several of the original Magonistas migrated to other revolutionary factions. Magonismo was also adopted, symbolically and retroactively, by elements in the labor movement and by the Partido Comunista Mexicana, the Mexican Communist Party, in the 1920s.[40]

For Magonistas, *la Revolución* was the people of Mexico "in open rebellion against their oppressors."[41] Ricardo Flores Magón in 1916 called it "the Social and Economic Revolution," which he defined as "the revolution of the downtrodden masses against their oppressors and exploiters; the revolution that chiefly aims to get control in common of the land, and thereby aims to free the Mexican people."[42] Madero was no revolutionary, his rebellion was no revolution, "because Madero did not struggle for the working class, but rather for the capitalist class." The same was true for Carranza and his rebellion, since he was "a bourgeois, a feudal lord, a hacendado himself." Villa, who had fought Magonistas by Madero's order, was no better: "he is a bandit, because he takes care of the interests of the bourgeoisie." Only Zapata qualified: "Zapata is an honorable and sincere revolutionary, because he snatches wealth from the hands of the bourgeoisie and gives it to its real owners: the poor."[43]

These incipient revolutionary traditions, discourses of memory and protest, constituted the counter-memory to the ever more dominant official memory of *la Revolución* constructed and imposed by Carrancismo. After 1915 the strains of Mexico's counter-memory of *la Revolución* became increasingly marginal, the property of fewer and fewer, disseminated in intermittent manifestos, a few pamphlets, books, and newspapers. The Convencionista government briefly published, in the winter and spring of 1915, for example, *La Convención*. Villistas published only two newspapers, both in Chihuahua. Of these, *Vida Nueva: Diario Político y de Información* was the official organ of Villismo and referred to itself as "the Voice of the Revolution."[44] The Zapatistas had no newspaper at all and made propaganda only through manifestos.[45] In February 1916, however, Zapata established the Centro Consultivo de Propaganda y Unificación Revolucionarias (Consultive Center of Propaganda and Revolutionary Unification) for the purpose of countering anti-Zapatista propaganda and convincing ordinary people that "*la Revolución* favors the people and cares for the protection of their rights."[46] The counter-memory survived, perhaps even thrived, however, in popular song and legend, what John Rutherford refers to as "the series of stories about the exploits and abilities of a particular revolutionary leader, which elevate him to the status of a hero in the eyes of his followers."[47] Only some of these stories, those in circulation before 1920, are available to historians.

Corridos presented both Villa and Zapata as popular caudillos, that is, leaders identified with the aspirations of the people in their struggle against the rich and powerful. Villa was predominantly portrayed in the early *corridos* as a violent, cyclonic force who inspired fear and terror in his enemies. He was also viewed during the struggle against Huerta, however, as an instrument of the popular will, as is reflected in this *corrido* recorded by John Reed: "Ambition will ruin itself / And justice will be the winner, / For Villa has reached Torreón / To punish the avaricious."[48] The struggle between Carranza and Villa was presented in a similar fashion. First Chief, warned one ballad, "don't fool yourself, you villain, with ambition for money. / Now we have begun to get rid of all these little traitors / and begun to trust in Villa and his supporters."[49] The Villa legend was even further enhanced following his attack in March 1916 on Columbus, New Mexico. The United States sent General John J. Pershing in command of an expeditionary force into northern Mexico to capture and punish Villa, but the caudillo eluded the gringos and became a symbol of national resistance.[50]

More than Villa, Zapata was presented in contemporary *corridos* as the personification and redeemer of the revolutionary ideals of land, liberty, peace, and justice. He "led the field as an inspiration for *corridos*."[51]

Con Zapata tendrá el pueblo
tierra, libertad y escuelas.[52]

With Zapata the people will have
land, liberty, and schools.

One *corrido* noted that the Plan of Ayala "defends religion / And gives land to those who ask."[53] Zapata's assassination in 1919 only enhanced the legend surrounding him and insured his remembrance: "The People of the South will never / forget in their souls / that General Emiliano / was their great Defender."[54]

While plans, pamphlets, and mainly *corridos* maintained the revolutionary counter-memory of the Villistas and Zapatistas, the Carrancistas in control of the federal government proceeded to impose their representation of *la Revolución* on the nation as the official memory. Carrancistas did this by several means. Throughout the country Carrancista generals established local offices of "Revolutionary Constitutionalist Propaganda and Information" and designated "Propaganda Agents of Revolutionary Action."[55] The director of the Puebla propaganda office informed Carranza, "our only objective is to publicize the ideals of the Constitutionalists, the liberties that are being given and the reforms that are being carried out by the decrees of the First Chief."[56] General Salvador Alvarado informed his propaganda agents, "it is necessary, as much for peons in the field as for workers in general, that they understand that the Constitutionalist Revolution is eminently on their side."[57]

A deluge of articles, pamphlets, and books poured from Carrancista pens and presses from 1913 to 1920.[58] This productivity was possible because, as Friedrich Katz writes, "the majority of intellectuals who participated in the revolution were in one way or another linked to the Carranza faction."[59] Throughout the country and outside of it, Carrancistas defended the cause, its heroes and martyrs, principles and ideals with great fervor and commitment. Carrancistas had learned from the Maderista experience. Part of the propaganda campaign was orchestrated by the leadership and published by official and semiofficial presses. The Carranza regime maintained subsidized, partisan newspapers: *El Constitucionalista* (1913–16), *El Pueblo* (1914–16), *El Demócrata* (1914–26), *El Mexicano* (1915), *La Opinión* from the press of the former Huertista *El País*, and in the provinces *El Paso del Norte* in Ciudad Juárez, *El Progreso* in Laredo, *La Revolución* in Monterrey, *Tierra* in Matamoros, and *El Pueblo* in Veracruz, among many others. (The regime also repressed dissident and opposition papers, arrested editors and journalists, and censored books and plays. The conservative *Mexican Herald*, for example, which had published in Veracruz during the American occupation in 1914, was denied permission to resume publication in any city in Mexico.)[60]

In 1913, the artist Geraldo Murillo, who rechristened himself as Dr. Atl, supported the Constitutionalist cause in Paris with the newspaper *La Revolution au Mexique*, whose editorials supposedly helped to prevent a French loan to the Huerta government.[61] He returned to Mexico in late 1913. During the fall of that year, Dr. Atl gathered together in Orizaba, Veracruz, a number of writers and artists informally known as the Jungle Group to support the Carrancista movement and to attract additional support. Dr. Atl obtained the support of the anarcho-syndicalist Casa del Obrero Mundial (House of the Workers of the World) and, with that help, shipped by train from Mexico City the printing presses and linotype machines of *El Imparcial*, the former official newspaper of Porfirismo. The group, which included José Guadalupe Zuno, Ramón Alva de la Canal, David Álfaro Siqueiros, and José Clemente Orozco—as well as the typographers of the Casa—published a revolutionary newspaper, *La Vanguardia*, and "set up presses and printed reams of literary and graphic propaganda."[62] Dr. Atl, Orozco later wrote in his memoirs, "would occupy the pulpit and preach the ideals of the Constitutionalist Revolution."[63]

When Carranza retreated to Veracruz in late 1914, the "Constitutionalist Government Press" began to issue pamphlets and books attacking Villistas and Zapatistas and praising the actions of Carranza. In Veracruz, and later in Mexico City, dependencies of the national government published pamphlets and books recounting and defending *la Revolución*, and Carranza and a number of his officials presented official interpretations of it.[64]

Also in late 1914, Obregón and a number of like-minded associates, notably Dr. Atl and Jesús S. Soto, formed the Confederación Revolucionaria (Revolutionary Confederation) to influence the ideological direction of the Constitutionalist movement and to promote its ideas and ideals through musical and literary programs as well as speeches and propaganda. The Revolutionary Confederation established a number of newspapers in provincial cities and even one on board a military train.[65] "I have confidence in [my] power to unite to our cause workers, students, and the middle class," Dr. Atl informed Carranza in January 1915. "He organized public meetings, dedicated schools, spoke to groups both large and small, arranged speaking engagements for Obregón and other revolutionary 'names,' and engaged in a wide variety of activities, all in the name of Carranza."[66] When the Carrancistas were back in Mexico City in early 1915 this group was able to convince the Casa del Obrero Mundial to support *la Revolución* (and the Carranza faction) with fighting "Red Battalions."[67]

"Teachers of revolutionary ideas" were drawn to Veracruz during the crisis, according to Félix Palavicini, Carranza's minister of public instruction and fine arts. Not knowing exactly what to do with them at first, the Constitutionalist government came to see the educators as political missionaries and dispatched them throughout the Republic in February 1915. These maestros were sent out, Palavicini stated, "as revolutionary propagandists and as liberal educators."[68]

It was also important to Carrancistas that the rest of the world, particularly the United States, understand the Mexican revolution the same way as they did. The Mexican Information Bureau was set up in the United States precisely for this purpose. No other revolutionary faction "matched the Carrancistas' capacity to initiate systematic, coordinated campaigns— in English and Spanish—at the national and international level."[69] Articles such as Carlo de Fornaro's "The Great Mexican Revolution" (*The Forum*, 1915) put forth the Carrancista line that "no compromise with the enemies of the Revolution, unconditional surrender were the watch words of Carranza."[70] Luis Cabrera in 1916 lectured the American Academy of Political and Social Science in Philadelphia, giving a scientific and objective interpretation of *la Revolución* that was also the Carrancista interpretation.[71] This meeting was just one stop on his speaking tours. Luis Bossero toured forty-two American colleges on behalf of Carranza. *Gales Magazine*, a Carrancista publication by the Marxist revolutionary Linn Gale, supported the cause in the United States, as did the Latin American News Association and the Columbus Publishing Company.[72]

Carrancistas also organized or sanctioned commemorations of significant revolutionary events, notably the assassinations of revolutionary martyrs (such as Serdán, Madero, and Pino Suárez) and the promulgation of the 1913 Plan of Guadalupe, to fix in memory a particular interpretation of the revolution. From 1915 to 1920 the Carrancistas clearly downplayed the significance of the first (Maderista) stage of *la Revolución* while emphasizing the second (Constitucionalista) stage of the "the Great Movement of Redemption." While due reverence was given to Madero as the "enlightened apostle and sublime martyr of the newborn Mexican democracy," Maderistas often came under severe criticism. With the assassination of Madero, noted *El Demócrata* in November 1915, "the 'official family' of the apostle fled cowardly."[73] In time, March 26—the date of the Plan of Guadalupe—came to outshine November 20 as the day of remembrance of *la Revolución* in the Carrancista calendar: "the most glorious date in the annals of our great Revolution."[74] No opportunity was missed, of course, to denigrate and condemn the "unfaithful Villistas" and the "Zapatista hordes" and to remind Mexicans that "there are many who have appeared to be revolutionaries but really are not."[75]

Numerous Carrancistas participated in the construction of the official memory of the revolution, yet their individual accounts were remarkably consistent. As discussed above, Carrancistas adopted and modified the Maderista collective memory of *la Revolución*. Díaz and *la Dictadura* were vilified, Madero and the other early martyrs were sanctified, and the political errors of Maderismo were identified.[76] Madero's errors and weaknesses, however, were presented as virtues: he preferred martyrdom rather than compromise of his democratic principles. "Madero, so good himself, believed that everyone else was as good, that everyone was as noble as he was, and that they were as incapable of evil doing as he was."[77]

La Revolución itself was reified, capitalized, and invested with enormous significance: "it has reached like no other revolution," Luis Sierra Horcasitas remarked, "an unusual importance and immense glory, because it has made us see its outstanding creativity."[78] To an even greater degree than in Maderista discourse, *la Revolución* for Carrancistas was the Prime Mover and the Great Signifier. According to General Silvino García, "*La Revolución* restores dignity to the peasant and the poor small farmer, and impels agriculture and raises the spirit of the worker."[79]

La Revolución according to Carrancistas was as significant as the French Revolution and was a continuation of Mexico's great revolutions of the nineteenth century. "Today we are imitating our big sister—France," declared the editors of the *Anuario Constitucionalista* in 1916.[80] "The Mexican Revolution," Antonio Manero noted, "is a social and economic Revolution, as justified and as comprehensive as the French Revolution."[81] "This revolution," an anonymous Carrancista wrote, "began with national independence."[82] For another, "the Constitutionalist Revolution is, then, the continuation of the Revolution of the Reform, interrupted by a prolonged plutocratic reaction."[83] It is nothing less than, according to General García, "the Mexican Revolution from 1810 to the present."[84]

The usurpation of power by Huerta represented the counterrevolution of the Reaction. Like Maderistas, Carrancistas defined this monster as a composite of *científicos*, plutocrats, and militarists. A number of Carrancistas, however, also added the clergy and privileged foreigners (particularly Spaniards and North Americans) to this list. In an interview in 1915, Obregón put the clergy in historical perspective:

Those who excommunicated Hidalgo and Morelos and applauded their murders, those who curse the memory of Juárez, those who allied themselves with Porfirio Díaz in order to make a mockery of the laws of Reform, those who applauded the assassin Huerta and came to terms with him, those who today acclaim Villa, will never be able to do good, ever. They will do nothing for our afflicted nation, which will curse them forever.[85]

Huerta was the supreme villain for Carrancistas: the Judas, the "new Santa Anna," the jackal, "the Zapotec Caligula," and "the legitimate son of Cain."[86] Ramón Puente, a Constitutionalist who would later become one of Villa's house intellectuals, saw him as "ugly, but a rare and cruel ugliness."[87] Huerta was, wrote an anonymous Carrancista, "the point of convergence of all reactionary interests."[88] Was this the betrayal of only one soldier? "No, it was the betrayal of all military chiefs, of all officials and even all federal soldiers."[89] By betraying Madero, Huerta unleashed the *torrente revolucionario*—the revolutionary flood—led by Carranza.

The Constitutionalist struggle against Huerta was nothing less than the people in arms against the Reaction. "The Army of *la Revolución* is the vote in arms."[90] With Carranza "was the soul of the people, the anonymous mass of the underdogs, of the exploited, of the enslaved."[91] The Plan of Guadalupe, "an austere and wise statute," gave the movement its legal character and wisely sought only the restoration of the constitutional order, the guarantee of human rights, and punishment for the crimes of 1913: it was "a war cry of plain ideas and a call to chivalry."[92] The Revolution of 1913, nevertheless, was more radical than was the Revolution of 1910, since "the ideal of 'class cooperation' of Madero went with him to the grave. With Carranza came the 'class struggle'."[93] The defeat of Huerta in the summer of 1914 did not yet signal the defeat of the Reaction nor the complete triumph of *la Revolución*.

"Militarism and clericalism would not accept defeat, and so the Reaction appeared with a new determination, and began to provoke division within the very ranks of the triumphant Revolution."[94] Carrancistas rarely described Villa and Zapata as reactionaries; these two caudillos were more generally depicted as instruments ("unconscious perhaps")[95] of the Reaction. Villa "was the most suited type to serve the machinations of those conservative henchmen. He obeyed with docility."[96] Luis Cabrera warned the convention at Aguascalientes in 1914 that Villa sought the reestablishment of order, not transcendent reform, therefore he "interprets *la Revolución* in a way completely contrary to the way both the soldiers and civilians present here understand it."[97] For Manuel Aguirre Berlanga, Villa "was no more than a figurehead [of the reactionary element]; the intellectual director was found elsewhere."[98] Pascual Ortiz Rubio traced Villa's treason against *la Revolución* to his brief but revealing disloyalty to Madero in the spring of 1911.[99] Another Carrancista, however, was able to link Maderismo and Villismo without defaming Madero. Antonio Manero charged that Villa was "unfaithful to Madero and to Carranza; the point of convergence of the reactionary interests that surrounded the administration of the Martyr President." Therefore: "Villa is the Maderista reaction."[100]

Zapatismo, likewise, "is nothing more than a service to conservative interests, hiding its betrayal behind a false revolutionary mask."[101] Some Carrancistas had difficulty portraying Zapata and Zapatismo as reactionary. For Dr. Atl, Zapatismo was genuinely revolutionary until it opposed Carranza, after which time "it had rapidly become a dangerous element of the reaction by providing direct help to the Division of the North and because elements of an intense religious fanaticism had developed within it."[102] For Alfredo Aragón, Zapatismo in 1910–11 was the party of "social redemption." After July 1914, however, "it degenerated into banditry."[103] Manuel Gamio distinguished three tendencies within Zapatismo: "banditry," "reactionary Zapatismo," and "legitimate and indigenous Zapatismo."[104] In most Carrancista accounts, however, Zapatismo was nothing but "hordes of bandits,"[105] the history of Zapatismo, nothing but "a long, frightfully criminal farce."[106] Zapatismo's "radical communism," argued González-Blanco not altogether logically, represented "the most absurd reactionary ideal."[107] Zapata and Villa belonged in the company of other reactionary counterrevolutionaries like Pascual Orozco, Félix Díaz, Felipe Ángeles, and even Victoriano Huerta.

Carrancistas did not simply denigrate the revolutionary credentials of their enemies; they were equally passionate in defending the revolutionary character of the "old man" and the cause. Carranza was "the immaculate caudillo, the humble and talented man; someone without personal ambition."[108] He was often compared to Juárez ("whose situation was identical to that of 1862"), since both fought to restore constitutional government in Mexico.[109] If Madero was the apostolic Juárez, "Carranza was the severe Juárez."[110] Carrancistas presented Carranza as stern, stubborn, austere, and incorruptible: "that integrity of his character, an integrity that even his enemies recognized."[111] His loyalists found this strength of character most attractive, but they were unable to transform Carranza into a popular hero. Contemporary *corridos* suggest that he failed "to capture the imagination of the people [el pueblo]."[112] Álvaro Obregón, the most popular and successful of Carranza's generals, did not have this problem.[113]

During the struggle against Villa, in December 1914 Carranza issued the Additions to the Plan of Guadalupe which, along with additional decrees and the actions of Constitutionalist caudillos, endowed *la Revolución* with its social and economic content. For Professor Lucio Tapia, this represented nothing less than Carranza, "Moses of the Mexican People," returning from "the Revolutionary Sinai" with "the brand-new Ten Commandments."[114] Carranza, according to Félix Palavicini, "designed a revolutionary program that the [Aguascalientes] Convention never could define. . . . The core of *la Revolución* was condensed in the Decree of December 12, called 'Additions to the Plan of Guadalupe.'"[115] The revolutionary strategy followed by Carranza was obvious: "first, war against the exalted criminals; then, the reform of our society."[116] Finally, some two years later, loyal Constitucionalistas wrote a new constitution for Mexico. Carranza noted that "the Constitution of 1917 entrusts the economic, political, and social ideals for which we have struggled."[117]

The speeches of the constitutional convention held in the city of Querétaro in late 1916 and early 1917, called by Carranza, revealed the consistencies and fissures within Carrancista memory. The past came up at the start of the sessions as *constituyentes*—convention delegates—judged each others' revolutionary qualifications. At issue was not the meaning or significance of *la Revolución* but how faithfully individuals followed, reflected, and adhered to it. (And, in the present, whether Carranza's closest advisors should guide the process of constitutional revision.) One controversy had to do with the Renovadores, the Maderista congressional deputies who accepted Madero's resignation in February 1913 and remained in the chamber following the coup. Were their intentions to save Madero and oppose Huerta or just the reverse? Others were accused of being Porfirista, Felicista (followers of Félix Díaz), Villista, even Zapatista. "You sir are a traitor, a Convencionista," Manuel Amaya accused Colonel Aguirre Escobar, "you are no friend of the revolution because you are no friend of the Chief [Carranza]."[118]

Alfredo Aragón in 1915 summarized the Carrancista perspective of recent history and politics in his "synoptic chart":

GRAL. PORFIRIO DÍAZ
The Great Dictator
Reelected, under the threat of Bayonets.
(30 November 1876–May 1911)

PARTIES OF UNCONDITIONAL SUBMISSION:

Porfirista, Born with the Plan of Tuxtepec

Científico, Formed by the plutocracy, the clergy and the favorites of the tyrant

Corralista, Initated to elevate to the Vicepresidency of the Republic a man who would prolong the Porfirian regime upon the disappearance of the Dictator

PREREVOLUTIONARY PARTIES:

Democratico, Composed of young people from all parties with the tendency to prepare for the future with a political institution

Anti-reeleccionista, Formed by elements contrary to the administration and by Tuxtepecanos deceived by Gral. Díaz

Nacionalista Democratico, Composed by workers under the direction of some intellectuals. This party was the first to view the social problem in the context of politics.

PARTIES WITH REVOLUTIONARY TENDENCIES:

Reyista, Headed by Free Masons and moderate Revolutionaries of good faith, who advanced Gral. Bernardo Reyes for the Vicepresidency, trusting in the forthcoming death of Gral. Díaz.

Maderista, Fusion of the Nacionalista Democratica y Antireeleccionista parties, openly revolutionary and reformist.

FRANCISCO I. MADERO
The Great Democrat
President Elect by the unanimous will of the people.
(6 November 1911–22 February 1913)

OROZQUISTA PARTY:
who initiated a revolution of personal ambition

REYISTA PARTY:
whose revolt aborted due to the prestige of its caudillo

FELICISTA PARTY:
which in union with dispersed elements of reyismo and porfirismo, and supported by the military and all manner of reactionaries, cowardly assassinated the leaders of the nation, don Francisco I. Madero and don José María Pino Suárez, and put Victoriano Huerta in power.

GRAL. VICTORIANO HUERTA
The Usurper
(22 February 1911–July 1914)

FELICISTA PARTY:
which died ridiculously upon the flight from the country of its chief

HUERTISTA PARTY:
composed of the most corrupt elements of the country

CONSTITUCIONALISTA PARTY:
headed by don Venustiano Carranza, who launched the armed

LIC. FRANCISCO L. DE LA BARRA

The White President

Elected to the Interim Presidency by the will of the Maderista Revolution following the Treaty of Ciudad Juárez.

(June–November 1911)

MADERISTA PARTIES:

Revolutionary

MADERISTA–PINISTA, Put forward by the Partido Constitucional Progresista

MADERISTA–VAZQUISTA, Put forward by former elements of the Partido Anti-reeleccionista

MADERISTA–IGLESISTA, Put forward by the Partido Liberal

Reactionary

MADERISTA–BARRISTA, Put forward by the Partido Católico

ZAPATISTA PARTY: for social reform

REYISTA PARTY:
President, Gral. Bernardo Reyes, Vicepresident, Lic. José Peón del Valle,
Formed by prominent elements of Freemasonry and the army and what was left from the Científico elite

VENUSTIANO CARRANZA

The Reformer

First Chief of the Constitutionalist Army, charged with Executive Power.

CONVENCIONALISTA PARTY:
Villista, composed of Científicos, reactionaries, the remains of the federal army and a very few revolutionaries

Zapatista, which degenerated into banditry

CONSERVATIVE PARTY:
formed in the United States under the patronage of the Ex-Archbishop of Mexico, José María Mora y Río.

INTERVENTIONIST PARTY:
integrated by pseudo-aristocrats and plutocrats, in agreement with the Conservative Party

CONSTITUCIONALISTA PARTY:
winner in the armed struggle against the usurpation, that day by day advances in the implementation of the reforms which cost so much blood to win

struggle in defense of our overthrown Institutions, our repressed rights and our wounded liberties, and formed by the revolutionary falange of the North, and some good elements of Maderismo.

From Alfredo Aragón, ¡A las Armas! 1916

The debates regarding revolutionary credentials dredged up a lot of history. The confusing vagaries of political alliances and shifting loyalties, particularly at the local and regional levels, forced a number of revolutionaries to explain away odd bedfellows. Only individuals "perfectly identified with the Constitutionalist revolution" were acceptable, which meant that delegates with excellent Maderista ties were not above suspicion and had to demonstrate their loyalty to the First Chief. Many disputes about the past were actually the first signs of a new fracture within Constitutionalism, a divide between rising Obregonistas and diehard Carrancistas.[119]

Constituyentes, despite their disputes over pedigrees, generally agreed that the Querétaro convention was the culmination of *la Revolución*. "The revolutionary spirit," stated Gerzayn Ugarte, "can inspire us to put in the Magna Carta those principles that the revolution demands." Francisco Múgica suggested at the beginning of the convention that the assembly constituted "the real triumph of *la revolución*, because at this moment the consummation of all the ideals of this august revolution and the attainment of all the conquests for which we have dreamed, fought for in the field of battle, and for which so many have given the supreme sacrifice, depends upon the judgment of these legitimate representatives of the Mexican people."[120]

When the 1917 constitution was promulgated, elections were scheduled and in May Carranza was elected constitutional president for the term 1917–1920. During his constitutional presidency, Carranza's revolutionary reputation practically disappeared. For Carranza, as Madero before him, the revolution was over, even though he viewed his government as one that "emanated from the revolution."[121] He repressed his former labor allies when they dared to go on strike and barely lifted a finger to redistribute land to peasant farmers, while returning confiscated haciendas to their former owners. The cautious Carranza sought order and progress and refused to enforce those articles of the constitution pertaining to the Catholic church and the foreign oil companies. Under his direction or by his order Emiliano Zapata and Felipe Angeles were murdered or executed.

By the time of his constitutional presidency, Carranza had begun to create a new official history that ignored Maderismo almost completely. In this version, *la Revolución* was divided into three periods: the armed struggle against Huerta, the struggle against the Villista and Zapatista reaction when the government was in Veracruz, and the reestablishment of the constitutional order and the reconstruction of Mexico. "The constitutionalist triumph gave [Carranza]," writes Eugenia Meyer, "the right to construct his own 'history', the history of the winner."[122]

In 1920 it appeared Carranza would impose a virtually unknown civilian, Ignacio Bonillas, the Mexican ambassador to the United States, as his successor in the presidential elections against opposition candidate Álvaro Obregón. "Meester Bonillas," as he was popularly known, was well known to Obregón and his closest supporters as a fellow Sonoran and a Maderista in 1910–11. Carranza desperately wanted to hand over power to a civilian, undoubtedly one he could influence or control. To nearly everyone else in Mexico, however, Obregón was the heir apparent. Carranza's political blindness and legendary stubbornness, and a conflict with the state of Sonora, led to a revolt by the state and the defection of much of the new revolutionary army. Carranza again, as in 1914, attempted a tactical retreat to Veracruz but was killed near Tlaxcalantongo in the state of Puebla.

At least one dogmatic Carrancista interpreted these events as the revenge of Maderismo. "In 1920 Maderistas, full of rancor and full of envy of the work they were unable to achieve and always inclined to militarism," Antonio Islas Bravo argued, "launched armed thrusts against the Chief of *la Revolución* and preached among the troops the urgent need to kill him." Once their purpose was achieved, "they danced in Tlaxcalantongo upon the corpse of the hero."[123]

Carrancismo had been defeated and, to a considerable extent, discredited. "Don Venustiano had too little appeal in the popular imagination for anyone to bother about embellishing his death scene," Todd Downing wrote in 1940. "I never heard a *corrido* in which he played the part of hero."[124] This changed not only the national political landscape but also the symbolic field: *la Revolución* was open to some revision. It resuscitated the Maderista tradition and placed the three predominant revolutionary traditions that had emerged from the anti-Huerta struggle, Zapatismo, Villismo, and Carrancismo, on a more equal playing field in the contest of shaping memory. These were now under the official supervision, of course, of one incipient tradition, Obregonismo. Revolutionary factionalism permeated the political scene and factional grudges were deeply felt, not least because they had a history. Mexico entered the newly proclaimed era of reconstruction divided by memory.

3 1920-1928

"Political domination involves historical definition." [1]

DURING THE 1920S, successive Mexican governments turned to *la Revolución* for legitimacy. *La Revolución*, as they received it, was indispensable but incomplete. The *voceros de la Revolución*, increasingly a part of the government bureaucracy, still worked on interpreting and defining the great event of their age. The Sonorans and their *voceros* provided two innovations in the continually developing discourse of memory. First, *la Revolución* was transformed into government ("la Revolución hecha gobierno") and was thus perceived as permanent and ongoing. Second, *la Revolución* was unified by a "revolutionary family" in which feuds would be forgotten if not entirely forgiven. The Sonorans worked to unify opposing revolutionary factions present and past and began to heal the wounds of memory. By 1928 *la Revolución*, under construction since 1911, was largely complete but for a few flourishes and some fine touches.

The Agua Prieta rebellion in 1920 brought to power at the national level the Sonorans, a regional branch of the Constitutionalist–Carrancista movement led by Obregón, Adolfo de la Huerta, and Plutarco Elías Calles. The Sonorans' newly obtained anti-Carranza credentials, and Obregón's reputation as a more radical politician than Carranza, facilitated the pacification of the country. Rebel groups long opposed to Carranza, such as the Zapatistas, seconded the rebellion. Interim president de la Huerta negotiated an agreement with Francisco Villa by which the rebel caudillo recognized the new government and in return was granted a hacienda, permitted an armed guard, and given a pension. Former Maderistas and Convencionistas who could not stomach Carranza, including José Vasconcelos and Francisco Lagos Chazaro, identified with the movement. "The death of Carranza," Vasconcelos wrote in 1920, "has been like a wave of peace. Carranza's disappearance has been enough for the enemies of yesterday to seek reconciliation; for all Mexicans of every opinion to once again feel like brothers." [2] In addition, the future secretary of education called upon "all of the intellectuals of Mexico to leave your ivory towers to sign a pact of alliance with the Revolution." [3]

Conciliation in the present was applied to the past. The Sonorans began the forging in official memory of the "Revolutionary Family," a term coined (or more likely popularized) by Obregón. The ambivalence that Carrancistas had held toward Madero and the Maderistas disappeared under the Sonorans. Madero once again became the unequaled revolutionary hero and Obregón his legitimate political heir. "To be Obregonista today," Vasconcelos remarked, "is the same as having been Maderista yesterday."[4] The Agua Prieta rebellion represented the "continuation of the popular movement initiated by Madero."[5] Congress made November 20, 1920, a "day of national celebration," and officials visited the tombs of Madero and Pino Suárez every February 22 on the anniversary of their assassinations. Madero's Plan of San Luis Potosí was again commemorated, while Carranza's Plan of Guadalupe was officially forgotten.[6]

In the new revision of official memory, Carranza and Carrancismo were reduced to an unfortunate deviation: "the tragic interim of the Carrancista period during which the values of *la Revolución* were transmuted and for a time defeated."[7] Obregón believed the Reaction had smothered and de-revolutionized Carranza. Calles, in a 1924 analysis of recent history, noted that Carranza "tried to turn away from the goals of *la Revolución* and was brought down as a result."[8] Carranza was often presented as an instrument of the Reaction and a traitor to *la Revolución* and was even placed alongside Díaz and Huerta in the national pantheon of despots. In this revision, it was Obregón who "consummated the victory of the Revolution in 1914." Finally, not even the achievements of the Constitution of 1917 were credited to Carranza: its agrarian and labor reforms were said to have been achieved by revolutionaries of good faith "in spite of the howling and stubborn manipulation of Carrancismo."[9] One marker of the new reordering was the 1921 renaming of Mexico City's Calle Jesús Carranza, which showed that even the surname, in this case attached to the former president's brother, was anathema.[10]

"Recently," Luis Olivares Sierra informed Juan Barragán in 1923, "Carrancistas have not been looked upon very favorably." This was, he continued, because "a majority of our old friends have joined de la Huerta."[11] Adolfo de la Huerta, who had rebelled against Obregón's impending imposition of Calles as his successor in 1923, similarly informed Barragán that "most Carrancistas like Generals [Manuel] Diéguez and [Cándido] Aguilar are with us."[12] The defeat of the De la Huerta rebellion further enhanced the power of Obregón and Calles and further tarnished the reputations of the Carrancistas. At the end of his term, however, in a conciliatory gesture Obregón awarded a pension to the children of Carranza because "Venustiano Carranza gave eminent services to *la Revolución* and to the nation." Julia Carranza and her brothers rejected the pension in a letter to Obregón that was signed, "Your loyal enemies." [13]

Zapatismo was finally accorded revolutionary status in official memory in the 1920s. High government officials attended the commemorations of Zapata's assassination, held in Cuautla and Cuernavaca every April, to praise the "apostle of agrarianism." Historical rehabilitation was such that the Porfirian-era iconoclast Francisco Bulnes in 1923 claimed that there existed "a cult of Zapata among revolutionaries." [14] In March 1923, President Obregón proclaimed in Cuernavaca that "the men of Morelos are, without a doubt, the best representatives of one of the ideals that came from the marrow of *la Revolución* and that is the agrarian ideal." [15] The Zapatistas returned the favor. At the first Congreso Nacional Agrarista (National Agrarian Congress) in June 1923, former Zapatista Soto y Gama praised Obregón as "the executor of the ideas of Emiliano Zapata." Before Zapata's tomb in April 1924 presidential candidate Calles declared that "this revolutionary program of Zapata, this agrarian program, is mine." [16] At that same ceremony former Zapatista Manuel Carpio sealed the bargain: "we have here today a man who will follow the road begun by the martyr Zapata: General Calles." [17]

The Magonistas, similarly, were retroactively incorporated as official actors in *la Revolución*. In 1922, Congress paid homage to Ricardo Flores Magón (who had died in a prison in the United States on November 21, 1922) and agreed to return his remains and to fly the national flag at half-mast. In the congressional chamber, Deputy Antonio Díaz Soto y Gama proclaimed that Flores Magón "is, for all of us, the teacher, the true founder, the intellectual author of *la Revolución Mexicana*." [18] For her part, Maria Flores Magón refused to permit the Mexican government to transport her husband's remains from Los Angeles and instead accepted the offer of transport by the Railroad Workers Alliance. [19] The national government honored Flores Magón when his body was returned to Mexico City hoping, his brother Enrique Flores Magón explained, "to win the love of the people." [20]

"The noble figure of Felipe Angeles," Francisco Madero's friend and a Villista general, was also rehabilitated in official memory in the early 1920s since he, like Emiliano Zapata, had been a victim of Carrancismo. It was, however, Angeles the Maderista and not Angeles the Villista who was re-membered and honored.[21] Official memory of Villa and Villismo under the care of the Sonorans during the 1920s differed little from that of the Carrancistas. Villa the instrument of the Reaction—"that terrible Genghis Khan"—became Villa the large landowner—"a comfortable bourgeois"—in the early 1920s.[22] Villa's assassination in July 1923 did little to soften the remembrance by Obregón and his followers.[23] In an address in 1927, Obregón said that the Reaction in 1914 "provoked a new betrayal within the ranks of *la Revolución*, and it was then when, headed by Francisco Villa, the hordes of that false revolution attempted to snatch away the rights and liberties of the people."[24]

Villa was a legend even before his death, and *corridos* following his assas-sination tended to idealize the image of the heroic caudillo. Villa was por-trayed as a fighter for justice with no personal ambitions. In "The Death of Francisco Villa," the caudillo was even described as benign: "Villa al-ways the loyal soldier, / always good and sincere, / came to revenge the be-trayal / that came to Madero."[25] In popular legend and the reminiscences of still loyal ex-Villistas or admirers such as Ramón Puente, Elías L. Torres, Rafael Muñoz, and Teodoro Torres, Jr., the Villista counter-memory per-severed and even thrived.

Former Carrancistas defended their absent leader and his place in his-tory against the disparagement of the Sonorans. General Marciano Gon-zález of Nuevo León proclaimed at the 1923 convention of the Partido Cooperativo (Cooperative Party), "I was, I am, and I will always be proudly Carrancista, and I am convinced that the black moon of the imposition of Bonillas will not darken the great work of Carranza."[26] Carrancistas still bucked the Madero cult. For Ygnacio Urquijo, for example, Carranza rep-resented "the most noble historical figure in our history. Superior to Ma-dero in character and in administrative skill."[27] Antonio Islas Bravo argued that "it was not anti-reelectionism that overthrew General Díaz, but *la Re-volución*."[28] Thus, a Carrancista counter-memory, one deprived of a pop-ular legend, arose in the 1920s to keep alive the revolutionary credentials of the First Chief.

During his term as president, Obregón added little to the discourse that framed the new official memory of *la Revolución* in the early 1920s. Like Madero and Carranza when they achieved power, Obregón generally re-ferred to the revolution in the past tense, as the armed struggle that had concluded and triumphed. The Reaction, however, while defeated by *la Revolución*, nevertheless still existed in the present tense, still opposed revolutionaries, revolutionary principles, and the revolutionary government. The revolution for Obregón was primarily destructive, whereas his government marked the beginning of the reconstruction of Mexico. Obregón, like Carranza before him, did see a causal relationship between *la Revolución* and his government: it was a government that emanated from *la Revolución*. And, of course, "the Program of the Revolution," if not the revolution itself, was alive and well in the present.[29]

The Obregón administration's most important effort to shape national memory came with the 1921 commemoration of the centennial of the achievement of independence. The regime put considerable time and money into this affair, which emphasized Mexico's revolutionary origins, its native roots, and mestizo character. The commemoration also produced dissension concerning the heroic or reactionary role of Agustín de Iturbide, the royalist officer who obtained Mexican independence in reaction to a liberal revolution in Spain. Nevertheless, by emphasizing the traditional themes of Mexico's liberal synthesis, but also events for workers and "the people" in general and downplaying the role and significance of religion in the commemoration of national history, the regime sought to encourage a spirit of revolutionary nationalism among Mexicans.[30]

During Obregón's presidency, the national government assumed little responsibility for the remembrance of revolutionary martyrs and anniversaries. Instead, rituals of commemoration in the early 1920s were organized by associations of citizens. The Pro-Madero Group (Agrupación Pro-Madero), for instance, organized the commemorations of November 20 and February 22.[31] Government officials attended, spoke, and laid floral wreaths, but they left the organizing of the events to others. As *El Demócrata* noticed in November 1922: "there was no official ceremony at all."[32] Political parties and labor unions also got into the act: the Constitutionalist Liberal Party commemorated the deaths of Benjamin Hill and Felipe Ángeles; the National Agrarian Party (along with the state government of Morelos) commemorated the assassination of Zapata; and the Federation of Labor Syndicates, along with the Mexican Labor Party, commemorated the assassination of the Yucatecan socialist Felipe Carrillo Puerto.

Obregón, a practical man little given to ideas and symbols, did not need to give much importance and emphasis to establishing a legitimizing official memory of *la Revolución*. He was, as Linda Hall explains, "the primary revolutionary hero, the embodiment of the Revolution." Obregón represented the unity of history and biography: the legitimacy of his authority and his government, therefore, was self-evident.[33]

Obregón's successor, Plutarco Elías Calles, on the other hand, possessed no such advantage. While his revolutionary credentials were excellent, he was not the Caudillo of the Revolution and, even more, was thought "totally lacking in charisma."[34] To a degree far greater than Obregón, Calles needed to justify his authority, and he sought that justification in *la Revolución*. As a result, Calles made several important lasting contributions to the official memory of *la Revolución*. First and foremost, he reactivated the transcendental and reified revolution in order to construct the permanent revolution that inhabited the past, present, and future. "The Revolution has placed in my hands," Calles proclaimed during the 1924 presidential campaign, "the sacred banner of a program of social reforms."[35] Second, the national government did not simply follow or even emanate from *la Revolución*, rather *la Revolución* became the government and the government was *la Revolución*: "la Revolución hecha gobierno," the Revolution becomes government.[36]

It is interesting to note the degree to which Obregón by 1927 was following the lead of Calles in viewing *la Revolución* as an ongoing enterprise. "The spiritual revolution, the constant revolution," he proclaimed in San Luis Potosí in 1927, "this can never end while good and evil exist." A year later, during his presidential campaign, the Caudillo of the Revolution stated, "we must never think that the revolutionary effort has won a final victory, because our struggle against the reaction will exist for as long as man is on earth."[37]

It was during the Calles presidency that the national government began to assume greater responsibility for commemorating *la Revolución*. The Ministry of Government, in cooperation with the Pro-Madero Group, for example, organized the ceremonies commemorating the assassinations of Madero and Pino Suárez in February 1925.[38] Beginning in 1926 celebrations were organized by the Official Committee of Patriotic Commemoration (later called the Organizing Commission of Civic Ceremonies), which was established by the municipal government of Mexico City.[39] Commemorations during the Calles presidency were becoming relatively nonsectarian: the government participated in ceremonies praising Madero,

Carranza, Zapata, Flores Magón, and Carrillo Puerto. Calles himself, quite unlike Obregón, rarely criticized or disparaged any of the major revolutionary caudillos, including Villa.

From the beginning of the Calles administration, Callistas pressed for the unification of all revolutionaries, "those of today and yesterday." Miguel Yépez Solórzano, a member of the Mexico City government, lamented the "deep divisions within the breast" of the Revolution and called for "solidarity and cohesion of the social class that directed *la Revolución* in Mexico."[40] In his New Year messages to the Mexican people in 1926 and 1927, President Calles urged citizens to "forget grudges."[41] Obregonistas had begun the process of historical reconciliation and Callistas intended to continue and complete that process.[42]

The most striking statements of history made during the Calles presidency were certainly "the sermons in fresco."[43] What later came to be known as the great mural movement, the core of a Mexican cultural renaissance, began in 1921 during Obregón's presidency under the patronage of Education Minister José Vasconcelos. Artists were commissioned to paint walls to reflect Vasconcelos's philosophical idealism. David Álfaro Siqueiros drew up a "social, political, and aesthetic declaration" in 1922 for the Syndicate of Technical Workers, Painters, and Sculptors to guide the mural painters. This manifesto proclaimed:

> We repudiate the so-called easel art and all such art which springs from ultra-intellectual circles, to destroy bourgeois individualism.
> We hail the monumental expression of art because such art is public property.
> We proclaim that this being the moment of social transition from a decrepit to a new order, the makers of beauty must invest their greatest efforts in the aim of materializing an art valuable to the people, and our supreme objective in art, which is today an expression for individual pleasure, is to create beauty for all, beauty that enlightens and stirs to struggle.[44]

The "greatest public revolutionary art of this century" had assumed its full ideological aesthetic (revolutionary nationalism with a nod to Marxism) by 1923 or 1924.[45] At this early date the murals "were considered to occupy the forefront of Mexican artistic and intellectual life."[46] Surprisingly, the mural movement had no ideological guidance from the Ministry of Education or any other part of the government. The manifesto of the syndicate, furthermore, was less revolutionary than simply avant-garde and of little guidance concerning subject and message. The muralists had been influenced by the *voceros de la Revolución* and through their art joined their ranks. This public art—Octavio Paz calls it "the painted apologia of the ideological dictatorship of an armed bureaucracy"—became a significant element of the Revolutionary Tradition.

Although a number of artists participated in the movement, the intense David Álfaro Siqueiros, the melancholy, one-armed José Clemente Orozco, and Diego Rivera—"the court painter to the Mexican government"[47]— produced the best-known and most explicitly didactic historical murals. The first revolutionary (in content) murals were Siqueiros's *Burial of the Worker* and *Call to Liberty* in Mexico City's Escuela Nacional Preparatoria, the country's most important secondary school. Rivera's work particularly glorified and romanticized *la Revolución* as a peasant and worker's revolution and frequently portrayed Zapata and Zapatismo in the most positive light. His biographer Bertram D. Wolfe observed that Rivera "painted what the Revolution should be, what it should become."[48] Orozco painted in a monumental style that especially suited the reified revolution:

> What this treatment does to history, to real events such as departing to fight a revolution, is to turn it into a natural (that is, of nature), inevitable, and timeless event, or not an event at all but a condition about which humans can do nothing to change since the condition is made of them and vice versa, to the point that it is impossible to determine cause, effect, motivation, or the possibility of human agency. History happens because it does, because it is no different than nature, and nature no different than people. This is myth-making of a subtle but powerful sort.[49]

Rivera's frescos at the new Ministry of Education (Secretaría de Educación Pública, SEP) building in Mexico City and the National Agricultural School at Chapingo, executed between 1923 and 1928, constitute an epic portrait of *la Revolución*. The new Mexico was a land of proud and unbowed peasants and workers. *The Liberation of the Peon* depicts heroic sacrifice in the revolutionary struggle, while *The New School* reveals one of the objectives of struggle and sacrifice. Other objectives, such as revolutionary justice in *Death of a Capitalist* and *The Festival of the Distribution of the Land*, and progress in *The Mechanization of the Country*, are also vividly presented. One of the most striking mythic statements, *The Blood of the Revolutionary Martyrs Fertilizing the Earth*, is found at the chapel at Chapingo. This panel presents two martyred heros, Zapata and the Zapatista ideologue Otilio Montaño, buried in red shrouds beneath a fertile cornfield.[50]

Orozco's frescos at the Escuela Nacional Preparatoria in Mexico City and the Industrial School (Escuela Industrial) in Orizaba, Veracruz, completed between 1923 and 1926, are monumental scenes that tell of the tragedy of the revolutionary struggle. *The Rich Banquet* has dissolute plutocrats enjoying themselves while workers fight one another. The critic Salvador Novo has said that Orozco's pictures aimed to awake in the spectator "an anarchistic fury if he was penniless, or if wealthy, to make his knees buckle with fright."[51] Orozco's most optimistic fresco in Orizaba is *Social Revolution*, a scene placed over a doorway and showing peasants and workers, rifles slung over their shoulders, building the new Mexico. Even here, however, tragedy is not far away. In the side panels below the builders are huddled women, crying, showing fear, with one wiping the face of an exhausted soldier.[52] *The Trench*, Orozco's most famous image, shows two men who have fallen and one on his knees, a revolutionary trinity against a red background. Art historian Leonard Folgarait reads the picture as a sequence of the falling poses of one man: "an armed soldier dies in battle, which leads to a state of spiritual purity and immortality, and finally is given new life, starting to rearm (the gun belt returns), starting to rise, about to come out from his shroud. The Revolution lives."[53]

La Revolución as defined by Callistas embraced three great episodes: the Maderista struggle of 1910, the reform of the constitution or "Magna Carta" in 1917, and the implementation of the revolutionary program after 1920, which embraced the current regime. There were setbacks, in 1913 and 1923, "by corrupt and ambitious men."[54] The great enemy of *la Revolución* in Calles's writings and speeches, still dangerous and treacherous in the mid-to-late 1920s, was the Reaction. In 1924, Yépez Solórzano called for a war to the death against the "pirates of public opinion."[55] Calles nearly obliged. The following year he forced Nemesio García Naranjo into exile when the former Huertista denigrated *la Revolución* in a series of newspaper articles. Law professor Educardo Pallares, another critic, lost his position at the national university partly because to him "the word *revolucionario . . .* is the term that divides."[56]

Calles viewed Mexican history as "a hundred years of civil war against a Proteus-like oppressor who is now Spaniard, now the clergy."[57] According to Calles, the Reaction, "hiding behind the mask of religion," once again had thrown the country into civil turmoil when the Church repudiated the revolutionary Constitution of 1917 and the government required compliance with that statement of fundamental law. In fact, the Cristero rebellion of the late 1920s developed into a massive peasant insurgency that rivaled the Zapatista movement in intensity and size. Official commemorative discourse, of course, never made such a comparison and, then and later, essentially ignored the episode.[58]

During the Calles presidency, Obregón and his followers made the necessary political preparations and constitutional modification to return the great Caudillo to office in 1928. Obregonistas warned that Mexicans faced the unhappy choice of "Obregón or chaos." The reelection campaign, however, polarized politics and irritated the wounds of memory that Calles had tried to heal. On the anniversary of Madero's assassination in 1926, Federico Cervantes, an old Villista, praised the Apostle Madero and his true successor, Obregón, and condemned Carranza's "use of the dictatorial 'hard line'."[59] Carranza's attempt to institute a civilian regime in 1920 appeared to opponents, on the other hand, as a legitimate effort to combat militarism. In November 1926 the antireelectionist bloc predicted that Carranza "will win his last battle in spite of death."[60] Antonio Islas Bravo, one of those opponents and a congressional deputy, was particularly disturbed by Maderista ("members of the Perpetual Veil of Madero") support for tyrants like Villa in 1914, Obregón in 1920, and—worst of all—Obregón in 1928. "After 1910 [the Maderistas] rabidly embraced militarism. Without a doubt the Maderistas today are not behind *la Revolución* as they were in 1910."[61] The national convention of the new Anti-reelectionist Party in June 1927 was as pro-Carranza as it was anti-Obregón: "the name of Carranza received applause, vivas, and cheers when it was announced."[62]

This new irritation of the wounds of memory reflected growing political uncertainty and disorder. The internal order "seemed to be just on the verge of breaking down in mid-1927."[63] The government was fighting one of the largest popular rebellions—the Cristero rebellion—in Mexican history, a struggle that ultimately claimed 90,000 lives. In October 1927 two of Obregón's closest comrades-in-arms launched a rebellion against Obregón and Calles in an attempt to prevent the reelection and, as they saw it, the establishment of a new dictatorship. The rebellion faltered on the first day and was followed by a murderous purge of enemies of the regime. "After the bloody purge of 1927 no candidate had even the slightest chance against Obregón. . . . In this climate, the undisputed election of Obregón on July 1, 1928 was no surprise to anyone."[64]

Two weeks later José de León Toral, a Catholic fanatic, shot and killed the president-elect. The country's political establishment was stunned. "And now what? Everyone, it seemed, asked themselves."[65]

1928	In September, in his last *informe* to the nation, President Calles calls for an end to personalist leadership.	León Toral, Obregón's assassin, makes a print showing revolutionary Mexico mourning the Caudillo of the Revolution.
1929	The Partido Nacional Revolucionario (PNR) is founded by Calles, and Pascual Ortiz Rubio is nominated to be its presidential candidate in the election to complete the six-year term of Obregón.	On the twentieth of November, Revolution Day, the first annual sports parade is held in Mexico City. On the same occasion, Obregón's name is inscribed on the wall of the national congress.
1929	Ortiz Rubio wins the national election against the candidate of the Anti-reelectionist Party, José Vasconcelos. The President is shot and wounded by a would-be assassin on his inauguration day.	Between 1929 and 1935, Diego Rivera paints murals in the National Palace that present a panoramic history of Mexico on three walls.
1928– 1934	In the Maximato, Calles, as Jefe Máximo de la Revolución, exercises more political influence than the elected presidents Pascual Ortiz Rubio (1929–32) and Abelardo Rodríguez (1932–34).	In 1930, Yucatecan socialist Felipe Carrillo Puerto becomes the third hero of *la Revolución* to have his name inscribed on the wall of Congress. One year later the names of Carranza and Zapata are added.

1934– 1940	Lázaro Cárdenas is elected president in 1934 and within two years puts an end to the Maximato.	In 1935 the monument to Obregón is officially inaugurated in San Angel.
1936	Former President Calles is forced into exile in the United States.	The first monument to Carranza, designed by Dr. Atl, is erected on the site of his assassination.
1938	The regional rebellion of General Saturnino Cedillo in San Luis Potosí is crushed. The PNR is restructured and renamed the Partido de la Revolución Mexicana (PRM).	The Monument to the Revolution is completed but not officially inaugurated.
1940– 1946	The administration of President Manuel Avila Camacho	In 1942, Carranza's remains are deposited in a crypt within the Monument to the Revolution. *Hora Nacional* (Hour of the nation), a Sunday night patriotic radio program, begins broadcasting.
1946	The PRM is restructured and renamed the Partido Revolucionario Institucional (PRI).	The remains of Ricardo Flores Magón are reinterred in the national pantheon of heroes in Mexico City.
1947	For the first time in history, a president of the United States visits Mexico City.	President Harry S Truman, on the centennial of the American occupation of the city, pays homage to the monument to the Child Heroes, who lost their lives in the war.

1946–1952	The administration of President Miguel Alemán Valdés	In 1949 the PRI sponsors a competition for the best history of the revolution.
1950–1951	The new University City, the modern campus of the national university (UNAM), is inaugurated, the most prominent lasting achievement of the Alemán administration.	In 1950, Octavio Paz publishes *The Labyrinth of Solitude*, the most important book on Mexico of the century.
1952–1958	The administration of President Adolfo Ruiz Cortines	In 1953 the government establishes the Instituto Nacional de Estudios Históricos de la Revolución Mexicana (INEHRM)
1957	A wave of labor agitation and strikes begin.	An earthquake in Mexico City topples the Monument to Independence.
1958–1964	The administration of President Adolfo López Mateos	In 1958, Carlos Fuentes publishes his novel *Where the Air is Clear*.
1959	With the Cuban Revolution, Dictator Fulgencio Batista goes into exile and the rebel forces of Fidel Castro take control of the island.	Fuentes's second novel, 1960's *The Death of Artemio Cruz*, depicts the corruption of the Revolution.
1959	Federal troops repress a railroad strike and imprison 10,000 strikers. Two union leaders are imprisoned for ten years.	In 1959 the National Commission for Free Textbooks, led by Martín Luis Guzmán, is created and authorizes national primary textbooks.

1960	President Oswaldo Dorticós of Cuba makes an official visit to Mexico and President López Mateos favorably compares the Mexican and Cuban revolutions.	In 1960 the nation celebrates the fiftieth anniversary of the beginning of the Mexican revolution.
1962	Peasant leader and dissident Rubén Jaramillo of Morelos, with his wife and children, is murdered.	President John F. Kennedy visits Mexico City and prays at the Basilica of the Virgin of Guadalupe.
1964–1970	The administration of Gustavo Díaz Ordaz	The National Museum of Anthropology in Chapultepec is inaugurated in 1964, an architectural and cultural triumph.
1965	Militants, following the example of Fidel Castro, attack a military barracks in Chihuahua.	Pablo González Casanova publishes *Democracy in Mexico*, which contains severe criticisms of the system. In 1965, President Díaz Ordaz uses the army to end a doctors' strike.
1966–1968	The student protest movement is provoked by the military takeover of the Colegio de San Nicolás in Morelia, Michoacán.	
1968	In August 1968, 100,000 students march to the Zócalo, Mexico City's central plaza, to protest the military takeover of the national university's preparatory school.	In May the Paris student uprising occurs. In August, Soviet tanks and troops invade Czechoslovakia and crush the "Prague Spring."

In September the federal army occupies the national university.

The Catholic Church of Mexico issues a declaration in favor of the Mexican revolution.

On the night of October 2 soldiers and police surround protesters in Tlatelolco Plaza and open fire on the crowd. As many as 10,000 students are arrested and hundreds are killed.

On October 10 the Olympic Games officially open in Mexico City. On October 11, Daniel Cosío Villegas writes, "The government will fall into a disrepute that nothing and nobody will ever wash away."

Fig. 1. An altar dedicated to Francisco I. Madero and the Serdán brothers in Puebla, 1914. Source: Archivo Fotográfico del Instituto Nacional de Estudios Históricos de la Revolución Mexicana, Caja 8, Número 365, Archivo General de la Nación, Mexico City.

Fig. 2. A grand demonstration in honor of the martyr Aquiles [Serdán], Puebla, 1914. Source: Archivo Fotográfico del Instituto Nacional de Estudios Históricos de la Revolución Mexicana, Caja 8, Número 347, Archivo General de la Nación, Mexico City.

Monumento a Zapata
Cuautla Mor. #5   Fot. Aguirre

Fig. 3. Monument to Emiliano Zapata by sculptor Oliverio Martínez in Cuautla, Morelos, April 10, 1932. Source: Period postcard purchased in Mexico City flea market.

Fig. 4. Monument to General Alvaro Obregón, designed by architect Enrique Aragón, with the two exterior sculpture groups sculpted by Ignacio Asúnsola. Inaugurated in 1935. Source: Period postcard purchased in Mexico City flea market.

Fig. 5. "Revolution Day." An idealized portrait of the Revolutionary Family including Carranza, Zapata, Angeles, Obregón, Calles, and Cárdenas, 1935. Source: *Calendario Nacionalista y Enciclopedia Popular* (Mexico, D.F.: Partido Nacional Revolucionario, 1934). Private collection of the author.

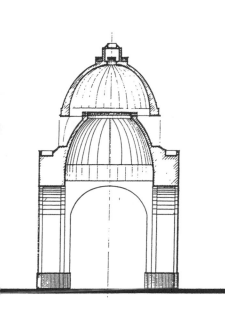

Fig. 6. The Monument to the Revolution.
Design of the double dome, 1933. Source:
*Catalogo de Monumentos Escultoricos y
Conmemorativos del Distrito Federal* (México,
D.F.: Oficina de Conservación de Edificos
Públicos y Monumentos, 1976). Private
collection of the author.

Fig. 7. The Monument to the Revolution,
Plaza de la República, Mexico City.
Architect, Carlos Obregón Santacilia.
Inaugurated 1938. Source: Period postcard
purchased in Mexico City flea market.
Private collection of the author.

Fig. 8. The Monument to the Revolution.
Sculpture group representing national
independence, located on the southeast
corner of the monument. Sculptor: Oliverio
Martínez. Photograph by Sharon Lee
House, 1995.

Fig. 11. Campaign poster: "From Madero to Cárdenas. For Effective Suffrage. November 20 in San Luis Potosí." In his presidential campaign of 1994, Cuauhtemoc Cárdenas sat in the jail cell which held Madero in 1910 to symbolize his solidarity with Madero's democratic struggle and with the Mexican Revolution. Photograph by Thomas Benjamin, 1994.

opposite

Fig. 9 (*above*). The remains of Venustiano Carranza are carried from the zócalo to the Monument to the Revolution, 1942. Source: Archivo Fotográfico del Instituto Nacional de Estudios Históricos de la Revolución Mexicana, Caja 8, Número 81, Archivo General de la Nación, Mexico City.

Fig. 10 (*below*). A meeting of the V. Carranza Association at the Monument to the Revolution on the 47th anniversary of the assassination of the president in 1947. Source: Archivo Fotográfico del Instituto Nacional de Estudios Históricos de la Revolución Mexicana, Caja 8, Número 75, Archivo General de la Nación, Mexico City.

Part Two
PERFORMANCE

In the summer of 1928 the *Caudillo de la Revolución* was assassinated. Obregón, not unlike Porfirio Díaz decades before, was not simply the strongman. He knew also how to play politics: how to balance interests and rivalries, how to conciliate and intimidate those individuals and groups he did not dominate. His abrupt disappearance from the scene led to the sharpening of knives, as another revolutionary schism of historic proportions threatened. President Calles tried to head off disaster by uniting all revolutionaries in one common political front, a national revolutionary party. Unity became the watchword of the era: in 1928 and after, this meant the unity of all revolutionaries and the political nation. Unity also included a historical dimension, the healing of the wounds of memory of 1911, 1914, and 1920. This was the purpose, first and foremost, of the Revolutionary Tradition: *la Revolución* transformed into remembrances, rites, celebrations, monuments, histories, and more. La Revolución hecha tradición.

The most immediate concern was presidential succession. In his last *informe*—the annual presidential address to Congress—in September 1928, President Calles declared the end of personalist rule in Mexico and the creation of a "nation of institutions and laws." The Revolutionary Family, he declared, had to unite to save itself and the country.[1] He stepped down at the end of his term of office in December and handed the presidency to a politician acceptable to both Obregonistas and Callistas, Emilio Portes Gil. The following year both factions agreed to the formation of a united party of all revolutionaries, the National Revolutionary Party (Partido

Nacional Revolucionario, PNR) and nominated Pascual Ortiz Rubio to be its candidate in the election of a president to complete the six-year term that was to have been Obregón's. Ortiz Rubio won the contest—his opponent was the Maderista true-believer José Vasconcelos—and occupied the office, but Calles, now the *Jefe Máximo de la Revolución*, exercised the greater power and authority.

During the period 1928 to 1934, known as the Maximato, the country saw a succession of three presidents. Mexico City residents wisecracked when they passed Chapultepec Castle, the president's residence, that "the president lives here, but the man who gives the orders lives across the street." Portes Gil negotiated an end to the Cristero rebellion and repressed the last serious military revolt against the national government. Ortiz Rubio got off to a bad start when he suffered a head wound as a result of an assassination attempt on the day of his inauguration. He had difficulty accepting the political direction of the Jefe Máximo and resigned in 1932. His successor, Abelardo Rodríguez, served the remaining two years of Obregón's term and knew how to take orders.

In 1934 the PNR nominated a young general who had fought in the revolution, Lázaro Cárdenas, as the party's candidate for the presidency. The official candidate searched for electoral support across the country to an extent not seen since Madero's 1910 campaign. As president, Cárdenas broke the Maximato and sent Calles into exile in the United States, redistributed more land than all of the previous regimes together, created a national peasant organization and a national labor confederation, and nationalized the foreign-owned oil companies. He reformed the official party, transforming it from an assembly of generals to a party of workers, peasants, bureaucrats, and soldiers organized corporatively: the renamed Party of the Mexican Revolution (Partido de la Revolución Mexicana, PRM). The Cárdenas administration reaffirmed the ideals of *la Revolución* more than any previous, or subsequent, Mexican government. At the end of his term he stepped down from power and did not seek a new Maximato. He set the pattern for the transfer of the office and the power of the presidency that is still followed today.[2]

From its formation, the official party and the government sought an influence broader than simply the political realm. This was not a new ambition but rather a more organized approach to cultural hegemony. Revolutionaries in the 1920s had attempted to revolutionize Mexican culture, as the conflict with the Church and militant Catholics demonstrated. The Ministry of Education under Vasconcelos sent cultural missions into the Mexican countryside to build schools, train teachers, organize recreation programs, and give instruction in agricultural techniques and personal hygiene.[3] As one critic explained in 1927, *la Revolución* had attempted to exercise an "irritating monopoly" over everything: art, science, politics, and the economy.[4]

The cultural program of the PNR was spelled out by the third party president, Portes Gil, in 1930. He proposed a "cultural hour" every Sunday, when revolutionaries in every *pueblo, ejido* (a revolutionary agrarian community), and labor union would gather to enjoy and learn from cultural programs of music, agricultural instruction, and simple presentations on hygiene, child care, and other topics of interest to the community. The PNR, it seems, was not willing to permit the Church to dominate Mexican culture, even on Sunday, without an effort. These Sunday programs and others through the week would be broadcast by radio to the entire country by new PNR-owned stations. One year later, President Ortiz Rubio reported that the Office of Central Broadcasting had given the people 6,758 cultural events and lectures.[5] The PNR also planned to take revolutionary culture to the people by means of cultural centers for workers and traveling social missions for campesinos (schools teaching reading and writing, music, sports, industrial arts and agriculture, as well as medical clinics and other useful services). Essentially, however, the goal of both the centers and the missions was the formation of "an advanced ideology consistent with the goals of *La Revolución.*"[6]

During his short term as party president (November 1930 to August 1931), Lázaro Cárdenas created the National Sports Confederation, which sought to organize the young, improve school attendance, and modernize customs. Mary Kay Vaughan has discovered that "in the 1930s politicians from Puebla city quickly perceived the role athletic events could play in incorporating local powers into the state political machine they were building."[7] As president of the nation, Cárdenas donated a radio receiver to every agricultural and workers' community in the country so that their residents could listen to the three state radio stations, one belonging to the Ministry of Education and the other two controlled by the official party.

In his famous "Proclamation of Guadalajara" of 1934, Jefe Máximo Calles declared that *la Revolución* was not over.

We have to enter a new phase, one that I would call the period of psychological revolution: we must enter and conquer the minds of the children, the minds of the young, because they do and they must belong to *la Revolución*.[8]

In the 1930s, writes Adrian Bantjes, "the Mexican revolutionary elite initiated a veritable cultural revolution."[9] The PNR's Six-Year Plan of 1934 stated that primary and secondary education should be based "in the orientations and postulates of the socialist doctrine that the Mexican Revolution supports." Under Cárdenas, "socialist education" sought to create for Mexico "the possibility of pulling itself together, culturally and economically, in revolutionary fashion."[10]

The official party's Committee of Propaganda and Cultural Action codified a new revolutionary calendar, a substitute for the old Christian calendar, that organized the year into new "holy days" that remembered, celebrated, and exalted the great events of the nation and *la Revolución*. Saints' days were replaced by nationalist and revolutionary anniversaries and fiestas, from Independence Day and Revolution Day to Day of the Precursors of the Revolution (June 11).[11]

The party and state also sought to shape political culture through the Revolutionary Tradition. The following chapters consider efforts to translate the past—*la Revolución*—into the present by means of festivals, monuments, and history.[12] Each of these are political tools that employ a performative language in different ways to different audiences. As Murray Edelman writes, "politics is in one sense a drama played simultaneously by and before many audiences in many different social settings."[13]

A political festival, of course, particularly a parade in this case, is the most dramatic of the three tools of tradition, although often the least commemorative. It was an important form of public entertainment—in the age before mass communication—imbedded with political symbolism and messages. As such, it draws the largest audience, one composed of both participants and spectators. A monument is no less a form of dramaturgy. The grandeur of a monument seeks itself to awe those who look upon it. A monument also communicates through symbols, but its messages are generally more serious and commemorative. Unlike the entertaining festival, a monument is a symbol and a place of reverence: a temple of a nation's civil religion. Official history is the least dramatic of these three tools, but it is the most intellectual and therefore is aimed at a quite small but influential audience. It is, or was, the foundation that authorized the messages, symbols, and historical representations portrayed in a more simple way by festivals and monuments. Certainly the government's official agency of revolutionary history, the National Institute of Historical Study of the Mexican Revolution, has exceeded its original and narrow role as the publishing house of official history. Since 1960 it has also participated in and guided the official commemorative anniversary festivals: those celebrating *la Revolución* but also Independence and the Reform. In the process, it has become perhaps the most important institutional sponsor of the Revolutionary Tradition.

Like political speech and performances generally, these three tools evoke and reinforce political reassurance, social solidarity, and quiescence among the citizenry at large. They were also aimed at the political class itself, which was divided by memory as well as interest. *La Revolución* in performance sought to heal those wounds of memory and, for a time, largely succeeded in doing so.

4 FESTIVAL

A Vigorous Mexico Arising

REVOLUTION DAY, the twentieth of November, is one of Mexico's most important patriotic festivals. On this day every year Mexicans remember and celebrate *la Revolución*. This day commemorates specifically November 20, 1910, the date selected by Francisco I. Madero for the popular uprising against the dictator Porfirio Díaz. As a commemorative festival, the twentieth of November became an instrument of civic education: "this experience constitutes one of the essential ties of our nationality," stated the civic yearbook of Mexico City. Through this annual celebration the people of Mexico were and are engaged "in the task of constructing a worthy and sovereign country."[1] In the rites and words devoted to this day, *la Revolución* was and still is integrated into the religion of the patria.

Civic holidays and celebrations serve a number of purposes. Commemorative festivals are designated, fundamentally, to present the past to the present. On these days orations, symbols, and rituals transmit the dominant myths of a society, reaffirming and reminding its members of their historic identity, shared values, and common understandings.[2] Mirabeau spoke to their power: the best way, he noted, "of acting powerfully on men in the mass is by means of public festivals."[3] Commemorative festivals also reshape the past (that is, the representation of the past) to meet the needs of the present. Collective memory is transfigured as well as transmitted so that the past can better sanction the particular (most commonly, the dominant political) arrangements of the present.[4] Official memory is rarely evenhanded in its recollection of the past. On the contrary, "commemoration silences the contrary interpretations of the past."[5] Holidays are thus used to strengthen patriotism and social solidarity, enhance the legitimacy of the state, and reinforce the popularity of a leader, a party, or a government.

Like their religious namesakes, civic "holy days" are separated from everyday, normal time. This temporal segregation, and the ritual activity marking the boundaries, divides the sacred from the profane. Historical events, heroes, and places are imbued with a store of profound collective meaning that the anthropologist Victor Turner calls "liminality," the scene and time "for the emergence of a society's deepest values in the form of sacred dramas and objects."[6] The regular recurrence of the special day, the symbolic communication of the day's rituals, and the festive celebrations staged in sacred centers affect popular memory, imagination, and emotions and constitute a powerful tool of political manipulation. It is not surprising, then, as Evitar Zerubavel writes, that "gaining control over the calendar has always been essential for attaining social control generally."[7]

Commemorative festivals in certain countries in the twentieth century have been transformed by states into mass political spectacles:[8] monumental symbolic dramas and visual performances that often include rituals, parades, festivals, and sporting events.[9] Rituals are nested within spectacles to invoke the "sacred" origins of such imagined communities as nations. Festivals encourage popular celebration and participation, while parades provide intense visual and sensual communication by means of colorful banners and flags, soldiers in formation, and bands playing stirring marches. Sporting events, finally, display a society's vigor in the present and promise for the future.[10] Spectacles are many-layered, complex acts of political persuasion.[11]

All of these elements in time became integral parts of the spectacle organized by the Mexican state to commemorate the anniversaries of the initiation of the Mexican revolution. This civic holiday, however, the twentieth of November, was born as a subdued day of remembrance. For nearly two decades, Revolution Day was nurtured by voluntary associations and virtually ignored, or at least neglected, by government. During the so-called institutionalization of the Revolution, at the end of the 1920s and the beginning of the 1930s, the Mexican state took control of and transformed the commemoration of *la Revolución*. Within only a few years the twin traditions of pilgrimage to the tombs of the martyrs and musical-literary *veladas* (soirées) were supplanted by what *La Prensa* in 1937 called "a great spectacle."[12] For more than sixty years the Mexican state has employed the language of symbols in impressive spectacles to present the picture of a nation created by its revolutionary history and unified in the realization of its revolutionary values. The dominant image in this history of spectacles is that of a vigorous Mexico arising out of a heroic revolution.

The early Mexican Republic had a hard time determining what to remember and celebrate. Its leaders, however, clearly recognized the need to do so, since few of the country's inhabitants understood the concept of Mexico as a nation. What most "Mexicans" remembered and celebrated, in fact, were saints' days. In the late seventeenth century one visitor to Mexico City counted ninety religious festivals. Each city, town, and village celebrated its own patron saint with music, fireworks, and a procession. The most important for many was the feast day of the Virgin of Guadalupe, the Mother of all Mexicans, on December 12. The idea of Mexico as a nation was new and generally unknown; Mexico as Christian, on the other hand, was deep and universal.[13]

The leaders of the new republic disagreed on the date of Independence Day. Liberals remembered and celebrated September 16, the day in 1810 on which Father Miguel Hidalgo called for an uprising. Conservatives, on the other hand, favored September 27, the day in 1821 on which General Agustín de Iturbide's army entered Mexico City and consummated independence. Depending upon who held power, celebrations were held on the sixteenth or the twenty-seventh of September, and occasionally other dates commemorating the abolition of slavery, or the signing of the act of independence, or some other notable event were celebrated. Curiously, it was the Emperor Maximilian, whom Mexican conservatives had supported, who in 1864 decreed September 16 to be the one official Independence Day.[14] The defeat of the empire, and with it the conservative cause, and the triumph of the liberal republic in 1867 definitively fixed Hidalgo's day in the official memory of Mexico and engendered many new patriotic holidays.

It was during the Porfiriato that patriotic commemoration of independence became a tradition. It was at the same time that France, seen by many Mexicans as their country's "big sister," began in 1880 to celebrate its own anniversary of revolution, Bastille Day. In an age when few in Mexico attended school and there was almost no mass media, civic festivals taught citizens the appropriate political values through hero worship. As a good liberal, Díaz viewed the Insurgency and the Reform as two stages of one ongoing revolution. As an intelligent politician, he portrayed his government as the culmination of both movements, he himself completing a patriotic trinity with Hidalgo and Juárez. In time, Díaz conjoined his personal history with the history of the nation by celebrating his birthday, September 15, as part of a now two-day Independence Day fiesta.

The Porfirian regime also celebrated other nationally significant days: February 5, anniversary of the proclamation of the liberal Constitution of 1857; May 5, "Cinco de Mayo," the date in 1862 of the Republican victory over the invading French army at Puebla; March 21, the birthday of the great national savior Benito Juárez in 1806; May 8, the day in 1753 on which the Father of the Country, Miguel Hidalgo, was born; April 2, the date of the Republic's and General Díaz's final victory over Maximilian, again in Puebla, in 1867; and July 18, date of the death of Juárez in 1872. Justo Sierra in the 1880s invented another new holiday, November 5, to honor the heroes of independent Mexico. The nation now had its secular saints and saints' days to unify all Mexicans.[15]

The Porfirian regime staged commemorative spectacles from time to time. The first great occasion came in 1887 and was the fifteenth anniversary of the death of Juárez. Since this took place at the same time that Díaz was arranging to amend the constitution to permit his reelection, and multiple terms were a trademark of Juárez, the timing was not coincidental. The regime also retrieved the parish bell rung by Hidalgo, now described as Mexico's Liberty Bell, and in 1896 installed it in a special tower in the National Palace. That year's September commemoration was particularly grand and added a new tradition: the ringing of the bell by the president in the manner of Hidalgo.[16] In 1906 the regime celebrated the centennial of Juárez's birth. Planning for this event had begun three years before with the appointment of a national commission. During the years of planning, and especially in 1906, cities and towns renamed streets and plazas and erected monuments. Books were published, patriotic orations abounded, and on March 22, 1906, festivities took place across the country. In Mexico City construction began on the great Juárez monument in Alameda Park on Avenida Juárez.[17]

The greatest of the Porfirian commemorations was also its last: the combined centenary fiestas of 1910, celebrating one-hundred years of independence, and the eightieth birthday of the president. Throughout September, Mexico invited visitors from around the world to its capital city. What in time would be seen as Mexico's most sacred patriotic monument, the Column of Independence (today called "the Angel" because of the golden statue standing at its top) was unveiled in the Paseo de la Reforma,

Mexico City's beautiful, central boulevard. Two days later the great white neoclassical Hemicycle of Juárez was dedicated. Public buildings and modern services were inaugurated, banquets and parties were held, parades were marched, and on the morning of September 15 the historic encounter between Moctezuma and Cortés was staged in full costume. That evening in the Zócalo, President Díaz gave the traditional *grito de independencia*— the "cry of independence" first issued by Hidalgo—and rang the Liberty Bell: "Long Live the Heroes of the Nation!" "Long Live the Republic!" "Viva Mexico!" The regime's preeminent intellectual, Justo Sierra, wrote at the time: "this country has not lost an ounce of its religious devotion to its history."[18]

By 1910, Mexico had institutionalized a full patriotic calendar of national holy days. Revolutionary regimes would honor them all and create new ones, and all were merged into one Revolutionary Tradition. One month after the centenary fiestas, Mexico's most famous exile made a new *grito*, which in time added a new day to the civic calendar.

SIX O'CLOCK ON SUNDAY NIGHT,
THE TWENTIETH OF NOVEMBER

In October 1910, following his escape from political detention, Francisco I. Madero issued a call for rebellion against the dictator Díaz. The Plan of San Luis—supposedly written in jail in San Luis Potosí but actually written in exile in San Antonio, Texas—proclaimed Madero to be provisional president in light of Díaz's recent fraudulent reelection. "I appoint six o'clock of Sunday night the twentieth of November next," Madero proclaimed in the plan, "as the time for an armed uprising of all the communities of the Republic."[19] Despite careful organizing on Madero's part, the revolution did not come off as intended.

A rebel conspiracy in the Puebla-Tlaxcala region was discovered by the government in mid-November, and arrests were made. This forced the rebel Aquiles Serdán to revolt two days ahead of schedule. A police detachment surrounded Serdán's house in Puebla on November 18 and made Serdán one of the first martyrs of the revolution. Further arrests in other cities in central Mexico extinguished the first sparks of revolt before they could flame and spread. Madero left San Antonio on November 18 and on the night of the nineteenth crossed back into Mexico, where he found neither arms nor supporters. "Without firing a shot," writes historian Charles C. Cumberland, "Madero retraced his steps into American territory. He was profoundly discouraged and heartsick."[20]

"The Mexican Revolution did not erupt," Paul Vanderwood writes, "it barely sputtered to a start."[21] But rebellion did break out here and there in rural backwaters, in Chihuahua and Morelos, Tlaxcala and San Luis Potosí, and elsewhere in the weeks and months to follow. Madero returned to Mexico in February 1911 and his rebel forces captured the border city of Ciudad Juárez in May. Under attack in dozens of regions and cities, Díaz resigned in late May, after his advisors made a deal with Madero for the establishment of a conservative interim government and the holding of a new presidential election. Madero was freely and overwhelmingly elected president and took office in November 1911.

One would surely be forgiven to note that little that was glorious took place on November 20, 1910, and that the political transition that occurred in 1911, while dramatic, was far from radical. Maderistas, however, immediately set about to convince Mexicans that the "Glorious Revolution of 1910" was a profound and historic rupture, as significant as Mexico's two great revolutions of the nineteenth century, of Independence and the Reform. *La Revolución* was made by "the people" and achieved nothing less than the conquest of liberty and the inauguration of democratic practices. The Plan of San Luis and its reference to November 20 became symbols of Madero's heroic resistance to Díaz and Mexico's glorious rebirth.

Revolution often reorders the symbolic system of a state, effecting "the removal of symbols of the old establishment and the introduction of those which represent the new ideology and the new political group which took over."[22] The Maderistas and their revolutionary successors did introduce new symbols but did not abandon the historical symbols upheld by the ancien régime. There was no need. Maderistas revered the same heroes and commemorated the same events as had the Porfiristas before them. The old and new regimes claimed continuity with the same nineteenth-century liberal tradition. Revolutionaries, however, contended that the Díaz regime had betrayed that tradition and that the 1910 revolution ended a generation of reactionary deviation. Maderistas, then, inherited a full calendar of patriotic holidays laden with great symbolic meaning. There was, as yet, no pressing need to invent new commemorative traditions.[23]

The first two anniversaries of the initiation of *la Revolución*, those that occurred during Madero's brief administration, elicited little attention or ceremony. Some government offices were closed on November 20, 1911, and, according to *El Tiempo*, "people in the streets cheered Madero."[24] *Nueva Era* published General Pascual Orozco's recollections of his activities in Chihuahua on November 20, 1910. The author of the interview concluded: "There it is, in short, the beginning of the great work that (who would have thought!) would come to shake, even undermine, a system that seemed indestructible, and open a new era of liberty and justice in our history."[25] In Puebla, admirers of Aquiles Serdán initiated an effort to erect a monument "so as to honor the immortality of the distinguished martyr of the reconquest of our political liberty."[26]

The following year on November 20, President Madero gave a banquet for members of the Congress. Speaking for the Chamber of Deputies, Luis Cabrera reflected on the meaning of anniversaries. July 14, 1789, he noted, is a glorious date since it signifies the struggle for liberty and reform. "The revolutionary movement begun on the twentieth of November, 1910, when we look back on it after half a century, may be seen as a day of national glory if we know how to lead our country to liberty; a day of infamy if it is simply an example of brothers fighting brothers."[27] Four days later Cabrera spoke at the laying of the cornerstone of the monument to Aquiles Serdán in the Plaza de Villamil. The statue, Cabrera proclaimed, "is placed upon its pedestal to speak to us and our children from there about what happened in his time and what was his deed, and to dictate his mandate to the generations to come."[28]

Maderistas used the first two anniversaries to recollect and inspire, to justify *la Revolución* and honor its heroes and martyrs, and to contrast the tyranny of the ancien régime with the liberty present in the new Mexico. A tradition of remembrance regarding the twentieth of November had begun, but it was as yet a weak tradition. As the decade wore on, however, as more revolts made revolutionary heroes, and many of these heroes became martyrs, *el veinte de noviembre* became the inauguration of something more and more momentous, more glorious but tragic, and more in need of justification.

"THE ANNIVERSARY OF THE DEMOCRATIC EPIPHANY"

The coup that overthrew the Madero government in February 1913, and the subsequent assassination of the president and vice-president, for many Mexicans transfigured everything related to the martyred president into sacred history. Religious connotations and imagery in revolutionary rhetoric were pervasive in the years from 1911 to 1920, and later still, as one way to communicate the profound nature of the nation's transformation to a people steeped in biblical stories and Christian symbolism. Madero became the "Apostle of Democracy," Huerta, who led the coup, became the Judas figure to Madero's Christ, *la Revolución* was characterized as "*la santa Revolución*," the holy Revolution, and the twentieth of November was described as the "anniversary of the Democratic Epiphany."[29]

The defeat of Huerta by the Constitutionalist movement, led by Carranza, by the summer of 1914 permitted the spontaneous and unorganized commemoration of Madero by revolutionary generals and political clubs. Madero's grave in the French cemetery in Mexico City became from July until October a site of obligatory pilgrimage, where hardened revolutionaries shed tears and reverentially placed flower wreaths on the grave.[30] For former Maderistas these ceremonies represented transparent efforts to honor Madero and to champion his ideals, while many individual revolutionaries no doubt declared (and publicized) their attachment to Madero and his ideals to underscore their revolutionary credentials.

The twentieth of November was not celebrated in 1914 in any organized way in the capital because of the factional rift within the revolutionary ranks that would soon thereafter lead to civil war. In the fall of 1914 the Constitutionalist movement fragmented into hostile factions and armies due, largely, to the distrust Carranza and Francisco Villa felt for one another. The military forces and government of Carranza began the evacuation of Mexico City in early November and by the twentieth of the month were settled in Córdova, in Veracruz. Villa's forces, and those of the agrarian revolutionary Emiliano Zapata, entered Mexico City in late November.

During 1915 the Carranza faction achieved the military victories necessary to form a national government in Mexico City. Between 1915 and 1919, the twentieth of November was commemorated and celebrated by groups of loyal Maderistas (and Obregonistas) but nearly ignored by the government of Carranza and by Carrancistas. Outside of Mexico City some state and municipal governments staged celebrations, the most grand, perhaps, occurring every year in Puebla to mark the death of Serdán. In Mexico City the tombs of Madero and his vice-president were adorned with flower wreaths ("symbol of the purity of the Patriotic Sentiment of the

People regenerated by the Revolution"[31]) during the day, and at night *veladas* were organized by local officials, school principals, and political parties. These *veladas* were organized programs of patriotic and commemorative orations, poetry readings, and music performances. Pilgrimages to the sacred tombs and dignified sedentary ceremonies constituted the traditions marking the twentieth of November from the mid-1910s until the 1930s.

In these years, the Carranza government organized or participated in the commemorations of the birthday of Benito Juárez (March 21), the United States seizure of Veracruz (April 21), the 1862 defeat of the French army at Puebla (May 5), and national independence (September 16). The twentieth of November, however, was given no special recognition. Indeed, in 1917 President Carranza ordered all government offices to remain open on that day.[32] Carrancistas emphasized the significance of the signing of Carranza's Plan of Guadalupe (on March 26)—"the most glorious date in the annals of our great Revolution"—over that of Madero's *grito* in the Plan of San Luis.[33]

Álvaro Obregón, Carranza's most important general during the battles against Villa in 1915 and a presidential candidate in 1920, with his followers affirmed their revolutionary credentials (and growing disaffection with Carranza) by emphasizing their continuity with Madero and his political ideals. Beginning in 1917, the Obregonista-leaning Constitutionalist Liberal Party (Partido Liberal Constitucionalista), for example, increasingly took responsibility for organizing *veladas* honoring Madero, Pino Suárez, and Serdán.[34] Following the rebellion that overthrew the Carranza government in 1920 and led to the president's death, Obregonistas (now in power) presented the "interregnum of Carranza" as a tragic interruption of the revolution, which had been initiated by Madero and was continued and concluded by his true political and spiritual heir, Obregón.[35] The Obregonista-dominated Congress in 1920 declared for the first time that the twentieth of November was officially a *día de fiesta nacional,* and members of the cabinet attended and participated in the *velada* of that year. In February 1921, on the anniversary of Madero's martyrdom, President Obregón led a procession from the National Palace to the French cemetery to lay a flower wreath on his grave.[36]

The national government, however, during the 1920s (with only two exceptions) still did not direct or organize the commemorative celebration of the twentieth of November. Congress each year declared it a day of national celebration, which closed government offices and all public schools, and high government officials laid wreaths and gave commemorative orations. Military cadets from the Colegio Militar provided honor guards for the graves. The responsibility for organizing ceremonies at the French cemetery and the programs of the *veladas* beginning in 1920 was assumed by the Pro-Madero Group, an unofficial association of activists and veterans.[37] The program of the *velada* of 1924, presented below, was typical of the time.[38]

The program of the 1924 *velada* obviously was intended for a cultured and exclusive audience. While the *veladas* of the 1920s included some revolutionary symbolism and a few references to the Revolution of 1910, they were still a long way from the more popular, and populist, *fiestas mexicanas* of parades and fireworks that the residents of many Mexico City neighborhoods, small towns, and state capitals enjoyed.[39] In order to "properly" honor the initiation of *la Revolución*, the new revolutionary leadership fell into a tradition of staid, elitist ceremonies which by their very nature excluded most Mexicans.

Beginning in the administration of Obregón's successor, Calles, the national government began to assume some responsibility for the commemoration and celebration of significant revolutionary events. In February 1925, for instance, the Ministry of Government cooperated with the Pro-Madero Group to formulate a program to commemorate the assassinations of Madero and Pino Suárez.[40] By November of that year the government had established the Official Committee of Patriotic Commemorations, which cooperated again with the Pro-Madero Group to organize the day's activities. Aside from the by then traditional graveside ceremony and evening *velada*, on this day the minister of government, Adalberto Tejeda, dedicated a bust to the martyred Yucatecan revolutionary Felipe Carrillo Puerto in the First of May Garden of the Villa de Tacuba.[41] By 1926 the official committee included representatives from the Pro-Madero Group, as well as representatives from the national Ministry of Government, the Federal District, and the municipal government of Mexico City. The official committee organized the commemorative ceremonies for the twenty-second of February and the twentieth of November.[42] By the end of the Calles administration, however, full responsibility for the commemorations had returned to the Pro-Madero Group. The national government's intervention in the remembrance of *la Revolución* had been brief

LA VELADA EN LA HIDALGO

19:30 HOURS, 20TH OF NOVEMBER 1924

Teatro Hidalgo

PART ONE

*1. Beethoven's Fourth String Quartet
performed by the Cuarteto Clásico Nacional.*

*2. A reading of the Plan de San Luis
by Lic. Calixto Maldona R.*

3. Puccini's Aria "Vissi D'Arte" from the Opera Tosca,
performed by Matilde L. Guevara.

4. An oration by Ramon Coy.

*5. A performance of "Golondrina Mensajera" by Esperanza Oteo,
presented by the Orquesta Típica, a workers' orchestra.*

*6. Saint-Saëns's "La Cloche"
performed by soprano Maria Luisa Escobar de Rocabruna.*

PART TWO

*1. Palmerin's "El Rosal Enfermo" and Talavera's "La Chinita,"
performed by the Agustín Caballero Choir.*

*2. Cesar Franck's "Scherzo del Cuarteto"
performed by the Cuarteto Clásico Nacional.*

*3. A performance of Ordaz's "Paso Doble"
by the Orquesta Típica.*

4. An oration by Manuel Gómez Morín.

5. An aria from Pietro Mascagni's opera Caballería Rústica,
performed by Madame Escobar de Rocabruna.

*6. Alverde's "El Clavelito" and Serrano's "El Carro del Sol,"
performed by the Agustín Caballero Choir.*

and temporary but anticipatory. In a short time the government would completely dominate and shape how Mexicans (*capitalinos*, residents of the Federal District, most of all) would remember and celebrate the initiation of *la Revolución Mexicana*.[43]

"A VIGOROUS MEXICO ARISING"

New traditions of commemorating and celebrating the twentieth of November were invented as the postrevolutionary state became increasingly institutionalized in the late 1920s and early 1930s. Government assumed almost complete responsibility for organizing the activities of the day and gave the civic holiday far more significance than ever before. In 1936, Congress decreed that henceforth the twentieth of November would be a *día de fiesta nacional*. Beginning in the 1940s the part of the day's activities devoted each year to commemorative ceremonies took place at the new Monument to the Revolution (see Chapter 5). The central event, however, of every Revolution Day since 1930 has been the athletic parade. Sports became a metaphor not for the historic 1910 revolution itself but rather for the benefits of *la Revolución* in the present and its promise for the future, as embodied in the forms of healthy, strong, and disciplined young people.

Sport became increasingly important in Mexico, and Western societies generally, between the wars. In Europe it became, as Eric Hobsbawm writes, "an expression of national struggle, and sportsmen representing their nation or state, primary expressions of their imagined communities."[44] In Mexico, as well, sport appeared to become more important and certainly obtained a higher visibility in society: teams were sent to the Paris (1924) and Amsterdam (1928) Olympic Games, the first Central American and Caribbean Games were held in Mexico in 1926, and Mexico joined the world soccer community in 1929. Beginning in 1928, the Federal District began to organize thousands of athletic events each year.[45] The promotion of sports and athleticism in Mexico reflected the temper of the times, but it was also supportive of both "revolutionary" and nationalist objectives: the promotion of Mexicans' physical betterment and the production of athletes capable of representing Mexico with success at international tournaments.[46]

In small-town Mexico team sports became associated with most civic holidays beginning in the 1930s. Schoolteachers viewed sports as an instrument for transforming peasant customs and values while promoting patriotism and history. Politicians saw local and regional teams as just another form of political networking. Thus, writes Mary Kay Vaughan, "local, regional, and national aspirants to power found in sports competitions a catalyst for legitimization and a mechanism of state formation."[47]

On November 20, 1929, President Portes Gil inaugurated the new Balbuena military complex and viewed the first sports parade, which consisted of allegorical cars and floats symbolizing the various sports cultivated by the different branches of the military.[48] Nearby, the head of the Federal District, J. M. Puig Casauranc, officially opened the Venustiano Carranza Social Sport Center for Workers. This impressive sports complex contained a gymnasium, running track, swimming pool, and several playing fields, as well as a library, cinema, medical clinic, and a day-care center.[49] Every twentieth of November thereafter would be identified to a considerable extent with sports.

The following year, an official of the Federal District (the director general of physical education of the central department) in coordination with the new official political party, the PNR, organized the first *desfile deportivo* (sports parade) through the symbolic center of Mexico City. (Thirty thousand athletes in the 1932 parade carried Mexican flags inscribed with the initials of the PNR.[50]) The various agencies of the national government, the federal states, and different elements of the military presented contingents of colorfully uniformed athletes, each representing particular sports and athletic activities: baseball, basketball, boxing, volleyball, tennis, cycling, polo, and football, among others. In this first year of the parade, as in all following ones, the rear was brought up by *mesnadas de charros* (horsemen or cowboys), dressed in the style of the region from which they came. Perhaps as many as 30,000 "athletes" (many of the participants, it was revealed years later, were government employees dressed in sports uniforms) paraded in front of President Ortiz Rubio, who was standing on the balcony of the National Palace in the Zócalo. The parade, noted *Excelsior*, "has been an augury for the future of our country, of what we can expect in the future with a generation healthy in body and spirit."[51]

From that day until the most recent *Día de la Revolución*, Mexico City, as well as the state capitals and many small towns, has witnessed each year a sports parade. During the 1930s and 1940s the parade organizers attempted continuously to outdo the parade of the year before. The parade became "*magno*," "*gigantesco*," and "*majestuoso*" as the numbers of participant athletes and the hours of entertainment increased. A spectacle was born. In 1935 it was reported that the parade continued for more than five hours and in 1939 it was estimated that 50,000 "sportsmen and women" participated in a parade that lasted six hours.[52] After the Second World War the parades were smaller but the participants, the organizers conceded, were now "authentic athletes," unlike "years before when we would see bureaucrats, peasants, and workers dressed as athletes parade."[53]

An erratic invented tradition that emerged with the sports parade, one that was less theatrical but no less a common structural element of festivals the world over, was the athletic contest.[54] In 1930 the organizer of the parade also held the Juegos de la Revolución (Games of the Revolution). The athletes, more than eight thousand, swore an oath of fair and quality competition to the president.[55] It was not until 1941, however, that the games reappeared as part of the festivities. Begun in 1930, the Juegos Nacional de la Revolución (National Games of the Revolution) was a competition for amateur athletes, male and female, with about twenty-five different sports included. "Besides honoring the Revolution and its goals of national development and international prestige," writes Joseph Arbena,

> the games were projected to improve coaching and playing skills,
> to raise national interest in sports, to build community solidarity,
> to strengthen ties of loyalty between citizens and all federal entities,
> and to instill in the masses the practice of organization and discipline
> which would prepare them for their obligatory military service. . . .
> After the event, Professor Graciano Sánchez declared that the life, joy,
> agility, and achievement associated with the festivities made a fitting
> contrast with the death and desolation associated with the memory
> of the Revolution.[56]

The revolutionary games were staged again in 1949. In 1951 and 1952, however, the Juegos Estudantiles (Student Games) were held in November to commemorate *la Revolución* and, in 1952, to inaugurate the stadium of the newly constructed "university city" of the national university.[57] Nearly two decades later, during the early 1970s, a series of "peasant youth cultural and sport games" was held for the athletes of Mexico's *ejidos*.[58] The Juegos de la Revolución were revived in the late 1970s and early 1980s.[59]

Why the organizers of the twentieth of November festivities adopted sports and athleticism as the primary symbol and manner to celebrate *la Revolución* can only be surmised. Over the years, however, a fairly consistent set of explanations has been voiced by politicians and journalists. The healthy, disciplined, competitive young men and women who paraded before the National Palace and the nation each year, according to those who wrote about them, demonstrated that the sacrifices of those who struggled in the conflict, as well as the efforts of the regimes of *la Revolución*, had not been in vain.[60] In 1931, President Ortiz Rubio told participants in the parade that they represented the "vigor and future of Mexico's national life." Former President Calles added that "this is the culmination of the work of the revolution."[61] On this day in Mexico City and in all of the state capitals, "there are grand parades of sports enthusiasts and athletes, organized by the National Revolutionary Party, that shows how the great revolutionary family has succeeded in crystallizing the yearning for social improvement," wrote Rafael E. Melgar in the *Calendario Nacionalista* of 1935.[62] "The parade was just brilliant," noted one cabinet officer in 1949. "It constitutes a demonstration of social progress. The degree of advancement that has been achieved in athletics symbolizes this stage of the Mexican Revolution."[63] The athletes and the parade itself symbolized *la Revolución* as a healthy, living force in Mexican history, confidently marching into the future. In the words of Luis I. Rodríguez, speaking for President Cárdenas in 1935, the parade inspired the president to anticipate "a vigorous Mexico arising, stronger and better tempered on the hard anvil of the Revolution."[64]

Certainly the parade through the Zócalo each year provided a striking contrast to the Revolution Day parade through Red Square in Moscow. Whereas the "revolutionary" face the Soviet Union presented to itself and the world each year was highly militarized, the Mexican "sports parade" was pacifist, if not antimilitaristic.[65] In 1939 contingents with "military-style uniforms" were excluded from the parade.[66] According to Adolfo Orive Alba, a cabinet official, the parade of 1950 "reflect[ed] that all Mexicans are dedicated to work and healthy diversions, like sport."[67] Federal Deputy Luis Farías in 1957 stated that the twentieth of November was not a date symbolizing "armed violence" but "a state of mind, such as aspiration and planning, more than as a warlike event."[68] For two journalists writing in 1984, "Mexico is the only country in the world that commemorates a war—which the Revolution of 1910 was—with a sports parade, like the one yesterday that was a manifestation of fraternity, nationalism, and solidarity."[69] Soldiers participated in the parades, not as uniformed soldiers carrying weapons, but rather as baseball players, boxers, and gymnasts carrying bats, balls, and gloves.

During the Second World War, on the other hand, organization of the parade was given to the command of the First Military Zone and the celebration became a "civic-military sports parade."[70] Soldiers took the place of athletes, battalions rather than contingents marched, and military uniforms substituted for sportswear. But just as bureaucrats, workers, and the party faithful paraded as "athletes" before the war, beginning in 1942 they put on the olive green and marched as "battalions." By November 1945 sportswear was back, and 25,000 athletes in 64 contingents paraded for four hours.[71]

The parades were also advertisements for each department of government and the entire state bureaucracy itself. On this day the traditional image of the gray paper pusher brightened considerably as anonymous bureaucrats were transformed by colorful uniforms into the appearance of vigorous athletes. Departments competed with one another to field the most impressive contingents and floats. In the disguise of athleticism it was the governing bureaucracy that was on parade.

Parades are living monuments. They are, Clifford Geertz writes, "stories a people tell about themselves."[72] A parade's route, its symbolic itinerary past historic monuments and through sacred centers, enhances its power, just as the parade itself lends new meaning to familiar, undistinguished space. "A parade is thus," writes Louis Marin, "an apparatus in the art of memory."[73] The twentieth of November parades in Mexico City have always followed "historic" routes. Parades begin in Avenida 20 de Noviembre (so named in 1933 and constructed over the next five years), from which they enter the Plaza of the Constitution, the Zócalo, Mexico's sacred center since Aztec times.[74] Within the Zócalo, parades pass by the central balcony of the National Palace, where the president and other members of the government review the many contingents of athletes. The parade exits the Zócalo through Avenida Cinco de Mayo, and takes Avenida Francisco I. Madero, then Avenida Juárez (past the monumental Hemicycle of Juárez) to the Monument to the Revolution. The parade is a procession through Mexican history, the dominant (liberal) version of that history.

After the completion of the Monument to the Revolution, located in the Plaza of the Republic, the solemn, commemorative rituals of the holiday began to take place there. Under the massive flag-draped dome of the monument, speakers extolled the virtues of *la Revolución* (and the current regime's faithful adherence to it), bands played the national anthem and revolutionary *corridos,* and presidents bestowed decorations and medals upon members of the military and aging veterans of the revolution.

Beginning in the 1940s a newly invented tradition, the "symbolic flame of *la Revolución,*" was added to the repertoire of the twentieth of November ritual events. Relay runners, often national champions, carried the Torch of the Symbolic Flame of the Revolution from Aquiles Serdán's house in Puebla to the Monument to the Revolution, a distance of 132 kilometers. This new *acto simbólico,* borrowed from the Olympic Games, emphasized the association between athleticism and *la Revolución,* as well as the permanence of the living revolution.[75]

The deposit of the remains of many of the most important revolutionary leaders in the piers of the Monument to the Revolution over the years has enhanced the meaning both of the monument and of the twentieth of November rituals staged under its dome. The remains of Venustiano Carranza were transferred to the monument in 1941 on the anniversary of the Constitution of 1917. The centerpiece of the 1960 commemoration was the transfer of the remains of Francisco I. Madero from the French cemetery to the monument. "Everyone filled with intense patriotic emotion," wrote *El Nacional,* "upon seeing the reverence and admiration by which Licenciado López Mateos took into his hands the urn and placed it in the crypt where the remains of the great enlightened one named Francisco I. Madero will, beginning yesterday, rest forever."[76] The later additions of the remains of Francisco Villa, Lázaro Cárdenas, and Plutarco Elías Calles only added to the sacred aura of the monument and the rituals conducted there.

CONCLUSION

The twentieth of November commemorations evolved from low-key civic rituals into a grandiose state-sponsored spectacle. A day of remembrance was transformed over the years into a showy advertisement for the state project and the bureaucracy itself. This transformation was but one more example of the political creativity of the men who engineered the "institutionalization" of *la Revolución*. The hard-headed realists who built institutions and disciplined factions also crafted what we call today a hegemonic discourse, communicated by means of commemorative holidays, public monuments, and official history. The twentieth of November spectacle was and is but one part of this discourse.

What does this festival mean? This question is not as simple or singular as it seems. Eric Van Young provides some guidelines for decoding the symbolic drama as text.[77] First, he asks, what does the civic ritual represent and how does it achieve representation? The twentieth of November festival represents *la Revolución*, of course, its past, present, and future. The ceremony at the Monument to the Revolution, with its historical allusions in speeches, *corridos*, veterans, and the imposing monument itself, looks from the present to the past. The sports parade, representing not *la Revolución* itself but the success of *la Revolución* in cultivating strong, healthy young people, looks from the present to the future.

Van Young's second question is more difficult to answer: What does the civic ritual do, that is to say, what social, cultural, and/or political function does it serve? Those who create or endorse it claim that the answer is self-evident: it does what it is. In the case of the twentieth of November, the holiday and its attendant rituals celebrate *la Revolución*, its ongoing implementation in the present, and its anticipated successes in the future. The nation pays homage to the past and is, as a result, stronger, wiser, and— above all—more unified. Students of civic ritual claim that there are "latent functions" embedded in it that serve more controversial purposes. Ritualized celebration is (in fact) authorization of the political status quo based on continuity and achievement. Revolution Day authorizes, justifies, and legitimizes the official party, the present regime, and the postrevolutionary state, since each of these institutions claims descent from *la Revolución* itself and proclaims itself to be implementing the Revolution's promises.

5 MONUMENT

From the Ruins of the Old Regime

FOR MORE THAN twenty years, the skeletal iron frame of the Palacio Legislativo Federal, the national capitol, designed to be one of the triumphs of Beaux-Arts architecture of the age of Porfirio Díaz, dominated the skyline of Mexico City. The most important building that the Porfirian regime planned to build was never finished. As Mexicans say, "¡Así pasan las glorias del mundo!"—*sic transit gloria mundi*. During the 1930s the ruin was transformed into a modern monument, a triumphal arch to commemorate *la Revolución*. Mexican history was refashioned, literally and physically, in iron, stone, and bronze. The Revolutionary Tradition assumed physical shape and form.

Commemorative monuments have as their most obvious purpose the evocation and celebration of the past in the present. They are constructed to memorialize heroes and events for various, but not always clearly evident, reasons. As exhortations to imitate worthy predecessors, monuments instruct citizens today and tomorrow what to believe and how to behave. As symbols of national glory and triumph, monuments promote horizontal and vertical solidarity, that is, they encourage persons of different locales, classes, and ethnicities, as well as different generations, to view themselves as one people, a nation. In this sense monuments are vital instruments in the invention and maintenance of a variety of "imagined communities." As initiatives by states and regimes, monuments emphasize the real or alleged continuity between present rulers and the seminal events and heroes of history, thereby bestowing upon those leaders the sanction and legitimization of a revered past.[1]

Certain monuments are designed to create a setting for ritual performances, for commemorations and celebrations. The creation of a special space sets the stage for a concentration of political suggestions. Some monuments become identified with recurrent calendrical celebrations. The monument, the setting, the performance, and the particular day combine to evoke symbolic reassurance that the state, the regime, or the leader is faithful to those considered the community's founding fathers, and that authority, therefore, is legitimate.[2] As stages for commemorative performances, monuments encourage people not simply to remember but to remember together, thereby affirming group solidarity and unity.[3]

Not unlike religious temples, certain commemorative monuments transform space so as to manifest sacrality. This transfiguration is effected by various symbolisms that bestow special meaning on the origin, construction, and history of the monument, and by recurrent rituals that stimulate the intersection of sacred time with sacred space, animating the monument and transforming visitors. A monument that becomes a sacred civic temple or shrine for a civic religion (based on nationalism or a particular political ideology) is a powerful political instrument capable of inspiring mass loyalty to the state, identification with the rulers, and sacrifice for those imagined communities called "the nation," "the people," or "the revolution."[4]

The past is often contested terrain in politics. Collective memory is constructed, James E. Young reminds us: "There are worldly consequences in the kinds of historical understanding generated by monuments." Commemorative monuments and civic celebrations shape, institutionalize, and disseminate particular versions of the past while at the same time excluding, suppressing, and devaluing other versions or traditions. When successful, they form part of a more comprehensive ideology or discourse that employs myths and symbols to promote loyalty and patriotism (read: conformity and obedience) to regime, state, and nation.[5]

The Monument to the Revolution is one of Mexico City's most prominent landmarks and the most impressive commemorative monument in Mexico. It is a giant text of iron and stone designed to reflect and shape the nation's collective memory. It embodies in its origins, construction, form, and sculpture almost every element of the two-decades-long revolutionary discourse of memory. The monument was built by the Revolutionary Family, according to a 1937 report, "to perpetuate the memory of the Mexican Social Revolution."[6] Today historians argue that it was built to enhance the legitimacy and authority of the postrevolutionary governing elite, "a tribute the institutional government made to itself."[7] These objectives, of course, are compatible one with the other, but they do not fully explain the monument.

The monument was built primarily to unify symbolically *la Revolución* and to heal the wounds of memory. This intention, more than anything else, explains why and when it was built. It represents one of the first official efforts to transform Mexico's discordant revolutionary traditions into a singular Revolutionary Tradition. The original design sought to erase personalism altogether from the idea of *la Revolución*. The Revolutionary Tradition, however, is not hostile to personalism and the cult of revolutionary heroes; it opposes the idea and practice of glorifying one hero above the rest. The monument came to embody the tradition fully when it later received the mortal remains of several revolutionary caudillos, when it became the pantheon of *la Revolución*.

HISTORY IN BRONZE

In both ancient Egypt and post-Soviet Russia, the smashing of statues marked the beginning of a new age. Dramatic political upheavals have often been accompanied by icon smashing, symbolic violence against the defeated regime.[8] The defeat and discrediting of the regime of Porfirio Díaz, however, was not accompanied by any outburst of iconoclasm. This absence of symbolic violence is particularly noteworthy and significant since the Porfiriato was the first great age of commemorative monument building in modern Mexican history. Mexicans forged their mythic history in bronze.[9]

The triumph of liberalism over its domestic and foreign enemies by 1867 allowed, finally, an unambiguous and unopposed celebration of Mexico's liberal past. By the time of the Porfiriato, argues Charles A. Hale, liberalism had become a unifying political myth. Porfirians viewed the struggle for independence of the 1810s and the struggles for reform and republican government during the 1850s and 1860s as two stages of an ongoing socio-political process. The Díaz regime embraced and encouraged this unifying political myth in order to reconcile the partisans of all liberal factions and to present itself as the worthy successor of the glorious liberal tradition.[10] It took time (and money), however, for this sensibility to become translated into stone and metal.

As late as 1885, Ignacio Manuel Altamirano complained that "we have a very small number of national monuments, whether due to internal wars, or whether the best materials have priority, or because the press and the artists themselves were not zealous enough in promoting the construction of public monuments to our heroes, and lastly, perhaps due to apathy, which is the very essence of our nature."[11] Altamirano listed only five monuments (incorrectly, since there were more, although not many more), all of them celebrating heroes of independence. The effort, however, was already underway. During the fertile quarter of a century between 1885 and 1910 Mexico's liberal tradition was immortalized in stone and metal. Mexico experienced, notes Carlos Monsiváis, "the invasion of statues."[12]

In 1877 the government decreed that three *glorietas* (traffic circles) on Mexico City's Paseo de la Reforma be reserved for monuments to Cuauhtémoc, the last Aztec king, the heroes of the struggle for independence, and those of the Reform.[13] The Cuauhtémoc monument was unveiled in 1887 and was modern Mexico's first great commemorative monument. Two additional statues of Aztec warriors (today popularly known as *los Indios verdes*, the green Indians, for their green copper patina) were erected on each side of the entrance to the Paseo in 1891.[14] Between 1889 and 1900, thirty-six statues of mostly Independence and Reform-era heroes were erected along the Paseo de la Reforma. Each province was invited to immortalize two of its native sons and thus share the cost of the project. On the centennial of the birth of Benito Juárez in 1906, construction began on the Hemiciclo de Juárez, located in the Alameda Park on Avenida Juárez. This Greek-style hemicycle, in which a sitting Juárez is flanked by white marble Doric columns, was inaugurated in 1910.[15]

"The mania for erecting statues," *El Universal* noticed in 1892, "is taking on the proportions of an epidemic in Mexico."[16] The establishment of the Fundición Artistica Mexicana (Mexican Artistic Foundry) during that same year contributed mightily to this "epidemic." Under the artistic direction of Jesús F. Contreras, the foundry produced twenty-four of the thirty-six statues that came to line the Paseo de la Reforma. In addition, Contreras himself produced many of the most impressive commemorative monuments erected in provincial Mexico in the late Porfiriato: the monument to Independence in Puebla (1898), the monument to Manuel Acuña in Saltillo, Coahuila (1897), the (equestrian) monument to General Jesús González Ortega in Zacatecas (1898), the (equestrian) monuments to General Ignacio Zaragoza in Puebla and Saltillo (1896–7), and the six busts of Benito Juárez that were widely distributed in the country.[17]

The mass production of public monuments was occurring at that time in Western Europe and the United States, as well as in Mexico.[18] Mexican monuments tended to be designed according to the fashion of the age: opulent allegorical decoration of a historical theme in classical, neoclassical, art nouveau, and sometimes a nationalist, neo-indigenist style.[19] "The country's greatest monument,"[20] the Column of Independence, for example, was modeled after the column in the place Vendôme in Paris. It was adorned with sculptures of the country's founding fathers, national eagles, one lion, seated women, and objects such as medallions, laurels, and escutcheons representing aspects of the nation, the liberal Republic and its history, and abstract ideas and values. A colossal bronze Angel of Independence, "Winged Victory," holding a laurel wreath in one hand and a shattered chain in the other, was placed at the top of the column.[21] Although envisioned in the 1877 plan for the Paseo de la Reforma, the column was not unveiled until September 16, 1910, appropriately the centennial anniversary of the commemorated event.[22]

Through commemorative monuments and civic celebrations, Aztec Mexico, Independence, the Reform, and the Díaz regime were symbolically superimposed, creating a unified liberal tradition. In this way the glorious past was marshaled to sanction the present. The Porfirian regime, as a result, did not erect monuments—self-conscious monuments—to itself.[23] There was, however, one frustrated exception. The Italian architect Adamo Boari drew up plans in 1900 for a monument glorifying Porfirio Díaz himself, although it is not known if the regime ever considered building it. It was a wonderful example of nineteenth-century excess: an Aztec pyramid base was decorated with angels and Mexican cacti, and it supported a neoclassical temple upon which an equestrian statue of Díaz stood. It was, the art critic Justino Fernández wrote, "una locurita romántica," a crazy little romantic thing.[24]

The regime's own monuments were not allegorical but utilitarian: railroads, bridges, and particularly grand public buildings that announced the power, progress, and style of Porfirian Mexico. The proposed Federal Legislative Palace was intended as the unequaled monument to Porfirian glory. The government initiated the project in 1897, budgeted five million pesos, and organized an international competition for the best design. The winner, Italian architect Pietro Paollo Quaglia, died before construction was begun. Five years later, the government selected a French architect, Émile Bernard, to design the building. Bernard's 1904 plan envisioned a grand structure in the neoclassical style of the United States Capitol, with characteristic touches of the French renaissance. The iron frame was to be covered with Italian marble and Norwegian granite. Grand stairways and rows of columns would face the front. An imposing dome rising from the center would be capped with a monumental sculpture of the national eagle. During the next six years the metallic frame was constructed, and during the centennial celebrations in 1910 President Díaz laid the first stone.[25] In the ceremony the federal deputy José R. Aspe noted that "today we place the first stone of what will be the true and superb temple of the Mexican legislature."[26]

Since the revolutionaries of 1910 and after saw themselves as the rightful heirs of Mexico's liberal tradition (and dismissed the Díaz regime as a deviation from it), they embraced the same pantheon of national heroes that had been glorified by the Díaz regime. Revolutionaries had no need to smash the statues and monuments of the old regime; on the contrary, they made them their own through annual celebrations and, in some cases, endowed them with new and greater meaning. The monument commemorating the centennial of the Siege of Cuautla, located in the Ciudadela Plaza in Mexico City, was begun during the Díaz regime, completed during de la Barra's administration, and inaugurated by President Madero on time on May 2, 1912.

Official revolutionaries gathered every year on the anniversary of Juárez's birth at the *hemiciclo* to honor the great reformer and to claim his allegiance for their cause.[27] During the 1920s the National Patriotic Organization of Popular Festivals, with official approval and assistance, employed the *hemiciclo* as the site for the annual ritual commemorating the signing of the revolutionary Constitution of 1917. The great liberal lawgiver of the nineteenth century in this way became linked to *la Revolución*, the revolutionary charter, and the political system it supposedly regulated.[28]

The mortal remains of Hidalgo, Allende, Aldama, Jiménez, and several other heroes of the struggle for independence were transferred from the national cathedral in 1925 to a newly constructed crypt within the Column of Independence. This ceremony was organized in part by the Pro-Madero Group. In 1929 the national government inaugurated an honor guard at the column. "In this way, the Column of Independence, *a simple monument in 1910*, was converted into the tomb of our liberators in 1925, and into an altar of the people's gratitude in 1929."[29]

The Porfiriato had left the nation a monumental commemorative legacy that revolutionaries embraced without a second thought. Independence, the Reform, and now *la Revolución* became the new trinity of Mexican national history, the three stages of the ongoing and unending struggle to make and mold Mexico. Revolutionary Mexico also accepted, incorporated, and, in one notable case, completed the great public buildings of the Porfiriato. The ancien régime left two palaces unfinished. The Madero regime continued construction of the Federal Legislative Palace in 1911–12 until funds for the project ran out. The construction of a national theater, designed by Boari and begun in 1904, was also interrupted in 1911. This building was much closer to completion, however, than was the legislative palace, with only its dome remaining unsheathed in marble. The building was finally finished, and the interior decorated, in 1932–4 and renamed the Palacio de Bellas Artes (Palace of Fine Arts). This glorious art nouveau monument was Boari's (and Mexico's) true monument to Porfirio Díaz.

CULTS OF MARTYRS

There was no similar "invasion of statues" in the two decades after 1911. Civil war, governmental instability, and competition for scarce pesos no doubt account for this inattention. State and national governments proclaimed that their social improvements and public works—schools, sports parks, *ejidos*, and irrigation works—were the real monuments to *la Revolución*. There was as well, perhaps, a reluctance based on a supposed revolutionary mentality. As one journalist noted, when revolutions begin to raise statues they demonstrate that they have lost interest in action, "they enter the [era of] drowsy boastfulness of bourgeois epilogues."[30]

During the 1910s and 1920s national governments remained largely unengaged in commemorating *la Revolución* in ceremony or stone. This aversion of Mexico's official culture to commemorative activity, however, did not mean that there was none. The official symbolic vacuum was filled by partisan and regional interests, which claimed *la Revolución* as their own while denying it to their rivals and enemies, past and present. The collective memory of postrevolutionary Mexico was shaped by the unregulated, multivocal expressions of competing revolutionary traditions. The revolutionary past itself became contested terrain.

During these decades commemorative activity became the responsibility by default of revolutionary factions and dedicated partisans. Followers of Aquiles Serdán in December 1911 proposed the first revolutionary monument, and they organized the first annual commemoration of the assassination of Madero on February 22, 1914.[31] In time this group became the Bloc of Precursors of the Revolution in the Years 1909, 1910, and 1913, which organized the most prominent commemorations of Serdán, Madero, and Carranza.[32] Later in the decade Maderistas organized the Pro-Madero Committee, which sponsored twentieth of November and twenty-second of February commemorations, while Carrancistas, through their control of government, commemorated each twenty-sixth of March the anniversary of the signing of the Plan of Guadalupe and virtually ignored November 20. Following Carranza's downfall, the Sonorans in turn ignored March 26 and made November 20 a national holiday. The (newly renamed) Pro-Madero Group, however, during the 1920s continued to organize the festivities for the twentieth of November, while some former Carrancistas commemorated the Plan of Guadalupe on March 26. Beginning in 1923, the Association of Querétaro Constituents began to commemorate the signing of the Constitution of 1917.[33]

Maderistas sought for many years without success to erect a monument to the Apostle of Democracy. The periodical *El Demócrata* began a monument fund in 1917 for a marble statue "as an enduring remembrance of the illustrious founder of this newspaper."[34] In 1920 the Pro-Madero Group began a campaign to erect a monument in every plaza in the Republic, "a monument of the immortal effigy of Madero in gleaming, imperishable marble."[35] On the tenth anniversary of the assassination of Madero and Pino Suárez, the Pro-Madero Group proposed the construction of a Madero monument in the Plaza of the Constitution in Mexico City. Although President Obregón laid the cornerstone on February 22, 1923, the monument was never finished.[36] The Madero and Pino Suárez tombs in Mexico City's French cemetery became de facto monuments, visited by thousands of mourners each February 22 and November 20, covered with flower wreaths, and sometimes marked by an honor guard. It was not until 1956 that the capital city erected a monument to Madero, a bronze statue by Fernández Urbina, which was placed at the intersection of Avenida 20 de Noviembre and Calle Fray Servando Teresa de Mier.[37]

During the 1920s and 1930s additional partisan cults dedicated to the martyrs commemorated the assassinations of Carrillo Puerto, Zapata, Obregón, and finally Carranza, and they constructed worthy tombs and monuments. These and other personalist tendencies, stemming from the factional struggles of the 1910s and 1920s, were of more than historical interest or concern. Writing in 1925, Juan Sánchez Azcona noted that "each split persists within the Revolution-converted-into-Government," and furthermore, these historical divisions "still burden us."[38] An example of the intertwined nature of politics and collective memory is found in a letter from Juan Barragán, an unreconstructed Carrancista, to presidential candidate Pascual Ortiz Rubio in August 1929. Barragán assured Ortiz Rubio that the majority of Carrancistas supported his candidacy. They could never support his opponent, Barragán continued, since Vasconcelos "has never missed an opportunity to denigrate the memory of Señor Carranza."[39]

Carrillo Puerto was perhaps the most memorialized revolutionary of the 1920s. His first monument, a bust on a tall base, was erected in Tacuba (in the Federal District) in 1925 and was the symbolic rallying point of the radicals in the new Calles administration.[40] Obregón unveiled a monument in Mérida, Yucatán, during his presidential campaign in the spring of 1928, "a temple and momento to unite always the people of the Peninsula to defend the precious legacy that [Carrillo Puerto] bequeathed with his blood."[41] In 1932 the government of Yucatán proposed to build, in anticipation of the tenth anniversary of the assassination, one of the greatest monuments in all of Latin America. "It will affirm for many years that the work of the Revolution and the work of its martyrs will not go unappreciated by future generations. For this reason the monument we will construct is of great dimensions."[42] A monument of considerably smaller dimensions was later erected.

Zapata's "humble grave" in Cuautla served each tenth of April as the setting for commemorations of the Apostle of Agrarianism. Throughout the 1920s Zapatistas, like Maderistas, pushed unsuccessfully for the construction of a monument. "To synthesize in bronze or stone the profound sentiment of gratitude that flows in the soul of the campesinos for the Martyr of Chinameca," wrote agraristas of the National Peasant League (Liga Nacional de Campesinos, LNC), "is no easy thing for sure." In 1927 the LNC proposed a monument to Zapata, not one with all the "vulgarity of bourgeois art" as in Porfirian times but a monument "very Mexican and very peasant at the same time"—a pyramid.[43] Even with Diego Rivera's support and design, the idea languished. Three years later the Central League of Peasant Communities marked the house Zapata occupied in Mexico City in 1914 with a marble plaque.[44] Finally, in 1932, a commemorative monument was erected in Cuautla by Zapatista veterans and the state government of Morelos. On April 10, 1932, the ashes of Zapata, placed in an urn, were deposited inside the base of the monument. This first monument to Zapata remains one of the finest. The equestrian statue was one of the first works of a young sculptor who very quickly became legendary, Oliverio Martínez. The composition shows Zapata on horseback, his right hand on the shoulder of a campesino, who looks up at the caudillo. "The new statue will speak of Zapata. Not the real Zapata but the one that little by little is being transformed into the symbolic Redeemer."[45]

The greatest single monument to an individual revolutionary was dedicated to Álvaro Obregón and stands in San Angel, in the Federal District. Unlike most other commemorative monuments of the day, the Obregón monument was constructed by order of the national government. Obregonistas, however, many of whom occupied some of the most important posts in government, managed to elevate their factional symbolic interest to official status. The monument, designed by Enrique Aragón, is reminiscent of an ancient temple: a stairway, bounded on each side by a large female figure in stone, leads to a doorway at the base of a short tower.[46] A two-story marble and granite chamber inside the monument holds a bronze statue of Obregón. Two magnificent exterior sculpture groups, the work of Ignacio Asúnsolo, display stone figures symbolizing Sacrifice on one side and Triumph on the other.[47] The monument, approved in 1930 and completed five years later, became the grandest revolutionary monument in the country. "Álvaro Obregón, in the place of your sacrifice," Aarón Sáenz declared at the inauguration ceremony, "the country consecrates to your memory this momento in stone."[48]

The death of Obregón permitted the symbolic rebirth of Carranza. Several former Carrancistas returned from exile abroad and a new martyr cult was organized. The apotheosis was soon underway. In 1929 the government named the military sports complex in Mexico City after Carranza and in 1931 his name (along with that of Zapata) was engraved on the wall of the Chamber of Deputies, and thus added to the official pantheon of national heroes. On November 20, 1932, the remains of Carranza were transferred from his "humble grave" in the Dolores cemetery, honored in the Chamber of Deputies for a period of twelve hours, and finally entombed again in the Dolores cemetery in the Retonda de los Hombres Ilustres.[49] Former Carrancistas paid for and erected a commemorative stele—designed and sculpted by Dr. Atl—at the site of Carranza's death, Tlaxcalan-tongo, Puebla, on February 9, 1936.[50]

The great revolutionary caudillos were gone by the 1930s and the new "institutional" political system and the "revolutionary" party more than ever before needed whatever symbolic support and historical legitimacy it could garner from the liberal and revolutionary past. Monuments to particular revolutionary caudillos were all the rage, but these symbols did not solve any of the political problems involved in the ongoing institutionalization of *la Revolución*. Beginning in 1929 and 1930 the ruling group and its associated intellectuals, journalists, and political hacks stressed the political unification of all revolutionaries. The squabbling political factions of the present became the Revolutionary Family, and the factional struggles of the past became *nuestra madre común: La Revolución*, "our common mother: the Revolution."[51] Unification in the present was dependent, in part, upon the mending of old but still bitter disputes. The factionalism perpetuated by the cults of martyrs, Juan Sánchez Azcona warned, undermined any "effective political organization of the revolutionary people."[52] The cults of martyrs, then, needed to be subsumed within an official, unified revolutionary tradition. "Unity," Moisés Sáenz declared in 1929, "is our crying need!"[53]

LA REVOLUCIÓN HECHA MONUMENTO

In 1932 workmen began to demolish the iron frame structure of the long-abandoned Federal Legislative Palace in Mexico City. Architect Carlos Obregón Santacilia immediately went to see Alberto Pani, the minister of the treasury, to stop the work. Obregón Santacilia grew up in the shadow of the structure, was fascinated by it, and developed an interest in architecture because of it. The site, its great metal corridors, huge marble blocks, and the space created by the great dome frame, had been his playground and still exercised his imagination. The man who went to see the minister had designed some of the most innovative and impressive public buildings in postrevolutionary Mexico. Nevertheless, his request to convert the frame structure into a massive monument to commemorate *la Revolución* was not approved. Obregón Santacilia left Pani's office, he later recalled, "almost without hope."[54]

Mexico rediscovered its enthusiasm for commemorative monuments in the 1930s. The caudillos of *la Revolución* were being immortalized in stone and bronze but there was no monument to *la Revolución* itself, nothing similar in purpose and function to the Column of Independence. The idea, however, was picking up speed. The official newspaper of the National Revolutionary Party editorialized in 1930, for example, that it was time to stop writing partisan history and building statues to the martyrs of revolutionary factions. One day, continued the editorial, a monument to *la Revolución* will be erected. "It will not be one that satisfies a faction, but rather something that consecrates the great success of our racial, cultural, and economic integration, an essential fact of our civilization. In such a monument there will not be agrarianism, nor Zapatismo, nor Carrancismo, nor Callismo."[55] One of the young turks of nationalist sculpture, Luis Ortiz Monasterio, was attracted to this idea in 1931. Although never built, his austere, modernist mock-up entitled "Monumento a la Revolución," a pantheon for all of the revolutionary heroes, reflected the thinking of official culture and anticipated the monument to come.[56]

In 1932 the erection of the Zapata monument in Cuautla sparked a public debate about the political wisdom and propriety of building monuments to individual revolutionary caudillos. The governor of Querétaro intervened in a dramatic manner; he proposed a national competition among artists to design a monument to *la Revolución* to be erected in his state, a monument that would crystallize in a definitive form its goals and ideals. In his decree, Governor Saturnino Osornio called on "all former Revolutionaries to forget their grudges, put aside their hateful motives and personal differences, yield to the voice of *la Revolución* and open their hearts, which beat to the same rhythm."[57] A few months later Obregón Santacilia proposed to transform the frame of the Palacio Legislativo Federal into a monument to *la Revolución*. The timing was right.

After overcoming his initial skepticism, Minister Pani took the idea to Calles, the Jefe Máximo, and on January 15, 1933, the pair announced the official Monumento a la Revolución project.[58] They proposed a monument of "extraordinary commemorative force," one that would honor "the greatest event of our history." Eight days later President Abelardo Rodríguez approved the idea and established the Grand Patronage Committee of the Monument to the Revolution, to be chaired by Calles, and he donated the metallic structure of the Federal Legislative Palace to the committee.[59]

Obregón Santacilia designed a massive domed tetra pylon, a structure set on four-columns. The four piers of the iron skeleton were encased in concrete, sheathed in light Mexican *chiluca* stone, then edged in porous black volcanic stone, producing four great arches, each over 18 meters wide and 26 meters high. Obregón Santacilia preserved the design of the original building, which placed a hemispheric dome on top of an elliptical one. This double dome prevents the tall arches from diminishing the monumental effect of the exterior hemispherical roof, which reaches a height of 65 meters. Two observation decks, one at the base of the exterior dome and the second on top of it, were provided, and two elevators were built into the piers in order to reach them. (From the upper deck, the pyramids of Teotihuacan were clearly visible in those days before smog.) The base of the plaza itself was gradually raised several meters, sloping toward the monument, enhancing the grandeur of the plaza and the monument itself. Below the raised floor of the monument, rooms were constructed whose function was to be determined later. The style of the monument was "modern regionalism"—a fusion of Mexican themes and materials with art deco lines.[60]

In September 1933 an open competition was held for the best design of the four sculpture groups to be placed, one on each corner, at the base of the monument's double dome. More than forty sculptors entered the competition and five were selected to make full-scale plaster models (11.5 meters in height); two of these models would be placed on the monument itself to determine the best design.[61] The winner, Oliverio Martínez, already known for his equestrian statue of Zapata in Cuautla, placed three figures in each group; the center figure in each is standing and the other two are sitting. The large size, clarity, and simplicity of these figures, and their distinctiveness in relief, make them visible and understandable to observers near and far. Their indistinct clothing give them a timeless quality. Martínez's figures are strong, proud, unbowed peasants and proletarians, soldiers and citizens, men and women, unmistakably Mexican—Indian and mestizo.[62] It is here, notes one critic, "where the definitive battle has been joined to authenticate the new sculptural ideal of postrevolutionary Mexico."[63]

Obregón Santacilia, Martínez, Calles, and Pani proposed, designed, and constructed a monument with a message, a text interpreting modern Mexican history in metal and stone. The revolution that the monument proclaimed and symbolized was popular and victorious, a continuation of earlier liberal-national struggles, and most importantly, permanent, singular, and whole, in short, *la Revolución.*

The monument's revolution was a people's revolution. It was described in the official initiative as a "collective work" and "the struggle of the people in the conquest of their rights." The "long-suffering mass of anonymous fighters," the proposal continued, were no less generous in their sacrifice than were the famous heroes, martyrs, and caudillos of *la Revolución*, and therefore, "this makes them deserving of national gratitude."[64]

Monumentality has long symbolized conquest and triumph. *La Revolución*, as it was interpreted in this grand edifice, was unambiguously triumphant, a victory of the people against the Reaction. In their formal proposal Calles and Pani referred to the intended monument as "un Arco de Triunfo," a triumphal arch. The very origin of the monument symbolized the triumph of *la Revolución* over the Porfirian regime. As Obregón Santacilia noted later: "From the ruins of the ancien régime, from the very building designed to perpetuate it, arose the Monument to the Social Revolution that defeated it."[65] The Monument to the Revolution, both massive and tall, was designed to be, as Calles and Pani wrote, "the greatest [monument] in the Capital of the Republic," one possessing "features of beauty and a magnitude of extraordinary commemorative force."[66]

This monument to the popular revolution was to be paid for by the people through a national subscription. "The monument should be the work of all and for all," Pani emphasized in his fundraising letter to state governors.[67] Newspapers often reported the small but onerous contributions of distant pueblos and poor *ejidos.* Governors and mayors organized bullfights and "authentic popular fiestas" to raise money. Army garrisons, primary schools, and private citizens sent in small donations.[68] The construction of the monument would also be of a popular, revolutionary character. Construction was deliberately begun on a revolutionary anniversary, and the stone for the building was cut by the workers of the Revolutionary Syndicate of Stonecutters of the Mexican Revolution, which, reportedly, had been the first labor union officially recognized by the new revolutionary government in 1911.[69]

The version of *la Revolución* embodied in the monument extended far into the past and continued into the present and the future. Calles and Pani argued, consistent with revolutionary discourse extending back to the 1910s, that the "great Mexican Revolution" developed in three stages: the first, "political emancipation," was the struggle for national independence in the 1810s; the second, "spiritual emancipation," was the Reform and the struggle against the French Intervention of the 1850s and 1860s; and the third, "economic emancipation," was the struggle of the people that began in 1910 and was directed against the privileged for popular government and a more equal division of wealth. The Monument to the Revolution would portray this continuity of struggle by means of the four allegorical sculpture groups.

Oliverio Martínez, unfortunately, never commented on the specific symbolism of the sculpture groups. They can, however, be "read," although some "passages" are a little obscure. The group located on the southeast corner symbolizes National Independence: a stoic indigenous figure is standing, flanked by a mother and child and a kneeling man holding a shattered chain. The group located on the northeast corner symbolizes the Reform: the standing figure is holding a sword, while the two sitting figures are each holding a book, perhaps representing the law. The group located on the southwest corner symbolizes the Redemption of the Peasant: the figures are clearly campesinos; the standing figure is holding what is probably a land grant title, while one of the sitting figures is reading a book and the other, a mother, is holding a child. The last group, located on the northwest corner, symbolizes the Redemption of the Worker: these are male, urban laborers, the standing figure holding machine parts, one of the sitting figures holding a hammer, and the last demonstrating the strength of his arms.

Since the Sonorans' postrevolutionary governments, and especially Calles himself, emphasized the idea of permanent revolution (*la Revolución hecha gobierno*, the Revolution converted into government and sustained by reform), Calles and Pani proposed that the monument "should prolong its commemorative action, also into an undefined future." This endeavor promised, then, *la Revolución hecha monumento*, the Revolution converted into a monument and sustained by commemoration. The Monument to the Revolution, therefore, was to be inscribed with these words: "To the Revolution of yesterday, of today, of tomorrow, of always." [70]

Finally, *la Revolución* portrayed by the monument was one: a singular revolution, not a heterogeneous mix of ideas, movements, factions, and caudillos. This message was related by omission of the obvious. The "fundamental characteristic" of the monument, noted Calles and Pani in their proposal, is that "it will not be erected to the glory of specific heroes, martyrs, or caudillos." On the monument, they continued, "there will be no names nor portraits of persons. It will glorify, in the abstract, the secular work of the people." The Monument to the Revolution, a reaction against personalism and factionalism in Mexican collective memory, would ignore the revolutionary factions and their chiefs altogether and glorify only *la Revolución* itself.[71]

Work on the monument began on August 14, 1933 (that date was chosen by the executive committee because it was the anniversary of the 1914 entry of the Constitutionalist army into Mexico City). The committee hoped to complete and inaugurate the monument on the twentieth of November the following year.[72] Three thousand workers, mostly masons and stonecutters, were employed on and off in the project. Obregón Santacilia reported that during construction he filled the 30,000 square meter plaza three times with stone for the monument. In 1936, with the construction still ongoing, Obregón Santacilia drew up plans to convert the rooms below the monument into a museum of the revolution with four galleries; this idea was not acted on at the time for lack of funds.[73] Funding, in fact, was the principal problem that delayed completion of all phases of the project.

The monument was supposed to be financed by public subscription, and the executive committee created an impressive public relations campaign that emphasized the numerous small donations of humble people, communities, and organizations. These moneys, however, never came close to financing even 10 percent of the project's cost. Every state governor pledged the enthusiastic support of his state, yet their contributions were also woefully inadequate. Funding campaigns were often interrupted as a result of natural disasters (which diverted monument funds to disaster relief) and the transition of the presidential administration in 1934–35. Most of the cost of the construction (estimated at approximately 500,000 to 600,000 pesos over five years) was shared by the PNR and the government of the Federal District.[74]

The Monument to the Revolution was completed on November 20, 1938, but there was no inaugural ceremony. Indeed, neither the Cárdenas regime nor its successor, that of Manuel Ávila Camacho, staged even part of the twentieth of November commemoration rituals at the monument. (Was it, one wonders, too closely identified in official circles with Callismo?) It is also possible that the monument, and revolutionary symbolism in general, became more important as the postrevolutionary regimes became increasingly conservative. Perhaps the reason the government kept its distance was the less than roaring popular approval of the monument's design. Some Mexico City residents said that it looked like the world's largest gas station. Newspaper cartoons made fun of its appearance. Alberto Pani later repudiated the design, saying that there should have been a competition among architects to select the best plan for the site.[75]

THE TOMB OF LA REVOLUCIÓN

A public monument is a continuing presence in a community,
but is it an active presence?[76]

In 1960, Carlos Obregón Santacilia declared proudly that the Monument to the Revolution had become "the indispensable scene of the most emotive acts of the country, where the largest numbers of citizens gather in order to forever feel like they belong."[77] This is clearly the image projected by a 1940 woodcut by Balmori, which shows President Cárdenas addressing a mass audience; the people with their banners are dwarfed by *la Revolución* as symbolized by the monument.[78] Official rhetoric was no less emphatic: "the great Monumento a la Revolución, stone symbol of the Mexican devotion to the causes of Democracy, Liberty, and Justice."[79] The commemorative and didactic function of the monument, it would appear, served the purpose designed by its creators.

Year after year the monument has served as the stage for official ceremonies remembering and honoring the Revolution and its heroes. Anniversary ceremonies of Madero's *grito* of 1910, the deaths of martyrs and caudillos, the Constitution of 1917, the expropriation of the foreign oil holdings in 1938, and other significant events in Mexican history, take place, according to official notices, "bajo la bóveda del Monumento a la Revolución" (under the dome of the Monument to the Revolution). "Under its dome and between its wide pillars," declared Jesús Silva Herzog in 1979, "we relive today the historic moments of our people."[80]

The successful monument, writes William Gass, has offspring, "it multiplies itself in images."[81] The image and outline of the Monument to the Revolution has multiplied as a result of the symbolic metonymy in which the edifice stands for *la Revolución*. The government agency responsible for disseminating revolutionary history has adopted the monument as its identifying symbol. The cover of Alberto Morales Jiménez's official history of the revolution, republished in 1961, shows the monument. The Authentic Party of the Mexican Revolution (Partido Auténtico de la Revolución Mexicana) has incorporated the image of the monument into its official emblem. In Mexico City, the subway station nearest the monument is named "Revolución" and is pictorially represented by an outline of the structure.

The monument's enduring evocative power has had less to do with its original design and symbolism than with a subsequent modification. In the early 1940s, perhaps at the suggestion of Congress, Obregón Santacilia designed a *panteón de los hombres ilustres* (pantheon of illustrious men) to be located in the base below the monument, an honored cemetery for the leaders of the Revolution.[82] This *panteón* was never realized, but by order of Congress a copper urn containing the ashes of Carranza was deposited in a crypt in one of the four piers in January 1942, on the twenty-fifth anniversary of the Constitution of 1917.[83] Over the next three decades the ashes or remains of Madero (1960), Calles (1969), Cárdenas (1970) and, finally, Villa (1976) were transferred to the different piers of the monument. Each entombment was the occasion for a massive popular tribute.

"The actual presence of martyrs," notes George Mosse, "was always important for the effectiveness of places of pilgrimage."[84] The placement of the ashes and remains of the five revolutionary leaders modified and enhanced the meaning of the monument. Originally designed to glorify, "in the abstract, the secular work of the people," it became identified with the great caudillos of *la Revolución*. The placement of the ashes and remains of leaders who were rivals, and in most cases bitter enemies, when alive breathed life into the concept of the singular and unified mythic revolution much more than did the previous cold, monolithic design. While partisan organizations, the separate civic associations of followers of Carranza, Madero, Calles, Cárdenas, and Villa, still maintain "the sincere veneration of our great patriots," orations since the 1960s have emphasized revolutionary unity.[85] Referring to the political differences between Calles and Cárdenas, Calles's son noted in 1971 that "when they were entombed in the same monument, the justice of *la Revolución* dissolved their differences." At the same ceremony, President Luis Echeverría Álvarez concluded, "we have consolidated one Mexican revolutionary thesis above the divergences of the past."[86]

The addition of these prestigious tombs has transformed the Monument to the Revolution into a sacred temple of the nation.[87] More than any other feature, the crypts have turned the monument into an active presence in the symbolic life (and commemorative calendar) of Mexico. On the anniversaries of the assassinations and deaths of the five leaders, the state organizes commemorative ceremonies at the monument (decorated for the occasion with huge Mexican flags, banners, and portraits), which involve orations, the laying of wreaths, music, and military honor guards. "Year after year," noted José González Bustamante in 1951 at a ceremony honoring Carranza, "we come to this monument, which the Mexican people have consecrated as the sanctuary of *la Revolución*, in order to remember the great caudillo who rests within these stones."[88]

Yet another afterthought has served to keep the monument an active presence in Mexican culture. Although Obregón Santacilia presented his plans for a museum of the revolution in 1936, it was not until November 20, 1986, that the National Museum of the Revolution became a reality. The museum is supported financially by the government of the Federal District; its content and historical narrative was organized by historians of the Dr. José María Luis Mora Institute of Investigation. The museum, which is open to the public free of charge, is composed of nine halls that exhibit documents, photos, clothing, tools, and weapons.[89]

CONCLUSION

"We must go on to ask how memorial representations of history may finally weave themselves into the course of ongoing events."[90] The Monument to the Revolution was built, primarily, to heal the wounds of memory that divided revolutionaries and retarded and weakened the development of a new institutional political order. The development of an official Revolutionary Tradition, of which the monument was a part, accomplished this goal, and over time the original problems of divisiveness became less important and therefore of less political concern. They have not, however, disappeared completely. The monument has emphasized as well the continuity between *la Revolución* and its heroes and present-day regimes. This element of the Revolutionary Tradition remains relevant and current. The monument's primary purpose has always been and remains the legitimization of state power and authority.[91]

Does it work? There is, of course, no way to test this proposition, but perhaps an anecdote can shed some light on the question. A few years ago I attended a ceremony at the Monument to the Revolution. It was a beautiful summer's day in July on the sixty-eighth anniversary of the assassination of Pancho Villa. Bands played, soldiers paraded, aging veterans were honored, and politicians placed a floral wreath at the door of the crypt holding the mortal remains of the caudillo. The event, it seemed, was another unremarkable example of official commemoration. After the ceremony, visitors were permitted to enter the small crypt to view the copper urn. Ahead of me in line were a father and his young son. The man was telling the boy about Villa and *la Revolución*. It was a serious history lesson. In the crypt the father stopped for a moment of silence, his head reverently bowed, and when he turned around to leave I saw tears on his face. Something small but profound had happened there. Some potent mixture of memory, myth, and history had been at work in what is the constant construction of nationhood. Scholars often refer to the process of sacralization that takes place at monuments. On that day I witnessed that process firsthand.

6 HISTORY

The Work of Concord and Unification

DURING THE 1960s veterans of *la Revolución* gathered every August to offer their political support to the president during what came to be known as the Breakfast of Revolutionary Unity. Unity in the present was projected upon the past. The bitter factional rivalries of earlier years were downplayed or forgotten as hundreds of *viejos revolucionarios*—the so-called spent cartridges of the Revolution—declared by their presence satisfaction with the revolutionary character of the present regime and the permanent revolution. "Our struggle was an authentic revolution," declared the featured speaker at the 1966 breakfast, General Baltasar R. Leyva Mancilla. "It was not a rampage of factions or political maneuverings for personal aggrandizement."[1]

The veterans who organized and attended these breakfasts subscribed to an interpretation that decades earlier had been constructed as the official memory of *la Revolución*. We have seen that many elements of this interpretation emerged quite early in the revolutionary discourse of memory. *La Revolución* was a genuine social revolution, a force of history itself, a continuation and expansion of the revolutions of Independence and the Reform, and victorious against a weakened but still dangerous Reaction. During the 1920s the idea of a continuing and permanent revolution, revolution converted into government and advanced through reform, was added to the interpretation. Most would agree with Rafael Nieto, who wrote in 1925 that "*la Revolución* of Mexico" had been "one revolution that manifested itself for more than a decade."[2]

Despite considerable consensus, the intense factionalism of the 1910s and the lingering factionalism of the 1920s and 1930s precluded the writing of a revolutionary history to which all revolutionaries could subscribe. "In the 1920s," writes Mary Kay Vaughan, the Secretaría de Educación Pública "published no textbooks to establish an official revolutionary vision of Mexican history."[3] Rival, even hostile, revolutionary traditions emerged from the multiple revolutionary schisms. As a result, amateur historians extolled the unimpeachable revolutionary credentials of their faction and portrayed their enemies as revolutionary impostors. The early histories of *la Revolución*—similar to early commemoration through festivals and monuments—were profoundly partisan, instruments in the developing cults of martyrs. "I know of no history of Mexico," noted one amateur historian in 1927, "that is written with any objectivity."[4]

Did it matter? Increasingly in the 1920s a number of voices said it did. In 1925, Juan Sánchez Azcona argued that the "schisms of *la Revolución*" extending from as early as 1910 and 1911 still undermined the power and solidarity of the revolutionary family. This problem, he continued, was responsible for the lack of "a suitable POLITICAL organization of the Revolutionary People."[5] This is an exaggeration, of course, but there is plenty of anecdotal evidence showing how bitterness from the past affected politics in the present.

One example is revealing. General Juan Barragán, Carranza's chief of staff and one of the opinion leaders of former Carrancistas in the 1920s and after, remarked in 1928 that he was loyal and devoted to the memory of Carranza and had maintained his animus against the authors (Obregón and Calles) of the overthrow of the First Chief. His political views were still hostage to the politics of memory. In considering the two possible presidential candidates who might run for the office the following year, José Vasconcelos and Aarón Sáenz, Barragán's position was based on an interesting logic. He rejected Vasconcelos out of hand because "he has been a bitter personal enemy of Señor Carranza, someone who has attacked him constantly." Sáenz, on the other hand, although a member of a faction hostile to Carranza and his followers, "has never fought Señor Carranza, neither during his life nor after this death. Furthermore, Aarón Sáenz remained on the margin of events in 1920." Barragán's choice, then, was Sáenz, the candidate least offensive to those still loyal to Carranza.[6]

Certainly one cannot say that the multiple wounds of memory that persisted even in the late 1920s dominated national politics. They were, however, part of the political equation and therefore a partial obstacle to the political unification of all revolutionaries. So long as Obregón remained the Caudillo, the political unification of all revolutionaries—while desirable—was unnecessary. Obregón's enormous prestige ensured that the divisions among revolutionaries past and present were generally kept under control. That is what Ezequiel Padilla was referring to in 1927 when he warned that Mexico faced a bleak choice in the upcoming election: "Obregón or chaos." Remove Obregón from the political scene, however, and his successors would need to employ every tool of political solidarity to hold the system together, including official history.

The last and perhaps most important concept in the definition of *la Revolución*, the complementary nature of the various struggles, movements, and contentious factions and therefore the essential singularity of *la Revolución*, while constructed in the 1920s was only truly honored in the 1930s. It was only then that all of the elements of Mexico's modern myth were put together for the first time.

TO SERVE THE HISTORIANS OF THE EPOCH

The first bibliography of *la Revolución*, Ignacio B. del Castillo's *Bibliografía de la Revolución Mexicana de 1910–1916*, appeared in 1918. This Ministry of Communications publication listed eight hundred books, pamphlets, revolutionary plans, and manifestos, as well as government documents and decrees.[7] Thirteen years later, another ministry published a second bibliography with a similar title. This one, by Roberto Ramos, more than doubled the number of works listed, to over eighteen hundred, "the greatest number of books and pamphlets related directly or indirectly to the revolutionary movements of 1910 to 1929."[8] Both bibliographers stated their desire to serve the historians of the revolutionary epoch.

While many were engaged in writing about the recent past, only a few competent historians were at work. The respected jurist, journalist, legislator, and government official Ramón Prida wrote one of the first and most objective histories of the revolution while in exile in the United States in 1914. He set the tone for the book with an epigram by Charles XII: "History is not a Flatterer but a Witness." In his introduction he notes, "Throughout, I judge deeds and men with the merciless and impersonal severity of the historian."[9] And so he did. Prida was critical of Porfirio Díaz for suppressing true democratic development of Mexico, of Francisco Madero who, despite his honorable nature and good intentions, was incapable of reconverting Mexico into a stable democracy, and of Victoriano Huerta for instituting a military despotism. He maintained that "the present revolution [led by Carranza] is fully justified because of the unspeakable acts committed by those in power.[10]

The few semiobjective early histories came from the pens of those who, like Prida, made their careers during the Porfiriato. Francisco Bulnes, Manuel Calero, Emilio Rabasa, and José López-Portillo y Rojas, all of whom published their histories in 1920–21, defended as well as criticized the Porfirian regime but saw little good gained against the terrible division and destruction of the preceding ten years. It was their belief in peaceful evolution, rather than violent revolution, that identified them as heretics in this new age.[11]

Most writers pursued other objectives besides understanding. Francisco Padilla González stated that his goal was to motivate those who fought in the struggle; Antonio Manero characterized himself as an "intellectual soldier" in service to the Constitutionalist movement; Isidro Fabela and Luis Cabrera sought to influence public opinion in the United States and Spain.[12] For nearly all these authors, books and pamphlets were simply weapons of a different kind. The official Carrancista history of "the revolutionary period" was written by Jesús Acuña for the Ministry of Government for presentation to the constitutional convention meeting in Querétaro in late 1916. Acuña's history included the most complete compilation of revolutionary plans and documents to that point in order to "prove" that the First Chief was the revolutionary champion of the Mexican people.[13] One of Mexico's most respected jurists, T. Esquivel Obregón, argued in 1919 that "as civil strife grows fiercer, those who narrate political events adhere more tenaciously to the idea that history is a tribunal, in order that they may lay the blame and curse of history upon their adversaries."[14]

Fewer histories were produced during the 1920s than in the previous decade. The passion of conflict was receding while the enthusiasm for commemoration, which comes only after the passing of time, had not yet grown strong. Factions that had been outside the developing official memory during the 1910s now sought respect after the fact. Anarchists and Marxists argued that their ideological predecessors in the late nineteenth century had contributed significantly to the outbreak of the social revolution and that their ideas and ideals were relevant still.[15] The new Ricardo Flores Magón Cultural Group published a number of volumes on Magonismo and its struggle against the dictatorship.[16] The first favorable Zapatista histories also appeared during the 1920s, portraying Obregón and Calles as Zapatistas and thus friends of Mexico's peasant farmers.[17]

In 1927 a Mexican historian stated that he knew of no objective history of Mexico. The "least bad," he continued, was Justo Sierra's *Historia Patria*.[18] Following one of Mexico's most violent and transformative episodes there was no recent history that Mexicans or even revolutionaries could recommend. In 1922, Education Minister José Vasconcelos republished Sierra's prerevolutionary history of Mexico. The old standard would have to do until something acceptable appeared.[19] Three years later a young revolutionary economist, Daniel Cosío Villegas, wrote: "*La Revolución* has created institutions, laws, public works, an ideology and even a language. The works, for the most part, are good; the institutions are just; but the language and ideology are confused." A new revolutionary culture needed a new history, one that would help Mexico to understand its revolutionary identity. Cosío Villegas proposed the unification of the immediate past and the present so as to permit the revolution to continue in the future. And, in an interesting suggestion notable for its prescience, he proposed the amalgamation of the factional struggles of the previous decade, converting them into *la Revolución*—"with a capital letter"—thus creating a revolutionary concept of social relations, of humankind, and of historical vision.[20]

REVOLUTIONARY UNIFICATION

Obregón's assassination presented the postrevolutionary political order with its greatest crisis. It signified, writes Tzvi Medin, "the disappearance of the only principle of unity and stability known in the Mexican political tradition until that moment."[21] President Calles and the fragile ruling coalition of Obregonistas and Callistas emphasized the need for the political unification of revolutionaries. "I insist that it is absolutely indispensable, if we want peace and an institutional order in Mexico," declared Calles in December 1928, "that we achieve revolutionary unification."[22] The National Revolutionary Party (PNR) was established in 1929 "in accordance with the plan of unification and organization of all the elements of the Revolution from the Maderista beginning to the present."[23] The PNR, noted one of its directors, desired "to obscure old rivalries, to forget hatreds."[24]

To overcome the divisiveness of the past, the PNR, under the leadership of Emilio Portes Gil, proposed in May 1930 to take control of revolutionary history. The party, it was announced, would establish an archive, a museum, and commission the writing of the history of *la Revolución*. Commissions, composed of individuals who had participated in the various revolutionary movements, would gather relevant documentation. For the periods of greatest intensity, such 1914–15, for example, various commissions would be named, each one composed of individuals who had belonged to the principal factions then in conflict: Villismo, Carrancismo, Zapatismo. The Historical Archive of the Revolution, led by Jesús Silva Herzog, would be the foundation upon which the history of *la Revolución* would be written. "It would not be a question, then, of writing the history of a faction; it would not be a sectarian labor in any sense; to write the history of the revolutionary social movement of Mexico in all of its generous vastness is what is desired."[25]

The new ruling party was not as culturally hegemonic as some of its leaders apparently desired: the PNR's history campaign never got off the ground. The plan was noteworthy, nevertheless, for affirming the "generous vastness" of *la Revolución*. This "brilliant conceptualization," noted *El Nacional*, was "created to support a specific course in politics today," namely, revolutionary solidarity.[26]

Mexico's mainstream political culture embraced the idea of historical conciliation enthusiastically, thereby obviating the need for the PNR to manage revolutionary history. In July 1931 the Chamber of Deputies simultaneously placed the names of Venustiano Carranza and Emiliano Zapata on its wall, alongside those of the heroes of the Independence and the Reform. (Madero had been so honored in 1925, the first of the revolutionary generation. He was followed by Alvaro Obregón in 1929 and Felipe Carrillo Puerto in 1930.[27]) For Jesús Corral of *El Nacional*, there was simply no fundamental reason for prolonging the "quarrel" that separated in life the great dead of the emancipation movement. "The enmity and distance that the vicissitudes of politics provoked between Madero and Zapata, between Zapata and Carranza, between Carranza and Obregón, matter not."[28]

Emilio Portes Gil later asserted that the "collective and impersonal interpretation of heroes" had become a "doctrine of the State."[29] This was emphasized in the PNR's annual *Calendario Nacionalista* of the 1930s, which celebrated commemorative holidays for every revolutionary caudillo (and presented a group portrait of the founding fathers of the Revolutionary Family). The General Committee of the Nationalist Campaign, which produced the calendar, embraced "the work of concord and unification."[30]

The writing of history remained hostage to discordant revolutionary traditions.[31] "Mexican historiography," wrote historian Luis Chávez Orozco, "has come to the point that many writers see in it the best means to manifest their passions and exhibit their political positions. The interpretations that they make about the past are converted into a weapon for combat in the present."[32] Partisan history, however, increasingly came under attack in the 1930s. For many critics partisan history was simply unreliable history. The history of *la Revolución*, according to one typical commentator, "has been audaciously adulterated by the partisans of this or that idol of their passions."[33] Another critic, on the eve of the first Mexican Congress of History in 1933, declared that "now is the time to end the spirit of battle in which our history has been written, and study it objectively."[34] For others, such as José Domingo Ramírez Garrido, partisan history served to divide the Revolutionary Family and furthered the political advancement of ambitious careerists and false revolutionaries.[35]

In 1931, Rafael Ramos Pedrueza provided "revolutionary suggestions" for the teaching of history. Although his primary interest was in promoting an economic interpretation of history, Ramos Pedrueza clearly opposed partisan factional history. *La Revolución* was made by Madero, Carranza, Zapata, Villa, and Obregón. The Sonoran caudillo was praised because "his government unified revolutionary elements, putting an end to the cycles of schisms." A revolutionary teacher, he concluded, "in his classes and presentations, in the press and in his books, in all of his intellectual activities, should promote the idea that *la Revolución* is alive and triumphant."[36]

J. D. Ramírez Garrido, a former Maderista, Constitucionalista, Obregonista, and Delahuertista, in 1934 began the first magazine devoted to revolutionary history, *La Revolución Mexicana*. "The purest eclecticism will inspire our labors," Ramírez Garrido wrote in the first number. "With the bitter and painful experience of years, now we have liberated ourselves from this or that ISTA."[37] Each issue included articles sympathetic to a wide range of revolutionary factions as well as regional movements.

Ramírez Garrido and *La Revolución Mexicana* also proposed and tried to organize a more ambitious historical project, a "true Monument of the Revolution." A comprehensive "historical, geographical, biographical, and bibliographical dictionary of the Mexican Revolution" was the goal. Like the PNR's "archive" four years earlier, the proposed historical dictionary would be the collective work of numerous "revolutionary writers," for the most part men of different and opposing factions. "Sectarians," however, were to be excluded from the project. While the officers of the project were all former Carrancista generals, the board included noted Maderistas, Villistas, and Zapatistas.[38] Nothing came of this project. The following year, however, a much less ambitious *Diccionario Biográfico Revolucionario* was published by Francisco Naranjo. His "little work," he wrote, was intended to "serve as a tie of union, as a fraternal bond, within the great revolutionary family."[39]

Beginning in 1929, simultaneous with the foundation of the ruling revolutionary party, agents of the new political order sought to heal the discord of memory within the Revolutionary Family. The new understanding emphasized the special contribution that each revolutionary faction made to the ideology of the Revolution. Madero, Zapata, Villa, Carranza, and Obregón became the founding fathers of this fragile family and state-information. The past was imaginatively reconstructed, just one tool among many, in order to put together and hold together a political alliance.[40]

SEMIOFFICIAL HISTORY

The third attempt to produce a collective, comprehensive, and nonpartisan history of *la Revolución* succeeded. In early 1935, President Lázaro Cárdenas received a letter from Senator Josue Escobedo and José T. Meléndez, who represented themselves as the editorial committee of the "History Book of the Mexican Revolution." They requested, and received, authorization to examine all documents related to *la Revolución* in government files.[41] Meléndez was a journalist loosely associated with the PNR's *El Nacional*, who, through Escobedo, had the backing of General Saturnino Cedillo. In a second letter to Cárdenas a month later, Escobedo and Meléndez explained the fundamental character of their "history book": "This is a project that seeks the collaboration of all revolutionaries without distinction of faction or category so as to produce a complete Work, worthy of the same nobility that inspired the Great Popular Movement."[42]

Meléndez's proposed history found favor with Cárdenas, who approved its publication by the government press later in the year. The president shared the basic premise of the project, namely, "the Revolution as a unitary phenomenon."[43] As Cárdenas wrote in his diary in 1937, the memories of Madero, Zapata, Carranza, and Obregón should be respected, for they were "caudillos that together were an epoch that struggled for social demands."[44]

Meléndez organized and edited what was undoubtedly the best history of *la Revolución* to date. The work, published under the title *Historia de la Revolución Mexicana*, was organized chronologically and divided into two volumes. The first, published in 1936, included essays on the Díaz regime and the origins of *la Revolución*, the crimes of Huertismo, the American intervention of 1914, and the Aguascalientes convention. This history portrayed the Porfiriato as "the dictatorship," the Flores Magón group was ratified as "the precursors," and each revolutionary faction was presented as making an essential contribution to the ideology of *la Revolución* and to the Constitution of 1917. This volume was dominated by three essays, on three key revolutionary leaders, written by men who had known and served their subjects. Juan Sánchez Azcona, President Madero's private secretary, wrote the essay on Madero; Dr. Ramón Puente, a Maderista who became one of Villa's advisors, produced the essay on Villa; and Octavio Paz Solórzano, a propagandist for the Zapatista cause in the United States, wrote on Zapata. (An essay on Venustiano Carranza by Manuel Aguirre Berlanga was planned for this volume but never completed.) In the prologue, Puente noted that Madero, Carranza, Zapata, and Villa sometimes were in conflict with one another, but he emphasized that all were genuine revolutionaries who struggled (each in his own way) on behalf of "popular redemption." As a result, "together they became a conglomeration of blood, of destruction, of greatness and heroism, and of that heterogeneous confusion that will secure a better future."[45]

The three central essays are classics of revolutionary historiography. Octavio Paz (the poet and son of Octavio Paz Solórzano), in his introduction to a 1986 reprint, noted that "these are not works of political theory but testimonies: they tell us what they saw and what they lived. More than historical studies, these three biographies are stories that oscillate between memoirs and chronicles. And therein lies their value: they are the primary sources of history."[46] Juan Sánchez Azcona eschewed hero worship. He contradicted the fanatical Maderista tendency "to attribute to Madero all of the glory for the initiation of the renovation of our social democracy."[47] His Madero was a genuine democrat but someone who overestimated the political capacities of the nation. This led Madero to his greatest mistake, according to Sánchez Azcona, the Treaty of Ciudad Juárez that preserved in large part the ancien régime and thus undermined the power and authority of the new revolutionary regime.

Ramón Puente, writes Paz, "portrays Villa with admiration but without illusions."[48] Puente's Villa was generous and cruel, sentimental and cold-blooded, a simple man of the people who was also a military genius. No one was more responsible for the military defeat of the reactionary Huerta regime than Villa and his División del Norte. He was the most genuine representative of the contradictions that are Mexico, "the representative of its ignorance, of its violence, of its courage, of its nobility, a surprising combination of virtues and defects."[49]

Paz Solórzano wrote the most hagiographic of the three essays. His Zapata was "the greatest of the Mexican revolutionaries."[50] This was, of course, due to Zapata's unwavering commitment to agrarian reform and the well-being of Mexico's campesinos. Paz Solórzano was not timid about criticizing Madero, Villa, and Carranza, but he denied all charges of Zapatista atrocities and excesses. As his son Octavio Paz noted, "given similar crimes, the author condemns those of the enemy and absolves those of his comrades."[51]

The second volume, published in 1940, includes sympathetic essays on Presidents Carranza, Obregón, Calles, Portes Gil, Ortiz Rubio, and Abelardo Rodríguez.[52] It was time, noted Vicente Peredo y Saavedra in the introduction, "to depersonalize the concept of the Revolution," to rise above all "*ismos personalistas*" in order to emphasize that *la Revolución* was and is the collective effort to create the nation. "Partisan zeal, one-sided factionalism is the seed of destruction, of annihilation, and of disintegration of national unity."[53]

The second volume was not nearly as good as the first in large part because it did not rise above *ismos personalistas*. General Francisco L. Urquizo's brief essay on Carranza was more eulogy than history or biography. Described in one-sentence paragraphs, Urquizo's Carranza was drenched in poetic metaphors: he was the mountain that endured, the sea that cleansed, the fire that purified. This Carranza was the unequaled patriot, reformer, and constitutionalist, "the symbol of the Revolution, the one who redeemed the country."[54] The essay on Obregón by General Rubén García was more substantial but only slightly less laudatory. Both Urquizo and García leveled severe criticisms at the enemies of their subjects and, in particular, at Francisco Villa. García, however, unlike Urquizo recognized the errors of Obregón ("great men are great even in their errors") of which the most serious was acceptance of reelection in 1928.[55] The best, and certainly the most critical, essay in the second volume is Ramón Puente's on Calles. Puente praised the former president's institutional reforms but characterized the Maximato as "the toughest dictatorship."[56]

Historia de la Revolución Mexicana was "the first history with an encompassing vision, one that does justice to the principal caudillos of the different revolutionary factions."[57] It is also described by Octavio Paz as "a little-known book that was soon forgotten."[58] This history was important, nonetheless, because it reflected the growing tendency of Mexico's political culture of the 1930s and 1940s to heal old wounds. In 1938, J. M. Puig Casauranc expressed this tendency very clearly: "The [revolutionary] movement of Mexico, with its numerous facets, its very different men, with its triumphs, with its bungling, with its crimes has to be judged as 'one and indivisible'—'*la Revolución Mexicana*'."[59] This tendency was semiofficial, since it was semi-independent of government. The writers and historians who participated saw themselves as revolutionaries and adherents of the postrevolutionary order.

What Meléndez began was soon followed by similar efforts. In 1936, Andrés Molina Enríquez finished *La Revolución Agraria de México*, arguing in it that all factions and ethnicities had made *la Revolución:* "criollos" and "criollos-mestizos" represented by the Maderistas and Carrancistas, and "indo-mestizos" represented by the Villistas and Zapatistas.[60] Revolutionary histories by Miguel Alessio Robles, Ramón Puente, and Alfonso Teja Zabre appeared in 1938, Jesús Romero Flores published his four-volume *Anales históricos de la Revolución Mexicana* in 1939, and the multiauthored history and contemporary survey coordinated by Félix F. Palavicini came out in 1945.[61] Agustín Casasola's five-volume photographic history of *la Revolución*, which appeared during the 1940s, was the ultimate in inclusive revolutionary history. Casasola, reported Vito Alessio Robles, "neither extols, nor censures, nor expresses judgments."[62] The first collection of historical documents relating to *la Revolución* declared that it was proper to remember the ideas of Madero, Zapata, Villa, Carranza, Obregón, and other revolutionaries. "At times, that body of thought seems incomplete, in others, contradictory. But it is the origin, the base and the force of the Mexican Revolution."[63]

The governor of Coahuila called in 1949 for a competition among Mexican historians to write the authentic history of *la Revolución*. One of the governor's supporters noted that "there are important contributions to the history of the Revolution, but almost all focus only on part of the story and many of them are almost totally discredited by passion and blind partisanship with regard to one or another of the factions that divided the Revolution." An authentic history, he continued, would be a "purified history" free of the superficial partisan rivalries that disparage and diminish *la Revolución* itself.[64] This idea was almost immediately taken up by the official party.

OFFICIAL HISTORY

Beginning in 1949 the Mexican state and its political party became much more closely involved in the construction of revolutionary history. In that year Baltasar Dromundo noticed how history was developing "an official character."[65] What was new was a competition sponsored by the recently established Institutional Revolutionary Party (Partido Revolucionario Institucional, PRI) for a work of history that best provided "an integrated, clear, and precise idea of the development of the principal events of the Mexican Revolution." On September 1, 1949, the party announced the History Competition of the Mexican Revolution, which would be coordinated with observances the following August of the thirty-sixth anniversary of the triumphal entry of the Constitutionalist army into Mexico City. The panel of judges, composed of Félix F. Palavicini, Diego Arenas Guzmán, Jesús Romero Flores, and Luis Chávez Orozco, selected the manuscript of a young teacher and journalist (on the staff of *El Nacional*), Alberto Morales Jiménez. In 1951 the PRI published his *Historia de la Revolución Mexicana*.[66]

This work by Morales Jiménez was classic official history. José López Bermúdez, secretary general of the central committee of the PRI, praised Morales Jiménez at the awards ceremony for understanding that history is "the science that defends the fatherland." He noted that the PRI did not want a scholarly history of *la Revolución*. "Our party wants a history of the Mexican Revolution that the people can read. A lively book, one open to the future since *la Revolución* has not ended."[67]

Historia de la Revolución Mexicana presented all of the basic themes of official revolutionary history. *La Revolución* was a reified force of history, the third phase of Mexico's national revolution that had begun with the War of Independence and continued with the Reform. It was popular, nationalist, and democratic. It began with the Precursors but triumphed in 1911 because of Francisco I. Madero's unshakable commitment to democracy. The military struggle in 1910–11, and again in 1913–14, was nothing less than a campaign of the people against the Reaction. The Reaction, unfortunately, time and again, proved capable of dividing *la Revolución*. This was the meaning of the Treaty of Ciudad Juárez, the Zapatista rebellion against the Madero government, and later the revolutionary schism within the Constitutionalist movement. All of the revolutionary factions, however, contributed to the synthesis that became the Constitution of 1917. And thereafter, *la Revolución* transformed itself into government and redistributed land, built health clinics and rural schools, organized workers to defend their rights and interests, modernized agriculture and industry, and continued to fulfill the promise of *la Revolución Mexicana*.

Morales Jiménez, declared López Bermúdez, "knew how to interpret, precisely, that organic unity of our social movement."[68] *La Revolución* was essentially an agrarian revolution according to Morales Jiménez. "All revolutionary groups —Carrancistas, Villistas, and Zapatistas—although divided for personal reasons, fundamentally desired agrarian reform." The three revolutionary caudillos "agreed upon the social program of the Revolution; nevertheless, since no clear concept of the reality of the moment existed, they fought among themselves." All of these currents of *la Revolución*, however, were synthesized ultimately in the Constitution of 1917: "the Mexican Revolution expressed itself in the supreme law."[69]

Twenty years after the ruling party first proposed a "history of the revolutionary social movement of Mexico in all of its generous vastness," one was finally published. Twenty-five thousand copies of the book were distributed for the first edition and twenty thousand each for the second and third editions in 1960 and 1961. In 1959 the Ministry of Education approved the history as a "work of consultation," thereby putting a copy of the book in every school in the country.[70]

Morales Jiménez's *Historia de la Revolución Mexicana* marks the beginning of the golden age of the construction of an official history of *la Revolución*. In 1952 the Sonoran state government and the University of Sonora proposed the formation of an archive of the Revolution and the preparation and publication of a history of Sonora. The project's director, Manuel

González Ramírez, noted that "the proposed history has the purpose of overcoming the factional differences and quarrels that were stirred up between the different revolutionary leaders and groups."[71] The Association for the History of Sonora over time published the most complete compilation of documents related to *la Revolución*.[72] "These books will make obsolete other works of history," wrote González Ramírez, "with the demonstration that this kind of historical study can be undertaken without subjecting it to rigid, partisan points of view."[73]

In 1953 the national government established the National Institute of Historical Studies of the Mexican Revolution (Instituto Nacional de Estudios Históricos de la Revolución Mexicana, INEHRM) as a dependency of the Ministry of Government. The mission of INEHRM was to collect documentation of *la Revolución* and publish works "of an official character, relating to the history of the Revolution."[74] The greatest merit of the collection of histories that have been published by the INEHRM, according to Javier Garciadiego Dantan, is that it is "absolutely plural in political terms: it made room for Magonistas, Maderistas, Carrancistas, Villistas, and Zapatistas, as well as other factions that shaped that very complicated process that was the Mexican Revolution."[75]

Under the leadership of Salvador Azuela, the INEHRM produced one hundred titles in the INEHRM Library collection, including biographies, chronologies, volumes of documents and testimonies, and, most importantly, regional histories of *la Revolución*. To commemorate the seventy-fifth anniversary of *la Revolución* in 1985 the INEHRM established the Library of Fundamental Works of the Mexican Revolution which reprinted twenty-six titles in forty volumes, all of them classic memoirs, political tracts, and histories first published between 1910 and the 1940s.[76]

Official history of *la Revolución* in the 1950s and 1960s was superseded by "objective" history. Gabriel Ferrer de Mendiolea, Jesús Silva Herzog, Berta Ulloa, and José C. Valadés in Mexico, as well as Frank Tannenbaum, Stanley R. Ross, Robert Quirk, and Charles C. Cumberland in the United States, produced sophisticated and impressively researched histories sympathetic to *la Revolución*. The next generation of historians, those raised during the "Mexican miracle," were less impressed with the benefits of *la Revolución* and revised its history. Revisionism, particularly in the form of regional studies, undermined the orthodoxy of revolutionary synthesis. *La Revolución* once again became plural, fragmented, and partisan: "a rampage of factions."[77]

The institutionalization of the postrevolutionary state gave birth to Mexico's official revolutionary party and official revolutionary history. Prior to 1929 governments shaped revolutionary history, of course, and sought to use the past to justify the arrangements of the present. A genuine, reified, historical, and ongoing revolution was invoked to induce consent. By 1929 that was not good enough. The crisis brought on by Obregón's assassination, most urgently the threat of civil war due to revolutionary disunity, led to efforts to unify revolutionaries in the present and historically. The various revolutionary traditions were submerged into *la Revolución*. The contributions of all of the different revolutionary factions were recognized, but *la Revolución* itself became greater than the sum of its dissonant parts. Official history repaired the fractured political foundation of the new state, at least that part sundered by memory.

Mexico's official revolutionary history was not dictated by cultural commissars and imposed on compliant masses. It emerged within the political culture, attended a specific political problem, and became politically popular as well as politically correct. Journalists, intellectuals, soldiers, politicians, teachers, and historians who identified with Mexico's new revolutionary political order were the authors of official history. Its "official" character was due to this identification, more than the result of governmental production or dissemination. Government sometimes (although not always) published its histories, and eventually put them in the schools, and government also celebrated this history in its commemorative ceremonies and monuments. The government's view of the history of *la Revolución* seemed to be the same as that held by society in general, which, of course, made official history all the more pervasive and persuasive.

This is no longer true. "Mexican scholars have found common ground," writes Allen Wells, "in their emphatic rejection of the revolutionary state's official mythology."[78] They have attempted to recover the real revolution, to "liberate it from the generation that is passing away and from the official ideologues who have taken it down a dead-end road."[79]

◦ℳ~ *Chronology of Events, 1968–Present*

1968–1969	In response to the massacre at Tlatelolco Plaza, Ambassador to France Carlos Fuentes and Ambassador to India Octavio Paz resign their posts in protest.	The Mexican City subway opens in 1969.
1970	Lázaro Cárdenas, the most respected citizen of Mexico, dies at age 74.	Cárdenas leaves a political testament that criticizes official Mexico's deviation from the true program of the revolution and the legacy of Madero.
1970–1976	The administration of Luis Echeverría Álvarez	
1971	On Corpus Christi, government thugs attack a demonstration march, killing several students. It is later learned that President Echeverría is behind the assault.	Historian Daniel Cosío Villegas is awarded the National Prize for Letters.
1973	The two largest television networks in Mexico merge to create the powerful TELEVISA network that comes to dominate national broadcasting.	The national government sets up a state-owned television network called IMEVISION.
1976	Over the course of its administration, the Echeverría regime has vastly increased the national debt, the size of the	President Echeverría engineers a coup at the independent newspaper *Excélsior* that removes the editorial staff.

government bureaucracy, and
the number of state-owned
enterprises.

1976–1982	The administration of José López Portillo	President López Portillo erects an equestrian statue of himself in Monterrey in 1980.
1978–1982	After two years of fiscal prudence, López Portillo uses Mexico's oil reserves to increase the national debt and embark on a massive program of public works.	In 1979, Pope John Paul II visits Mexico, the first ever visit of a pontiff to Mexico.
1982	Oil prices decline, reducing Mexican revenues and pushing the country to the brink of bankruptcy. The president responds by expropriating the banks.	During the López Portillo administration, the Mexico City police chief amasses a fortune from racketeering amounting to several hundred million dollars.
1982–1988	The administration of Miguel de la Madrid	By 1982, Mexicans are referring to the previous twelve years as "the tragic dozen years."
1983	The opposition Partido de Acción Nacional (PAN) wins several municipal elections in the state of Chihuahua, including control of Ciudad Juárez.	In 1984 the journalist Manuel Buendía is machine-gunned to death.
1985	In September, the worst earthquake in Mexican history occurs in Mexico City, killing 50,000 people.	Super Barrio Gómez, a former wrestler, becomes a spokesman for the urban poor.

1987–1988	A "democratizing faction" within the PRI leads a major defection from the party. Its leader, Cuauhtémoc Cárdenas, son of the former president, becomes a candidate for president in 1988. Many believe he wins the election, although the official count gives the PRI candidate 50.1 percent of the vote.	On the night of July 6, 1988, the evening of the presidential election, the national election commission announces that an unexplained computer malfunction had occurred in the counting of the votes. Several days later the official candidate, Carlos Salinas de Gortari, was declared the winner.
1988–1994	The administration of Carlos Salinas de Gotari	In 1993, Peruvian novelist Mario Vargas Llosa, on a national television broadcast, refers to the Mexican political system as the "perfect dictatorship."
1993	Representatives of Mexico, Canada, and the United States sign the North American Free Trade Agreement. The U.S. Congress ratifies the treaty in November 1993.	Also in 1993, Education Minister Ernesto Zedillo authorizes the revision of national history textbooks which question the authenticity of the legend of the Niños Héroes, positively reevaluate the Porfiriato, and suggest that the army was responsible for the Tlatelolco massacre in 1968. Protest by the army, politicians, and teachers leads to the recall of 6.8 million books.
1994	On January 1, Zapatista rebels in the state of Chiapas seize the city of San Cristóbal de las Casas.	

In March the presidential candidate for the PRI, Luis Donaldo Colosio, is murdered in Tijuana.

1994–
2000

The administration of
Ernesto Zedillo Ponce de León

CONCLUSION

Affirming and Subverting the Revolution

If Carranza would only marry Villa,
And Zapata marry Obregón,
If Adelita would only marry me,
Revolution would be dead as a stone.
"Adelita" [1]

DURING THE LATE 1940s some of Mexico's most prominent intellectuals pronounced *la Revolución* dead. No revolution, they argued, is immortal, and Mexico's more conservative turn under President Miguel Alemán Valdés (1946–52) certainly marked the end of an era in modern Mexican history. These critics did not repudiate the historic revolution but rather the continuing revolution: la Revolución hecha gobierno. Their evidence was found in words as well as deeds. "In recent years," José Iturriaga wrote in 1947, "one could observe that the phraseology used by the Revolution has lost its seductive power, the enchantment like force, which it previously possessed." Two years later Jesús Silva Herzog noted that "Revolutionary language gradually lost its meaning and efficacy. Spent and empty words ceased to have a galvanizing effect." [2]

This criticism (some said self-criticism) from the liberal-left, from "within the Revolution," marked the first significant challenge to the mature Revolutionary Tradition. It was not left unanswered, of course, by the true believers, the new *voceros de la Revolución*. In his study of Mexican intellectuals in 1956, Charles Haight found that "the Mexican Revolution was still, after forty-five years of unfoldment, the topic of topics in its native land." [3] Partisans of *la Revolución* as alive and well were numerous and vociferous. Some conceded that perhaps governments made errors and politicians were unfaithful but these were the failures of individuals and not of *la Revolución*. Manuel Germán Parra, a government economist, spoke for many when he stated:

the Mexican Revolution has neither died nor failed. It cannot die so long as its two great historical objectives have not been consummated: the economic independence of the nation and the development of capitalism in the country. And a social movement cannot have failed if in almost half a century it has established the bases for national liberation, destroyed feudalism and slavery, and is constructing, by means of industrialization, a modern society that should be capable of providing the people with better living conditions.[4]

"It would seem useless to deny that there is a popular Revolutionary 'mystique' abroad in the land, however vague its nature," Charles Haight noted in 1956.[5] Ten years later Stanley R. Ross borrowed Mark Twain's phrase and wrote that "the reports of the death of the Mexican Revolution have been greatly exaggerated."[6] This mystique, the Revolutionary Tradition, was taught in schools, reaffirmed during every national holiday, given special attention during anniversaries, glorified in murals in the seats of power, and even reinforced in the movies and on television.

Curiously, subsequent dissent and protest against the direction and policies of particular regimes often affirmed the Revolutionary Tradition, indeed used it symbolically against successive governments. Monuments and rituals became places and occasions for emphasizing the discrepancy between the revolutionary ideal and the unhappy reality of contemporary Mexico. La Revolución—and the Revolutionary Tradition—was affirmed, while its original purpose, the legitimization of power and the unification of revolutionaries, was subverted. It had outgrown the state.

Beginning in the 1960s historical revisionism subverted nearly every tenet of the Revolutionary Tradition. La Revolución in official symbolism, history, and ritual became increasingly divorced from Mexico's intellectual and academic culture. Not only was the permanent revolution, la Revolución hecha gobierno, pronounced dead, but the historic revolution, la Revolución itself, was declared a fraud. Its unequivocal triumph, popular nature, continuity to past struggles (as its discontinuity with the Porfiriato), permanence through reform, and essential unity were all illusory. Official history, although still produced today, is almost completely discredited.

HISTORY

During the 1960s, in contrast to the Cuban experience, the Mexican pattern of transformation was the "preferred revolution" in the eyes of Mexican and North American conservatives (and many liberals). To a new generation of Mexican students and historians, however, the Cuban revolution was a real revolution while the Mexican one was "frozen."[7] Official pronouncements about "revolutionary progress" were contradicted by the poverty of millions of Mexicans and quantified by a respected social scientist. Pablo González Casanova's devastating critique of the system, *La democracia en México*, published in 1965, demonstrated the great social, economic, and political failures of the so-called progress of the revolution.[8] Second thoughts about *la Revolución* were generated also by repressive actions taken by successive regimes. In 1959 federal troops attacked striking railroad workers and the government arrested its leaders. In the fall of 1968 the army killed hundreds of student protesters in Tlatelolco Plaza in Mexico City to put an end to a growing popular democracy movement before the start of the Olympic Games to be held in Mexico that year. For many, the Tlatelolco massacre symbolized the bankruptcy of *la Revolución*.[9] It also "changed the interests and orientation of those interested in history."[10]

Pessimism concerning the present was projected onto the past. Modern revisionism was born. "Specialists are sharply divided over its merits," David C. Bailey wrote in 1978, "and probably the only common ground left is the acknowledgment that there is less agreement today about the nature and meaning of the Mexican Revolution than at any time since scholars first turned their attention to it more than fifty years ago."[11] Some revisionist historians were guided by definitions and analyses of revolution by Marx and Lenin, while others found the sources of their disillusionment in the archives. Revisionism was not confined only to Mexican historians; scholars north of the border (in both the United States and Canada), as well as those from Western Europe, the Soviet Union, and Australia, contributed to the assault on official history.

Luis González researched the history of his hometown in 1968 and found that the revolution was not the glorious affair presented in official texts but little more than an unpleasant intrusion of hunger, brigandage, and immorality that effected little lasting change. John Womack's history of Zapatismo emphasized the revolutionary nature of the Morelos movement and highlighted the conservatism and failures of Maderismo and Carrancismo. Adolfo Gilly in 1971 further disaggregated *la Revolución* by portraying the Zapatista and Villista peasant revolutions as the genuine Mexican revolution.[12]

Revisionism put the Porfiriato in a new light. Following the path laid out by Alexis de Tocqueville's take on the French Revolution, historians now came to see more continuity than change between the old and new regimes. Donald Keesing maintained in 1969 that the revolution interrupted the development of the Mexican economy more than it changed its essential nature. In a series of interesting histories of ideas published in the 1970s, Arnaldo Córdova argued that the ideology of capitalist development was sustained as the dominant ideology in both the Porfirian and revolutionary regimes by the national bourgeoisie. Historians of politics argued that the revolution simply modernized authoritarian rule. Ultimately the Institutional Revolutionary Party, Peter H. Smith wrote in 1979, has not institutionalized the Mexican revolution. "What it has done is to find a new formula for re-institutionalizing the essence of the Porfiriato."[13]

Local, regional, and provincial studies in the 1970s and 1980s discredited the image of the singular and unified revolution and contributed to the revisionist interpretation of the Mexican experience as a failed popular revolution or as a triumphant bourgeois movement. Studies of Tlaxcala, Hidalgo, the Veracruz Huasteca, Guerrero, Jalisco, Michoacán, Chiapas, and other states and regions have revealed that agrarian struggle and class conflict took a back seat to factional disputes among landowners and the rise of new caciques.[14]

In 1979, on the fiftieth anniversary of the founding of the ruling political party, the weekly news magazine *Proceso* published a telling cover illustration. It shows a couple celebrating their golden wedding anniversary. La Señora appears as a plump, rather gaudy thing wearing a too-tight red, white, and green dress and jewelry inscribed with the letters PRI. El Señor, in contrast, has clearly been dead for some time, a skeleton in tattered clothing with two bandoleers. The unmistakable message expresses a simple, yet bitter truth: the government party has become a nouveau riche grand dame while her "partner," the Mexican revolution, has been dead for decades, although not yet buried. The image sums up better than any book the revisionist message of the time.[15]

It would be dishonest at this point not to mention the minirevival of the "popular revolution" thesis in the 1980s. Two massive histories taking two quite different perspectives countered the revisionist interpretation of "the great rebellion." Alan Knight and John Mason Hart attempted to restore our faith in the Mexican revolution if not *la Revolución* itself.[16] Mexican historians, however, appear not to be following their lead.

Historical revisionism has not destroyed the Revolutionary Tradition within Mexican political culture. It survives not simply in official symbolism and rhetoric. Opponents of the postrevolutionary system have reclaimed pieces of the tradition and often find it useful to compare the corrupt present with the pristine past. Symbols and rituals still have meaning for both friends and foes of the system.

MONUMENT

In recent decades the image of the Monument to the Revolution has been appropriated by cartoonists critical of the "regime of the Revolution." In 1977, Rius portrayed the twentieth of November anniversary ceremony at the monument. In his portrayal, one of the participants, admitting some confusion, asks whether "This is the anniversary of the triumph *of* the Revolution or the triumph *over* the Revolution?" For another cartoonist, Rocha, "years later" the plutocracy have taken the places of honor on the monument while ordinary Mexicans, once represented and honored by the four sculpture groups, are now on the street selling fruit to survive. On the seventy-fifth anniversary of the Revolution of 1910, cartoonist Naranjo captured the PRI's ridicule of the real revolution and its symbols. Three years later he portrayed the Revolution—in the form of the monument—as an obedient lapdog of Mexico's capitalist elite.[17]

For opponents of the postrevolutionary political system the Monument to the Revolution stands as a reproach; its purpose (for them) is the delegitimation of state power and authority. The monument has served as a place of pilgrimage, protest, and confrontation for proponents of reform, as well as for opponents of the successive administrations in office and of the political system itself. In 1959 striking railroad workers marched to the monument and were attacked by the police. In November 1975 perhaps as many as 150,000 supporters of the Tendencia Democrática (TD), an independent union of electrical workers, marched to its plaza. A second convocation at the monument in March 1976 provoked the government to call out 27,000 policemen, 15 riot tanks, and 25 army tanks. The president of the PRI denounced the TD for using the monument ("the least appropriate site") as the backdrop for its agitation. In October 1979 the newly formed national syndicate of university workers chose the monument as the site at which to announce to the nation the creation of their union. In late 1980 the national teachers union organized a massive meeting at the monument to pressure the government to agree to its demands. And in March 1987 independent unions organized a massive demonstration at the monument to demand an emergency increase in salaries and suspension of debt payments. In each of these protest demonstrations, and many more since, opponents of the regime affirmed the mythic image of the Monument to the Revolution and attempted to use this symbol against regimes that in their eyes had betrayed *la Revolución.*

The Monument to the Revolution just as plausibly can be said to commemorate the rise of an authoritarian and Machiavellian state, rather than a popular revolution and its political progeny. It is, Gustavo de Anda wrote in 1967, "the emblem of the consolidation of political power in Mexico, by means of the Institutional Revolutionary Party." The monument, in de Anda's view, symbolizes not *la Revolución* and the government's faithful or unfaithful adherence to it, but the disfigurement, death, and interment of the revolution itself.[18]

The public meaning of a memorial like the Monument to the Revolution is, like the meaning of all symbols, never permanently established. We must speak instead of "meanings," which evolve over time and differ according to the observer—layers of meanings, like sediments, that are deposited by each passing age. This is ironic, of course, since the massive "monumentality" of monuments is designed by their creators to make permanent and everlasting a particular interpretation of the past. Usually it is government that defines the first "meaning" of a monument in its need to shape public memory. Yet, as James E. Young remarks, "once created, memorials take on lives of their own, often stubbornly resistant to the state's original intentions."[19] A monument erected for the purpose of legitimating state power can be perceived anew and its purpose recast to one that rebukes state power. The Monument to the Revolution does both, and in so doing it reflects the disagreements of Mexican society today.

FESTIVAL

Every twentieth of November, politicians still speak at the Monument to the Revolution, presidents still honor the ever-fewer and more ancient surviving revolutionaries, and thousands of athletes still parade through the sacred center of Mexico representing, the regime no doubt hopes, "a

Mexico on the move." The *parada deportiva*, Daniel Esparza Hernández writes, "combines the colors, icons, and symbols of a country that admires and represents vigorous, developing youth."[20] Over the years, however, another image and a quite different interpretation of the traditions of *el veinte de noviembre* has emerged. As early as 1950, *Excelsior* noticed that the anniversary "has come and gone almost without notice." It had become a "fiesta de obligación, desfile 'deportivo' de ritual," merely obligatory ritual.[21] Forty-three years later Aurora Serrano González noted that "the institutional fiesta has not changed in years."[22] On November 20, 1968, not quite two months after the massacre of protesters in Tlatelolco Plaza, Alfonso Martínez Domínguez assured the nation that "the Revolution is not just talk, it is not only rhetoric."[23] To the cartoonist Rius some years later, however, revolutionary rhetoric was an imposing wall separating the politicians from the people. The image of a youthful and vigorous Mexico "on the move" appeared to some as petrified as the statues of its heroes. The parade, as depicted by Rius in 1984, was similarly motionless except for the corrupt politicians running away with their loot.[24] The twentieth of November anniversary cover of *Siempre!* in 1992 shows a butler opening a closet to dust off Madero, Carranza, Zapata, and Villa. The message is clear: every year the government highlights its revolutionary icons for a few days, only to return them, and the principles they symbolize, to storage, forgetting about them for another year.[25]

The traditional events of the twentieth of November increasingly have come to be viewed as only form without content. In 1978 the parade, according to *Unomásuno*, was simply "a spectacle Las Vegas style." To *Siempre!* "each year, we present to the Mexican people and our visitors a revolution reduced to a spectacle. *La revolución* as a show."[26] This show, noted one agrarian leader and protester in 1993, the athletic parade, "has no relation whatever with the Mexican Revolution."[27] For most Mexicans the real celebrations follow the official ones. The twentieth of November, Manuel Moreno Sánchez wrote in 1982, "was one more of official orations before bored audiences which quickly dispersed so that each could have his own fiesta."[28] After the speeches and the parade, families picnic in parks, children play, musicians sing and couples dance, young men play baseball and soccer.

If the official rituals of Revolution Day have lost their power and significance for many Mexicans, the day itself continues to hold meaning. Critics and opponents of the postrevolutionary regime often choose the twentieth of November to highlight the undemocratic nature of the official party and the "anti-revolutionary" policies of the current government. In 1993, for example, the Council of Agrarian Organizations and other independent campesino organizations organized a march from the Monument to the Revolution to the Zócalo to protest the reform by the government of President Carlos Salinas de Gortari of Article 27 of the Constitution and "to struggle for the redemption of the social agrarian content of the Mexican Revolution."[29] That same year, the conservative National Action Party held its national party convention on the twentieth of November to remind Mexicans that Panistas are the genuine heirs of Madero and his democratic revolution and that the monopoly Institutional Revolutionary Party is the new manifestation of the Díaz dictatorship. On the left, Cuauhtémoc Cárdenas Solórzano, the presidential candidate for the Party of the Democratic Revolution, traveled to San Luis Potosí on the twentieth of November to sit in the cell that had held Madero in 1910 and to rally his supporters.[30] Political posters throughout the country portrayed Cárdenas as the new Madero with an old demand: "Por Sufragio Effectivo!" For Effective Suffrage. The symbolism embedded in commemorations and monuments, like a double-edged sword, can cut two ways: it can subvert as well as sanction.[31]

The twentieth of November commemorations evolved from low-key civic rituals into a grandiose state-sponsored spectacle. A day of remembrance was transformed over the years into a showy advertisement for the state project and the bureaucracy itself. This transformation was but one more example of the political creativity of the men who engineered the institutionalization of the revolution. The hard-headed realists who built institutions and disciplined factions also crafted what we call today a hegemonic discourse, one that communicated by means of commemorative holidays, public monuments, and official history. The twentieth of November spectacle was and is but one part of this discourse.

Revolution Day authorizes, justifies, and legitimizes the PRI, the present regime, and the postrevolutionary state, since these institutions are descended from the revolution and are implementing its promises. Protest on that day, on the other hand, affirms the opposite (discontinuity and failure) and thus turns the symbol against its handlers. Representation, celebration, authorization, subversion: *el veinte de noviembre* is a busy day.

The anonymous balladeer who added the marriage verse to "Adelita" during one of the revolutionary campaigns speculated on and no doubt wished for the unification of all the revolutionary factions. He was surprisingly prescient. One of the central tasks of the postrevolutionary state and its *voceros* was precisely that, unification of factions in the present and past. The Revolutionary Tradition, the symbolic manifestation of the institutionalization of the revolution, sought to heal the wounds of memory that resulted from the bitter divorce of Carranza and Villa and the others. In festivals, monuments, and history, the Revolutionary Tradition remarried Carranza and Villa, Zapata and Obregón, and celebrated and transmitted to later generations the one revolution, the revolution as a bloc, "the indivisible combination of popular aspirations." [32]

La Revolución is not dead as a stone, however. José Revueltas noted in 1947 that a process of symbiosis had taken place: "Revolution and nationality are consubstantial." [33] Long after the PRI regimes are a distant memory, *La Revolución* will be honored in memory, myth, and history.

Notes

1. Sáenz, quoted in a lecture by Ramón Beteta delivered on July 22, 1930, "The Moving Forces in Mexican Life," in *The Mexican Revolution: A Defense* (Mexico: DAPP, 1937), p. 8.

2. These *voceros de la Revolución* were intellectuals inasmuch as they gave an explanation of the world, but they cannot be described as "great" intellectuals in the mold of Justo Sierra and Antonio Caso or "organic" intellectuals from the local communities, as described by Alan Knight. They fit better into the category of *clase media intelectual*, middle-class intellectuals, who possess a certain educational preparation, as noted by Gloria Villegas Moreno. See Villegas Moreno, "La Militancia de la 'Clase Media Intelectual' in la Revolución Mexicana," and Alan Knight, "Intellectuals in the Mexican Revolution," both in Roderic A. Camp, Charles A. Hale, and Josefina Zoraida Vázquez, eds., *Los intelectuales y el poder en México* (Los Angeles: El Colegio de México and UCLA Latin American Center Publications, 1991), pp. 211–12, 141–71.

3. Alphonse de Lamartine, "Declaration of Principles," quoted in Clifford Geertz, "Ideology as a Culture System," in Geertz, *The Interpretation of Cultures* (New York: Basic Books, 1973), p. 221.

4. Statement attributed to Wilson by Carlos Pereyra and quoted in Peter Calvert, *Mexico* (New York: Praeger, 1972), p. 153.

5. Luis Cabrera, "México y los mexicanos," in Cabrera, *Obras Completas. Obra Política* (México: Ediciones Oasis, 1975), Tomo III, p. 398. Around the same time, Carlo de Fornaro noted that "one is too apt to see only a wanton destruction of property, a needless sacrifice of lives." See Fornaro, "The Great Mexican Revolution: An Analysis," *The Forum* 49 (November 1915): 532.

6. One contemporary observer noted that the production of books rose during the decade. Henry C. Schmidt writes: "The decade 1910–1920 was shot through with intellectuality." See Schmidt, "Power and Sensibility: Toward a Typology of Mexican Intellectuals and Intellectual Life, 1910–1920," in Roderic A. Camp, Charles A. Hale, and Josefina Zoraida Vázquez, eds., *Los intelectuales y el poder en México* (Los Angeles: El Colegio de México and UCLA Latin American Center Publications, 1991), p. 173.

7. Hans Kellner, *Language and Historical Representation: Getting the Story Crooked* (Madison: University of Wisconsin Press, 1989), p. 208.

8. Isaiah Berlin, "The Bent Twig: On the Rise of Nationalism," in Henry Hardy, ed., *The Crooked Timber of Humanity: Chapters in the History of Ideas* (New York: Vintage, 1992), p. 244.

9. Ernest Renan, a lecture delivered at the Sorbonne, March 11, 1882, "Qu'est-ce qu'une nation?" reprinted as "What is a Nation?" in Homi K. Bhabha, *Nation and Narration* (London: Routledge, 1990), p. 19.

10. Benedict Anderson, *Imagined Communities: Reflections on the Origin and Spread of Nationalism*, revised edition (London: Verso, 1991), p. 195.

11. Jean Meyer, "History as National Identity," *Voices of Mexico*, October–December 1995, p. 33.

12. Linda Colley, *Britons: Forging the Nation, 1707–1837* (New Haven: Yale University Press, 1992), p. 5.

13. Yael Zerubavel, *Recovered Roots: Collective Memory and the Making of Israeli National Tradition* (Chicago: University of Chicago Press, 1995), pp. 6–7.

14. A nation, according to William Pfaff, is "a community with a common memory—a people which has suffered together." See Pfaff, *The Wrath of Nations: Civilization and the Furies of Nationalism* (New York: Touchstone, 1993), p. 58.

15. Lord Acton, "Nationality," *The Home and Foreign Review* 1 (July 1862): 170.

16. Beatriz Pastor Bodmer, *The Armature of Conquest: Spanish Accounts of the Discovery of America, 1492–1589* (Stanford: Stanford University Press, 1992), pp. 50–100; José Rabasa, *Inventing America: Spanish Historiography and the Formation of Eurocentrism* (Norman: University of Oklahoma Press, 1993), pp. 83–124.

17. René Jara, "The Inscription of Creole Consciousness: Fray Servando de Mier," in René Jara and Nicholas Spadaccini, *1492–1992: Re/Discovering Colonial Writing* (Minneapolis: University of Minnesota Press, 1989), pp. 349–79; D. A. Brading, *Los orígenes del nacionalismo mexicano* (México: SepSetentas, 1973), pp. 59–148.

18. D. A. Brading, *The First America: The Spanish Monarchy, Creole Patriots, and the Liberal State, 1492–1867* (Cambridge: Cambridge University Press, 1991), pp. 576–602, 634–47.

19. Enrique Florescano, "Creole Patriotism, Independence, and the Appearance of a National History," in Florescano, *Memory, Myth, and Time in Mexico: From the Aztecs to Independence* (Austin: University of Texas Press, 1994), pp. 184–227.

20. Enrique Krauze, "Founding Fathers," *The New Republic*, November 28, 1994: 58–66.

21. Robert A. Potash, "Historiography of Mexico Since 1821," *Hispanic American Historical Review* 40:3 (August 1960): 389–91.

22. David R. Maciel, "Los Orígenes de la Cultura Oficial en México: Los Intelectuales y el Estado en la República Restaurada," in Roderic A. Camp, Charles A. Hale, and Josefina Zoraida Vázquez, eds., *Los intelectuales y el poder en México* (Los Angeles: El Colegio de México and UCLA Latin American Center Publications, 1991), p. 579.

23. Edmundo O'Gorman, "La Historiografía," *México: Cincuenta Años de la Revolución* (México: Fondo de Cultura Económico, 1960), pp. 423–26; Thomas Benjamin and Marcial Ocasio-Meléndez, "Organizing the Memory of Modern Mexico: Porfirian Historiography in Perspective, 1880s–1980s," *Hispanic American Historical Review* 64:2 (1984): 323–64.

24. Maurice Halbwachs, *La Mémoire collective* (Paris: Presses Universitaires de France, 1950); Halbwachs, *On Collective Memory*, Lewis A. Coser, ed. and trans. (Chicago: University of Chicago Press, 1992).

25. Kammen, *Mystic Chords of Memory: The Transformation of Tradition in American Culture* (New York: Vintage, 1991), p. 10.

26. Leon Wieseltier, "After Memory," *The New Republic*, May 3, 1993: 18.

27. The *voceros de la Revolución*, it should be noted, did not monopolize Mexican collective memory. Revolutionary soldiers and other "everyday" participants rarely held a global image of the revolution or understood it as a unified entity. See Luis González y González, "La Revolución Mexicana desde el punto de vista de los revolucionados," *Historias* 8–9 (enero–junio 1985): 5–13.

28. Stephen C. Ausband, *Myth and Meaning, Myth and Order* (Macon, GA: Mercer University Press, 1983), p. 114; William McNeill, "Make Mine Myth," *The New York Times*, December 28, 1981: A19.

29. Nina Tumarkin, *The Living and the Dead: Rise and Fall of the Cult of World War II in Russia* (New York: Basic Books, 1994), p. 8.

30. Natalie Zemon Davis and Randolph Starn, "Introduction" to the special issue on "Memory and Counter-Memory," *Representations* 16 (Spring 1989): 2.

31. Carl Becker, "Everyman His Own Historian" (1931), in Becker, *Everyman His Own Historian: Essays on History and Politics* (Chicago: Quadrangle Books, 1966), p. 248; Francois Hartog, "Memory and Time," *The UNESCO Courier*, March 1990: 15; and Patrick H. Hutton, "Collective Memory and Collective Mentalities: The Halbwachs–Ariès Connection," *Historical Reflections/Reflexions Historiques* 15:2 (Summer 1988): 312.

32. The term is Foucault's; see his *Language, Counter-memory, Practice: Selected Essays and Interviews*, trans. and ed. Donald F. Bouchard (Ithaca: Cornell University Press, 1977); it is discussed and employed by George Lipsitz, *Time Passages: Collective Memory and American Popular Culture* (Minneapolis: University of Minnesota Press, 1989), p. 213; and Zerubavel, *Recovered Roots*, pp. 10–12.

33. Popular Memory Group, "Popular memory: theory, politics, method," in Popular Memory Group, eds., *Making Histories: Studies in History Writing and Politics* (Minneapolis: University of Minnesota Press, 1982), p. 208.

34. Hume quoted in John H. Schaar, "Legitimacy in the Modern State," in William Connolly, ed., *Legitimacy and the State* (New York: New York University Press, 1984), p. 128.

35. "In the modern world, national identity much more than any other, has been such a generalized identity. Its framework, nationalism, thus has been the framework of the modern social consciousness. It was religion, by contrast, that formed the framework of social consciousness in the premodern world; nationalism has

replaced religion as the main cultural mechanism of social integration." Liah Greenfield, "The Modern Religion?" *Critical Review*, 10:2 (Spring 1996): 171.

36. It is interesting to note that the same was true during the Porfiriato. The liberal synthesis, and political discourse in general, Charles A. Hale writes, reflected the obsession for "union" and "reconstruction" of the liberal party. See Hale, "Los Mitos Políticos de la Nación Mexicana: El Liberalismo y la Revolución," *Historia Mexicana* 46:4 (abril–junio, 1997): 830.

37. Michael Walzer, "On the Role of Symbolism in Political Thought," *Political Science Quarterly* 82:2 (June 1967): 194.

38. Pierre Nora, "General Introduction: Between Memory and History," in Nora, dir., *Realms of Memory: The Reconstruction of the French Past*, Vol. I: *Conflicts and Divisions*, trans. Arthur Goldhammer (New York: Columbia University Press, 1996), p. 5.

39. John Gunther, *Inside Latin America* (New York: Harper and Brothers, 1940), p. 55.

40. Samuel G. Inman, "The Mexican Revolution," *Southwest Review* 23:3 (April 1938): 271. "En México, Revolución y nación son conceptos indivisibles, que se influyen y determinan de manera permanente." *Curso, balance y perspectivas de la Revolución mexicana* (México: PRI, Comisión Nacional de Ideología, 1983), pp. 7–8.

41. "Finally, we come to the question of nationality, to the identification of liberalism of the nineteenth century and the revolution of the twentieth century with the destiny of the nation." Hale, "Los Mitos Políticos de la Nación Mexicana," p. 834.

42. Vicente Lombardo Toledano, *Definición de la Nación Mexicana* (México: Universidad Obrera de México, 1943). The French Third Republic after 1871, in addition, "had to forge a civic consensus and a national community in the aftermath of three revolutions, an empire, a short-lived republic, a civil war, and a major military defeat all in the span of one short lifetime. They succeeded because they had a story to tell about France that could bind the past and future into a single narrative." See Tony Judt, "A la Recherche du Temps Perdu," *The New York Review of Books*, December 3, 1998: 58.

43. President Miguel de la Madrid, "Third State of the Nation Report by the President of Mexico, Halfway Along the Road," *Mexico Today* 34 (September 1985); *Análisis Ideológico de la Revolución Mexicana, 1910–1971*. México, CEN del PRI, 1972.

PART ONE. CONSTRUCTION

1. El C. Bolaños, November 27, 1916, quoted in *Diario de los Debates del Congreso Constituyente 1916–1917*, Tomo I (México: INEHRM, 1960), p. 140.

2. Historians have generally viewed *la Revolución* as a postrevolutionary construction. Referring to the 1920s, David A. Brading writes, "What until then had

been viewed as a disastrous series of civil wars fought out between barbaric caudillos and regional caciques now became reified as *The Revolution,* defined as a watershed in national life, with a Constitution expressing the social aspirations of the Mexican people." See Brading, "Mexican Intellectuals and Political Legitimacy," in *Los intelectuales y el poder en México,* p. 838. Luis Anaya Merchant sees it as a post-1940 construction. See his "La Construcción de la Memoria y la Revisión de la Revolución," *Historia Mexicana* 44:4 (abril–junio 1995): 526.

3. Dror Wahrman, *Imagining the Middle Class: The Political Representation of Class in Britain, c. 1780–1840* (Cambridge: Cambridge University Press, 1995), p. 14.

4. Henry C. Schmidt long ago (1981) identified the need to study regional literary life, which "comprised a subculture that often developed a connection with the Revolution." See Schmidt, "Power and Sensibility," in *Los intelectuales y el poder en México,* p. 181.

5. Quoted in Colin M. MacLachlan and William H. Beezley, *El Gran Pueblo: A History of Greater Mexico* (Englewood Cliffs, NJ: Prentice Hall, 1994), p. 285.

1. 1911–1913

1. Joseph Brodsky, "Profile of Clio," *The New Republic,* February 1, 1993: 62.

2. Edmundo O'Gorman, *The Invention of America: An Inquiry into the Historical Nature of the New World and the Meaning of its History* (Bloomington: Indiana University Press, 1961), pp. 9, 124, 51. Also see Neil Larson, "Phenomenology and Colony: Edmundo O'Gorman's *The Invention of America,*" in Larson, ed., *Reading North by South: On Latin American Literature, Culture and Politics* (Minneapolis: University of Minnesota Press, 1995), pp. 110–16.

3. A recent rendering of this idea is taken from Hans Kellner: "Historians do not 'find' the truths of past events; they create events from a seamless flow, and invent meanings that produce patterns within that flow." From Kellner, *Language and Historical Representation,* p. 24.

4. This is, as Nelson Goodman puts it, a kind of "worldmaking." See Goodman, *Ways of Worldmaking* (Indianapolis: Hackett Publishing Co., 1978).

5. Mariano Azuela, *The Underdogs* (1915; reprint, New York: Signet Classic, 1996), p. 71.

6. The term "Maderista" and those that follow ("Zapatista," "Carrancista," etc.) are necessary simplifications for an essay of this length. Each of these names disguises the political rivalries, social complexity, fluctuation in membership, and ideological contradictions that existed within each camp at any one point and over time.

7. Reinhart Koselleck, *Futures Past: On the Semantics of Historical Time* (Cambridge: The MIT Press, 1985), p. 40. Enrique Krauze refers to the "magic word" in "Y el Mantel Olía a Pólvora," *Vuelta,* julio de 1995: 9.

8. Anne Staples, "El rechazo a la Revolución francesa," in Solange Alberro, Alicia Hernandez Chavez, and Elías Trabulse, eds., *La Revolución Francesa en*

México (México: El Colegio de México, 1992), pp. 161–67; and Charles A. Hale, "The Revival of Political History and the French Revolution in Mexico," in Joseph Klaits and Michael H. Haltzel, eds., *The Global Ramifications of the French Revolution* (Cambridge: Cambridge University Press and the Woodrow Wilson Center Press, 1994), pp. 164–66.

9. D. A. Brading, *The First America*, pp. 645–49; Charles A. Hale, *Mexican Liberalism in the Age of Mora, 1821–1853* (New Haven: Yale University Press, 1968), pp. 17, 31; José María Luis Mora, *México y sus revoluciones* (México: Editorial Porrua, 1950), Tomo III, p. 15.

10. Enrique Krauze, "Prólogo," in Magu and Enrique Krauze, *Hidalgo y sus Gritos* (México: Sentido Contrario, 1993), p. 16.

11. For a specific example, see Michael P. Costeloe, "A Pronunciamiento in Nineteenth Century Mexico: '15 de julio de 1840'," *Mexican Studies/Estudios Mexicanos* 4(2)(Summer 1988): 245–64. Luis Cabrera noted in 1920 that in the nineteenth century "se ha profanado el nombre de Revolución." From *La herencia de Carranza* (1920), reprinted in Cabrera, *La Revolución es la Revolución. antología* (México: Comisión Nacional Editorial del CEN del PRI, 1985), p. 228.

12. A Nuevo León government circular announcing amnesty in 1876 made no distinction between "revolutionaries" and "insurrectionaries." For similar examples, see Laurens Ballard Perry, *Juárez and Díaz: Machine Politics in Mexico* (DeKalb: Northern Illinois University, 1978), p. 208.

13. Donald Fithian Stevens, *Origins of Instability in Early Republican Mexico* (Durham: Duke University Press, 1991), p. 10.

14. Michael P. Costeloe, *The Central Republic in Mexico, 1835–1846: Hombres de Bien in the Age of Santa Anna* (Cambridge: Cambridge University Press, 1993), p. 256.

15. Enrique Plasencia de la Parra, *Independencia y nacionalismo a la luz del discurso conmemorativo (1825–1867)* (México: Consejo Nacional para la Cultura y las Artes, 1991), p. 131.

16. David A. Brading, *Mito y profecía en la historia de México* (México: Vuelta, 1988), p. 141.

17. Antonia Pi-Suner Llorens, "La Prensa, Disfusora de los Ideales de Ayutla," in *La Revolución Francesa en México*, p. 176.

18. Jacqueline Covo, "La Idea de la Revolución Francesa en el Congreso Constituyente de 1856–1857," *Historia Mexicana* 38:1 (julio–septiembre, 1988): 69–70.

19. Juárez quoted by Brian Hamnett, *Juárez* (London: Longman, 1994), p. 109.

20. Francois-Xavier Guerra, *México: del Antiguo Régimen a la Revolución* (México: Fondo de Cultura Económica, 1988), Tomo I, p. 169; Jean-Pierre Bastian, "El paradigma de 1789. Sociedades de ideas y revolución mexicana," *Historia Mexicana* 38:1 (julio–septiembre, 1988): 79–88.

21. Plasencia de la Parra, *Independencia y nacionalismo a la luz del discurso conmemorativo*, p. 99.

22. Hamnett, *Juárez*, pp. 112–13.

23. Robert Gildea, *The Past in French History* (New Haven: Yale University Press, 1994), pp. 36–39; Charles A. Hale, *The Transformation of Liberalism in Late Nineteenth-Century Mexico* (Princeton: Princeton University Press, 1989), pp. 38–41.

24. Bastian, "El paradigma de 1789," p. 79.

25. Nicole Giron, "Ignacio M. Altamirano y la Revolución francesa: una recuperación liberal," in *La Revolución Francesa en México*, pp. 209, 212.

26. Guy P. C. Thomson, "Bulwarks of Patriotic Liberalism: The National Guard, Philharmonic Corps and Patriotic Juntas in Mexico, 1847–1888," *Journal of Latin American Studies* 22:1 (February 1990): 31–32; Covo, "La idea de la revolución francesa," pp. 69–81; Bastian, "El paradigma de 1789," pp. 82–110.

27. Andres Lira, "La Revolución francesa en la obra de Justo Sierra," in *La Revolución Francesa en México*, pp. 179–200; Sierra's essay on Mexican history first appeared in *México: Su evolución social* (1900–02). This quotation is taken from Sierra, *The Political Evolution of the Mexican People*, trans. Charles Ramsdell, Intro. and notes by Edmundo O'Gorman (Austin: University of Texas Press, 1969), pp. 248–49.

28. Eric Hobsbawm, "Mass-Producing Traditions: Europe, 1870–1914," in Hobsbawm and Ranger, eds., *The Invention of Tradition* (Cambridge: Canto Edition, 1992), pp. 270–72.

29. *Bola* is defined as a "widely used word referring to large mobs in disorder." From Francisco J. Santamaría, *Diccionario de Mejicanismos*, segunda edición (Méjico: Editorial Porrua, 1974).

30. Rabasa quoted in Max Aub, "De algunas aspectos de la novela de la Revolución mexicana," *Dialogos* 7:37 (enero–febrero 1971): 4–5.

31. "Discurso pronunciado por don Francisco I. Madero, al colocar la primera piedra al monumento destinado a Aquiles Serdán . . ." [23 de Noviembre de 1912], reprinted in Isidro Fabela, ed., *Documentos Históricos de la Revolución Mexicana: Revolución y Régimen Maderista* (México: Fondo de Cultura Económica, 1965), Tomo IV, p. 212. (Hereafter cited as DHRM:RRM, with volume, year of publication, and page number.)

32. Jose María Pino Suárez, "Al Pueblo Yucateco," abril 21 de 1911, reprinted in DHRM:RRM, I, 1964, p. 320.

33. Lic. Blas Urrea [Luis Cabrera], "La Revolución es Revolución," 20 de julio de 1911, reprinted in *Obras políticas del Lic. Blas Urrea* (México: Imprenta Nacional, 1921). In time the phrase was transmuted into "La Revolución es la Revolución." Cabrera referred to that article and its meaning in "La Revolución de Entonces (y la de ahora)," 26 de noviembre de 1936, reprinted in Eugenia Meyer, *Luis Cabrera: teórico y crítico de la Revolución* (México: SepSetentas, 1972), p. 156.

34. Ernst Cassirer, *An Essay on Man* (New York: N.p., 1946), p. 142. John Dewey and Arthur F. Bentley argue that naming may be viewed "as itself directly a form of knowing," since it places what is named in a class of objects that then allows comparison and judging. From Dewey and Bentley, *Knowing and the Known* (Boston: Little, Brown, 1960), p. 147.

35. Fernando Solís Cámara, *La Reconstrucción de Nuestra Patria* (Nueva York, 1915), p. 8.

36. J. H. Plumb, *The Death of the Past* (Middlesex: Penguin Books, 1973), p. 33.

37. Paul Connerton, *How Societies Remember* (Cambridge: Cambridge University Press, 1989), p. 7.

38. "La Solución del Conflict," reprinted in *Obras políticas del Lic. Blas Urrea*, p. 178.

39. Antonio P. González (Kanta Klaro) y J. Figueroa Domenech, *La Revolución y sus Héroes. Crónica de los sucesos políticos ocurridos en México desde Octubre de 1910 á Mayo de 1911*, quinta edición (México: Herrero Hermanos, 1912), p. 7.

40. Rafael Martínez, Carlos M. Samper, Gral. José P. Lomelín, *La Revolución y sus Hombres (apuntes para la Historia contemporánea)* (México: "El Tiempo," 1912), p. 6.

41. Hernández quoted by T. F. Serrano in *Episodios de la Revolución en México* (El Paso, TX: Modern Printing, 1911), pp. 305–06; Rogelio Fernández Güell, *El moderno Juárez. Estudio sobre la personalidad de Don Francisco I. Madero* (México: Tipografía Artística, 1911).

42. "Discurso pronunciado por don Francisco I. Madero," [23 de Noviembre de 1912], DHRM:RRM, VIII, 1965, pp. 212–15.

43. Madero's Veracruz address of September 23, 1911, is quoted in Charles Cumberland, *Mexican Revolution: Genesis under Madero* (Austin: University of Texas Press, 1952), p. 211.

44. John Mason Hart, *Revolutionary Mexico: The Coming and Process of the Mexican Revolution* (Berkeley: University of California Press, 1987), pp. 258–59.

45. Guillermo Palacios, "La idea oficial de la 'Revolución Mexicana'," Tesis de Maestría, Centro de Estudios Históricos, El Colegio de México, 1969, p. 7.

46. Roque Estrada, *La Revolución y Francisco I. Madero* (Guadalajara: Imprenta Americana, 1912), pp. ii–iii.

47. Cabrera, "La Revolución es la Revolución" [20 de julio de 1911] in Lic. Blas Urrea, *Obras políticas*, pp. 240–41.

48. Serrano, *Episodios de la Revolución en México*, p. 307.

49. "Another way of saying this is that reification is the apprehension of the products of human activity as if they were something else than human products—such as facts of nature, results of cosmic laws, or manifestations of divine will." Peter L. Berger and Thomas Luckmann, *The Social Construction of Reality: A Treatise in the Sociology of Knowledge* (New York: Anchor Books, 1967), p. 89; and Burke C. Thomason, *Making Sense of Reification: Alfred Schultz and Constructionist Theory* (London: The Macmillan Press, 1982), pp. 88–93.

50. Peter Berger and Stanley Pullberg, "Reification and the Sociological Critique of Consciousness," *History and Theory* 4:2 (1965): 206–07.

51. Alfred Schultz, *Collected Papers*, Vol. I: *The Problem of Social Reality*, Maurice Natanson, ed. (The Hague: Martinus Nijhoff, 1973), p. 285.

52. "El cambio del Gabinete Díaz," *México Nuevo* 8 (29 de marzo de 1911) and 9 (30 de marzo de 1911).

53. Martínez, Samper, and Lomelín, *La Revolución y sus hombres*, p. 9. "González, Moya, and Guillermo Baca" refers to Abraham González, José Luis Moya, and Guillermo Baca, all revolutionaries.

54. Cabrera, Nota Preliminar, "La Revolución dentro del Gobierno" [27 de julio de 1911], in Cabrera, *Obras políticas*, 244.

55. Ramón Puente, *Pascual Orozco y la revuelta de Chihuahua* (México: Eusebio Gómez de la Puente, 1912), p. 62.

56. Thomason, *Making Sense of Reification*, p. 7.

57. The Renovators, quoted in Stanley R. Ross, *Francisco I. Madero: Apostle of Mexican Democracy* (New York: AMS Press, 1970), p. 277.

58. Estrada, *La Revolución y Francisco I. Madero*, p. 487; Cabrera, "La Revolución dentro del Gobierno," [27 de julio de 1911], Urrea, *Obras políticas*, p. 279; Alan Knight, *The Mexican Revolution*, Vol. 1: *Porfirians, Liberals and Peasants* (Cambridge: Cambridge University Press, 1986), p. 467; and "Memoria Presentado por el 'Bloque Liberal Renovador' a Don Francisco I. Madero," pp. 10, 15.

59. Knight, *The Mexican Revolution*, Vol. I, p. 335. Knight, however, in the epigraph of the book quotes Bernardo de Sahagún and compares the Mexican revolution to an ancient Mexican god: "He created, he brought down all things." The temptation of reification is almost irresistible.

60. Those who had supported the Díaz regime and opposed Madero's insurrection, naturally, unleashed a barrage of criticism. See, for example, Jorge Vera Estañol, *Partido Popular Evolucionista* (México: N.p., 1911). For an analysis of the criticism of one opposition newspaper, see Ariel Rodríguez Kuri, "El discurso del miedo: *El Imparcial* y Francisco I. Madero," *Historia Mexicana* 40:4 (1991): 697–740.

61. "Manifiesto de los Flores Magón para definir su actitud anarquista en relación con la Revolución. 23 de septiembre de 1911," in *Planes de la Nación Mexicana* (México: Senado de la República, 1987), Vol. 7, p. 149. (Hereafter cited as PNM.)

62. "Plan de Tacubaya que reforma al de San Luis Potosí. 31 de octubre de 1911," PNM, Vol. 7, p. 155.

63. Zapata in a letter to Madero, August 17, 1911, quoted by Cumberland, *Mexican Revolution*, pp. 177–78.

64. Quotation from "Ley Orgánica de la Revolución del Sur y Centro de la República, noviembre de 1911," PNM, Vol. 7, p. 191. Also see "Plan de Ayala, Campamento de las Montañas de Puebla, 11 de diciembre de 1911," PNM, Vol. 7, pp. 187–89.

65. Clifford Geertz, "Learning with Bruner," *The New York Review of Books*, April 10, 1997: 24.

2. 1913–1920

1. Plumb, *The Death of the Past*, p. 34.

2. Pesqueira in 1913 quoted in Edmundo González-Blanco, *Carranza y la Revolución de México*, segunda edición (Madrid: Imprenta Helénica, 1916), p. 517.

3. Jose C. Valadés, *Historia general de la Revolución Mexicana*, Vol. II: *Los hombres en armas* (México: Edición Conmemorativa del 75° Aniversario de la Revolución Mexicana, 1985), p. 312.

4. Francisco Bulnes refers to "the deified figure of Madero" and "a veritable idol in the eyes of the people." See Bulnes, *The Whole Truth About Mexico* (New York: N.p., 1916), p. 156.

5. Fabela, "El apóstol Madero," *La Voz de Sonora*, 14 de septiembre 1913. This article compares Madero's martyrdom to that of Christ.

6. Gonzalo de la Parra, *De como se hizo revolucionario un hombre de buena fe* (México: N.p., 1915), pp. 12–13. Stanley R. Ross writes that "his martyrdom accomplished, at least for a time, what he had been unable to do while alive: unite all the revolutionists under one banner." See Ross, *Francisco I. Madero*, p. 340.

7. Luis F. Seoane, *Méjico y sus luchas internas* (Bilbao: Viuda e Hijos de Hernández, 1920), p. 13.

8. "Ayer fue Glorificado el Presidente Madero por una gran Muchedumbre," *El Demócrata*, 19 de septiembre de 1914. General Álvaro Obregón, one month earlier, had led a commemorative celebration of Madero. See, "Grandioso homenaje de los vengadores al mártir de la revolución," *El País*, 18 de agosto de 1914.

9. Friedrich Katz, *The Life and Times of Pancho Villa* (Stanford: University of Stanford Press, 1998), pp. 459–60.

10. Alfonso Taracena, *Historia Extraoficial de la Revolución Mexicana* (México: Editorial Jus, 1987), p. 163.

11. Ernest Gruening, *Mexico and Its Heritage* (New York: The Century Co., 1928), p. 647. Todd Downing argued that *corridos* "take the place of newspapers, movies, radio, since they furnish news, fiction, gossip, drama, history, jokes, political speeches." Downing, *The Mexican Earth* (New York: Doubleday, 1940), p. 232.

12. Merle Simmons, *The Mexican Corrido as a Source for Interpretive Study of Modern Mexico (1870–1950)* (Bloomington: Indiana University Press, 1957), pp. 87, 91.

13. "Manifiesto a los habitantes de Sonora, Primera División del Ejército Constitucionalista del Estado de Sonora, 12 de marzo de 1913," in PNM, Vol. 7, p. 245. Identical sentiments are expressed in "Pronunciamiento de la guarnición de Campeche en adhesión al constitucionalismo, 10 de junio de 1913," and "Proclama del general Felipe Angeles al Ejército Mexicano para que se une a la revolución, para combatir a Huerta, 17 de octubre de 1913," in PNM, Vol. 7, pp. 259, 261.

14. Teniente Coronel David G. Berlanga, *Pro-Patria* (Aguascalientes: N.p., 1914), p. 58.

15. "Comentario a cada uno de los artículos del Plan de Guadalupe y a un programa político que se elaboro en una convención preliminar de constitucionalistas en El Paso, Texas, Piedras Negras, Coahuila, 10 de abril de 1913," PNM, Vol. 7, p. 251.

16. "Manifiesto del General Lucio Blanco a los soldados constitucionalistas de las Estados de Nuevo León y Tamaulipas, Tamaulipas, agosto de 1913," PNM, Vol. 7, p. 260.

17. "Declaraciones del Primer Jefe del Ejército Constitucionalista," reprinted in Isidro Fabela, ed., *Documentos Históricos de la Revolución Mexicana: Revolución y Régimen Constitucionalista* (México: Fondo de Cultura Económica, 1960–70), Tomo I, 1960, pp. 501–03. (Hereafter cited as DHRM:RRC, with volume, year of publication, and page number.)

18. "El problema agrario," *El Renovador*, reprinted in DHRM:RRC, I, 1960, p. 291.

19. Arnaldo Córdova, *La ideología de la Revolución Mexicana: La formación del nuevo régimen* (México: Ediciones Era, 1973), p. 136.

20. "La Revolución no Debe Detenerse," *El Renovador*, segunda época, 1 (10 de marzo de 1914). Enrique Amado noted that Madero's cabinet was infected by "el virus limanturista." From Amado, *La revolución mexicana de 1913* (Valencia: Prometeo, 1914), p. 10.

21. Francisco Padilla González, *Perfiles Rojos* (Veracruz: Imp. del Gobierno Constitucionalista, 1915), p. 34.

22. "Jerges Azota al Mar," *El Renovador*, 12 de Mayo de 1914.

23. Dr. Atl, *Confederación Revolucionaria: Conferencias Públicas* (México: N.p., 2 de Febrero de 1915), p. 5.

24. T. F. Serrano y C. del Vando, *Ratas y Ratones o Carranza y los Carrancistas* (El Paso, TX: N.p., 1914), p. 38. Identifying with Madero has never gone out of style. At the November 20 celebrations in 1995 the Secretario de Gobernación compared the government of President Ernesto Zedillo to that of Madero. See Ciro Pérez Silva and Roberto Garduño Espinosa, "Acto casi priísta en la Plaza de la República," *La Jornada*, 21 de noviembre de 1995.

25. Knight, *The Mexican Revolution*. Vol. 2: *Counter-revolution and reconstruction* (Cambridge: Cambridge University Press, 1986), pp. 113–14.

26. Ibid., pp. 36, 96. "'¡Esta Revolución no tiene nada que ver con la de 1910!' decía el C. Carranza, afanado en desvincularse del Apóstol Madero." From *El conflicto personal de la Revolución mexicana*, México: N.p., n.d. (circa early 1915).

27. "Abajo Caretas. los hombres de Don Venustiano Carranza. El Gral. Álvaro Obregón," El Paso, Texas, 9 de mayo de 1914, Broadside from Colección Documental del Instituto Nacional de los Estudios Históricos de la Revolución Mexicana, Archivo General de la Nación, Caja. 11, Expediente 6, Foja. 11. (Hereafter cited as CD-INEHRM and identifying information.)

28. "Manifiesto de Francisco Villa al pueblo Mexicano. Chihuahua, Chi. Septiembre de 1914," *PNM*, Vol. 7, pp. 317–18. In 1917, Villa declared that he struggled against Carranza "por haber traicionado a la Revolución." From "A La Nación. Programa del Partido Reconstructor Nacional," Río Florido, Chihuahua, Octubre 11 de 1917, Manuscript Division, Library of Congress (Hereafter cited as LC), No. 114.

29. Enrique C. Llorente, *General Francisco Villa. His Policy in Dealing with Certain of the Clergy and the Reactionary Element in Mexico—Its Justification* (Washington, DC: N.p., 1915), p. 10.

30. "Acta de Ratificación del Plan de Ayala," San Pablo Oxtotepec, 19 de julio de 1914, Manuscript Division, LC, No. 87a.

31. "Manifiesto a la Nación del general Emiliano Zapata, estado de Morelos, 20 de octubre de 1913," and "Manifiesto de los Zapatistas al pueblo mexicano. Milpa Alta, México, Agosto de 1914," *PNM*, Vol. 7, pp. 275–77, 312–14.

32. "Acta de Ratificación del Plan de Ayala," 1914. LC.

33. "Exposición al Pueblo Mejicano y al Cuerpo Diplomático," 1 de Octubre de 1916, reprinted in *Méjico Revolucionario. A los pueblos de Europa y America. 1910–1918* (Habana: N.p., n.d., circa 1918), p. 59.

34. Robert E. Quirk, *The Mexican Revolution, 1914–1915: The Convention of Aguascalientes* (Bloomington: Indiana University Press, 1960), p. 110.

35. Leon J. Canova to Secretary of State William Jennings Bryan, quoted in Quirk, *The Mexican Revolution*, p. 110.

36. Villareal quoted in Katz, *The Life and Times of Pancho Villa*, p. 381.

37. See, for example, "Programa de Reformas Político-Sociales de la Revolución aprobado por la Soberana Convención Revolucionaria. Jojutla, Morelos 18 de abril de 1916," *PNM*, Vol. 7, pp. 353–55.

38. "Una corriente revolucionaria sectaria con un limitado ascendiente sobre la población" is how Arnaldo Córdova describes the PLM. See Córdova, *La ideología de la Revolución Mexicana*, p. 135.

39. Ramón Eduardo Ruíz, *The Great Rebellion: Mexico 1905–1924* (New York: W. W. Norton, 1980), p. 170.

40. Donald C. Hodges, *Mexican Anarchism After the Revolution* (Austin: University of Texas Press, 1995), pp. 7–32.

41. Ricardo Flores Magón, Librado Rivera, Anselmo L. Figueroa, Enrique Flores Magón, "Manifiesto a todos los trabajadores del mundo," *Regeneración*, 3 de abril de 1911, reprinted in *Regeneración 1900–1918. La corriente más radical de la revolución mexicana de 1910 a través de su periódico de combate*, Prólogo, Selección y Notas de Armando Bartra (México: Ediciones Era, 1977), p. 287.

42. "Address of Enrique Flores Magón in Federal Court, Los Angeles, June 22, 1916," reprinted in Colin M. MacLachlan, *Anarchism and the Mexican Revolution* (Berkeley: University of California Press), pp. 128–29.

43. R. Flores Magón, "El rebaño inconsciente se agita bajo el látigo de la verdad," *Regeneración*, 4 de marzo de 1911; R. Flores Magón, "La necesidad del momento," *Regeneración*, 8 de enero de 1916; and R. Flores Magón, "Zapata y Villa," *Regeneración*, 11 de julio de 1914, all in *Regeneración 1900–1918*, pp. 282, 380, 349.

44. See the section entitled "Villista Propaganda" in Katz, *The Life and Times of Pancho Villa*, pp. 423–26; and Necah S. Furman, "*Vida Nueva*: A Reflection of Villista Diplomacy, 1914–1915," *New Mexico Historical Review* 53:2 (April 1978): 171–192. It is possible that *Vida Nueva* was also published in cities under Villista

control. When Villa occupied Mexico City in late 1914 his faction took over a number of newspapers. See Walter F. McCaleb, "The Press of Mexico," *Hispanic American Historical Review* 3:3 (August 1920): 448.

45. Samuel Brunk, *¡Emiliano Zapata! Revolution and Betrayal in Mexico* (Albuquerque: University of New Mexico Press, 1995), pp. 334–35; and John Womack, Jr., *Zapata and the Mexican Revolution* (New York: Vintage Books, 1969), pp. 417–18.

46. From a Zapatista document from the Archivo Jenaro Amezcua, quoted by Gloria Villegas Moreno, "La Militancia de la 'Clase Media Intelectual' en la Revolución Mexicana," p. 227.

47. John Rutherford, *Mexican Society during the Revolution: A Literary Approach* (Oxford: Clarendon Press, 1971), p. 132.

48. Quoted in John Reed, *Insurgent Mexico* [1914] (Reprint, New York: Penguin Books, 1983), p. 67.

49. Vicente T. Mendoza, *El Corrido de la Revolución Mexicana* (México: UNAM, 1990), p. 94.

50. Simmons, *The Mexican Corrido*, pp. 250–84. Also see Donald Fogelquist, "The Figure of Pancho Villa in the Corridos of the Mexican Revolution," *Hispanic-American Studies* 3 (1942): 11–12.

51. Downing, *The Mexican Earth*, p. 233.

52. Mendoza, *El Corrido de la Revolución Mexicana*, p. 53.

53. Simmons, *The Mexican Corrido*, p. 291.

54. Ibid., p. 301.

55. Francisco Coss, for example, established such an office in Puebla on April 25, 1915. Colección Documental del INEHRM, AGN, Caja 1, Exp. 6/4, F. 1; Salvador Alvarado, *Cartilla Revolucionaria para los Agentes de Propaganda de la Causa Constitucionalista* (Mérida de Yucatán: N.p., 1915).

56. Guadalup Narváez, Puebla to Carranza, Veracruz, 31 de julio de 1915, Colección Documental del INEHRM, AGN, Caja 1, Exp. 6/4, F. 4.

57. Alvarado, *Cartilla Revolucionaria*, p. 6.

58. Ignacio B. del Castillo, *Bibliografía de la Revolución Mexicana de 1910–1916. Historia, Legislación, Literatura, Cuestiones Sociales, Políticas y Económicas, Documentos, etc. Marzo de 1908 a Junio de 1916* (México: Talleres Gráficos de la Secretaría de Comunicaciones y Obras Públicas, 1918).

59. Katz, *The Life and Times of Pancho Villa*, p. 280.

60. Knight, *The Mexican Revolution*, Vol. 2, p. 447; McCaleb, "The Press of Mexico," pp. 448–50; Engracia Loyo, "La lectura en México, 1920–1940," in *Historia de la lectura en México* (Mexico: El Colegio de Mexico, 1988), pp. 246–47. Michael S. Smith, "Carrancista Propaganda and the Print Media in the United States: An Overview of Institutions," *The Americas*, 52:2 (October 1995): 155–74; Pablo Yankelevich, "Némesis: Mecenazgo Revolucionario y Propaganda Apologética," *Boletín* 28 (mayo-agosto de 1998): 1–32.

61. MacKinley Helm, *Modern Mexican Painters: Rivera, Orozco, Siqueiros and*

Other Artists of the Social Realist School (Reprint, New York: Dover Publications, 1989), p. 13.

62. Helm, *Modern Mexican Painters*, pp. 16–17; Alma Reed, *Orozco* (New York: Oxford University Press, 1956), p. 39.

63. José Clemente Orozco, *An Autobiography*, trans. Robert C. Stephenson (Austin: University of Texas Press, 1962), p. 52.

64. The definitive Carrancista history of the revolution, compiled and written for the constitutional convention to meet in Querétaro, is Jesús Acuña's *Memoria de la Secretaría de Gobernación correspondiente al período revolucionario comprendido entre el 19 de febrero de 1913 y al 30 de noviembre de 1916* (México: Revista de Revistas, 1916).

65. Gabriel Ferrer Mendiolea, "Año de Carranza," *El Nacional,* 18 de octubre de 1959; Linda B. Hall, *Álvaro Obregón: Power and Revolution in Mexico, 1911–1920* (College Station: Texas A & M University Press, 1981), pp. 140–44.

66. Dr. Atl telegram to Carranza and the subsequent quotation are from Charles C. Cumberland, "'Dr. Atl' and Venustiano Carranza," *The Americas* 13 : 3 (January 1957): 288.

67. John M. Hart, *Anarchism and the Mexican Working Class, 1860–1931* (Austin: University of Texas Press, 1978), pp. 135–36.

68. C. Palavicini, November 28, 1916, in *Diario de los Debates del Congreso Constituyente, 1916–1917,* Tomo I, p. 227.

69. Smith, "Carrancista Propaganda and the Print Media in the United States," p. 173. For the view in South America, see Pablo Yankelevich, *Miradas australes. Propaganda, cabildeo y proyección de la Revolución mexicana en el Río de la Plata, 1910–1930* (México: SRE-INEHRM, 1997).

70. Fornaro, "The Great Mexican Revolution," p. 535.

71. "I sincerely believe that the United States needs to study the Mexican Revolution." Luis Cabrera, "Mexico y los Mexicanos," 10 de noviembre de 1916, in *Tres intelectuales Hablan sobre México* (México: N.p., 1916), pp. 3–27, quotation on p. 26.

72. Douglas Richmond, *Venustiano Carranza's Nationalist Struggle, 1898–1920* (Lincoln: University of Nebraska Press, 1983), pp. 190–91.

73. "La Victoria de la Revolución significa el Triunfo de un Pueblo," *El Demócrata,* 26 de noviembre de 1915.

74. "El Plan de Guadalupe, Firmado Hoy Hace Cuatro Años," *El Demócrata,* 26 de Marzo de 1917; "Conmemoración del 5° Aniversario de la Firma del Plan de Guadalupe," *El Demócrata,* 26 de marzo de 1918.

75. "Quienes Son los Verdaderos Revolucionarios," *El Demócrata,* 23 de noviembre de 1915.

76. Referring to the agreement of Ciudad Juárez, Ing. Pascual Ortiz Rubio wrote: "Gravísimo error, debido principalmente, al magnánimo corazón del mártir." From Ortiz Rubio, *La Revolución de 1910. Apuntes históricos* (México: Herrero, Editores, 1919), p. 234.

77. L. Rivas Iruz, *La situación mexicana* (México, Octubre 26 de 1914), reprinted in DHRM:RRC, I, 1960, p. 381.

78. Luis Sierra Horcasitas, *Patria. Obra Histórico-Revolucionaria* (México: Talleres Gráficos de la Sría. de CYOP, 1916), p. 91.

79. Gral. Silvino García, *Vibraciones Revolucionarios (Prensa y Tribuna)* (México, 1916), p. 7.

80. *Anuario Constitucionalista* (Puebla: La Nacional, 1916), p. 33.

81. Antonio Manero, *Por el honor y por la gloria. Cincuenta editoriales escritos durante la lucha revolucionaria constitucionalista en Veracruz* (México: Imprente T. Escalante, 1916), p. 40.

82. *La Revolución libertaria y la Reacción en México* (México: N.p., 1915), p. 12.

83. Manero, *Por el honor y por la gloria*, p. 119.

84. Gral. Silvino García, "Luz y Sombra," in García, *Vibraciones Revolucionarias*, p. 115.

85. Obregón quoted in David C. Bailey, "Álvaro Obregón and Anticlericalism in the 1910 Revolution," *The Americas*, 26:2 (October 1969): 189–90.

86. Padilla González, *Perfiles Rojos*, p. 27.

87. Ramón Puente, *La Vox de Sonora*, 13 de septiembre de 1913.

88. This included Porfiristas, banker thieves, aristocrats, and pernicious clergy. See "Semisalvaje y Carnicero," *Boletín de Veracruz*, julio 1915.

89. Alfredo Aragón, *El desarme del Ejército Federal por la Revolución de 1913* (Paris: N.p., 1915).

90. Pierra-Purra [Pedro Lamicq], *La Parra, la Perra y la Porra* (México: Editorial Azteca, 1915), p. 213.

91. Salvador Martínez Alomia, "Venustiano Carranza y el Constitucionalismo" [Noviembre de 1913], in Félix F. Palavicini, ed., *El Primer Jefe* (Mexico, 1916), p. 32.

92. M. Aguirre Berlanga, *Revolución y reforma. Génesis legal de la Revolución Constitucionalista* (México: Imprenta Nacional, 1918), pp. 28–29.

93. Pierra-Purra, *La Parra, la Perra y la Porra*, p. 85.

94. José N. Macias, "¿Quién es Carranza? [Diciembre de 1915], in Palavicini, *El Primer Jefe*, p. 47.

95. Francisco Azcona B., *Luz y Verdad: "Pancho" Villa, el Cientificismo y la Intervención* (New Orleans: Coste and Frichter, 1914), p. 19.

96. Acuña, *Memoria de la Secretaría de Gobernación*, p. 149.

97. Luis Cabrera, *Discurso pronunciado ante la Soberana Convención Revolucionaria de la Ciudad de México el 5 de octubre de 1914* (Nueva York: Edgar Printing and Stationery Co., 1914).

98. Berlanga, *Revolución y Reforma*, pp. 58–59. Edmundo González-Blanco argued that reactionaries were responsible for Villismo more than the 'illiterate bandit Villa' himself. See González-Blanco, *Carranza y la Revolución de México*, pp. 556–64.

99. Ortiz Rubio, *La Revolución de 1910*, pp. 220–23.

100. Manero, *Por el honor y por la gloria*, pp. 44–45. C. Trejo Lerdo de Tejada wrote that "en el Villismo convergia el Maderista personalista." From Lerdo de Tejada, *La Revolución y el Nacionalismo* (Habana: N.p., 1916), p. 210. Members of the Madero family "ha tenido una funesta influencia sobre el general Villa," writes Federico P. Robeledo in *El Constitucionalismo y Francisco Villa a la Luz de la Verdad* (Matamoros: El Demócrata, 1915), p. 24.

101. Acuña, *Memoria de la Secretaría de Gobernación*, pp. 202–03.

102. Dr. Atl, *Confederación Revolucionaria*, p. 10. This passage is also quoted by González-Blanco, *Carranza y la Revolución de México*, pp. 568–70. Also see M. C. Rolland, *Carta a mis conciudadanos* (Mexico: N.p., 1916).

103. Aragón, "Cuadro Sinóptico de los Partidos Políticos desde la época dictatorial hasta la emancipación constitucionalista," in Alfredo Aragón, *¡A Las Armas!* (México: N.p., 1916).

104. Manuel Gamio, *Forjando Patria (Pro Nacionalismo)* (México: Edicciones Porrua, 1916), pp. 315–16.

105. "Lo que Dijo el 2 de Enero en Querétaro el Señor Carranza," in Palavicini, *El Primer Jefe*, p. 258.

106. Parra, *De como se hizo revolucionario*, p. 122.

107. González-Blanco, *Carranza y la Revolución de Mexico*, p. 189.

108. L. Suárez, "Nuestros Enemigos Pigmeos," México, agosto 12 de 1915, in DHRM:RRC, v. 4 del Tomo I, 1969, p. 205.

109. Robledo, *El Constitucionalismo y Francisco Villa*, p. 55. Antonio Rivera de la Torre, *Paralismo de Hombres y Caracteres. Juárez = Carranza, Asuntos Varios del Constitucionalismo* (México: Oficina Impresora de Hacienda, 1918).

110. González-Blanco, *Carranza y la Revolución de México*, p. 578.

111. Guillermo Mellado, *Tres Etapas Políticas de Don Venustiano Carranza* (México: N.p., 1916), p. 35.

112. Simmons, *The Mexican Corrido*, p. 133.

113. Feliciano Gil, *Biografía y Vida Militar del General Álvaro Obregón* (Hermosillo: N.p., 1914).

114. Prof. Lucio Tapia, and Dr. Krumm Heller, *Trilogía Heróica: Historia condensada del último movimiento libertario en México* (México: Andres Botas, 1916), pp. 49–50.

115. Félix F. Palavicini, "El Primer Jefe," in Palavicini, *El Primer Jefe*, p. 10.

116. Berlanga, *Revolución y Reforma*, p. 30.

117. Carranza, "Manifiesto a la Nación," México, mayo 5 de 1920, DHRM:RRC, v. 6 del Tomo I, 1970, p. 415.

118. *Diario de los Debates del Congreso Constituyente*, Vol. I, pp. 161–62.

119. "En la política del señor Carranza . . . ha habido, como hay siempre en esa clase de instituciones, divergencias de criterio y dificultades personales," C. Palavicini, November 28, 1916, in *Diario de los Debates del Congreso Constituyente*, Tomo I, p. 166.

120. C. Ugarte, December 6, 1916, and C. Múgica, November 30, 1916, in *Diario de los Debates del Congreso Constituyente*, Tomo I, p. 377, 499.

121. El C. Primer Jefe, December 1, 1916, in *Diario de los Debates del Congreso Constituyente*, Tomo I, p. 394.

122. Eugenia Meyer, "Cabrera y Carranza: Hacia la Creación de una Ideología Oficial," in Roderic A. Camp, Charles A. Hale, and Josefina Zoraida Vásquez, eds., *Los intelectuales y el poder en México*, pp. 237–58 (Los Angeles: El Colegio de México and UCLA Latin American Center Publications, 1991), p. 256.

123. Antonio Islas Bravo, *La Sucesión Presidencial de 1928* (México: Imp. Manuel Léon Sánche, 1927), pp. 41–42. Islas Bravo was referring to José Vasconcelos, Juan Sánchez Azcona, Jesús Urueta, Antonio Villareal, José Inés Novelo, Roque Estrada, Hilario Rodríguez Malpica, Fernando Iglesias Calderón, Eduardo Hay, Alberto J. Pani, Enrique Bordes Mangel, "and many others we will not mention so as not to make this account interminable."

124. Downing, *The Mexican Earth*, p. 260.

3. 1920–1928

1. Popular Memory Group, "Popular memory: theory, politics, method," in Popular Memory Group, eds., *Making Histories*, p. 213.

2. José Vasconcelos, *La caída de Carranza, de la dictadura a la libertad* (México: N.p., 1920), p. 246.

3. Vasconcelos, quoted by Mary Kay Vaughan, *The State, Education, and Social Class in Mexico, 1880–1928* (DeKalb: Northern Illinois University Press, 1982), p. 142.

4. Ibid., p. 62.

5. "No Contra-Revolución Sino Ultra-Revolución," *El Demócrata*, 1 de noviembre de 1921.

6. "Se Declara Día de Fiesta Nacional el Décimo Aniversario de la Revolución," *El Demócrata*, 12 de noviembre de 1920; "Solamente Fueron Recordados y Venerados los Mártires de la Revolución de 1910," *El Demócrata*, 21 de noviembre de 1920; "Como Se Conmemorará el Asesinato de los Sres. Madero y Pino Suárez," *El Demócrata*, 20 de febrero de 1921.

7. "El Veinte de Noviembre," *El Demócrata*, 20 de noviembre de 1920.

8. "El Sr. General Calles Analiza la Historia de México," *El Demócrata*, 27 de febrero de 1924.

9. "Fue Glorificada Ayer la Memoria de los Mártires de la Democracia," *El Demócrata*, 23 de febrero de 1921.

10. Esther Acevedo, "Las decoraciones que pasaron a ser revolucionarias," in Acevedo, ed., *El nacionalismo y el arte mexicano* (México: UNAM, 1986), p. 184, n. 31.

11. Luis Olivares Sierra, México, to Juan Barragán, 4 de noviembre de 1923, Archivo Juan Barragán (hereafter cited as AJB), Caja XVII, Exp. 18.

12. A. De la Huerta, Veracruz, to Juan Barragán, New York, 3 de enero de 1924, AJB, XVII, 15.

13. John W. F. Dulles, *Yesterday in Mexico: A Chronicle of the Revolution, 1919–1936* (Austin: University of Texas Press, 1961), p. 268.

14. Francisco Bulnes, "El Culto a Zapata," *El Universal*, 30 de abril de 1923.

15. "El Problema Agrario en el E. de Morelos," *El Universal*, 18 de marzo de 1923.

16. "Homenaje al Caudillo del Sur," reprinted in Carlos Macias, ed., *Plutarco Elías Calles. Pensamiento político y social. Antología (1913–1936)* (México: Fondo de Cultura Económica, 1988), p. 97.

17. "El Programa Agrarista de Zapata es el Mio, Dijo Ayer en Cuautla El General Elías Calles," *El Universal*, 11 abril de 1924.

18. "Serán Traidos a México los Restos del Socialista Ricardo Flores Magón," *El Universal*, 23 de noviembre de 1922; "La Memoria de Ricardo Flores Magón Honrada en la Cámara," *El Demócrata*, 23 de noviembre de 1922.

19. Diego Abad Santillán, *Ricardo Flores Magón. El Apóstol de la Revolución Social Mexicana* (México: Grupo Cultural 'Ricardo Flores Magón,' 1925), p. 131; MacLachlan, *Anarchism and the Mexican Revolution*, p. 109.

20. *Conversaciones con Enrique Flores Magón. Combatimos la Tiranía. Un Pionero Revolucionario Mexicano Cuenta su Historia a Samuel Kaplan* (México: Biblioteca del INEHRM, 1958), p. 322.

21. "La Noble Figura de Felipe Ángeles," *El Demócrata*, 26 de noviembre de 1922; "Solemne Velada de Ayer Para Conmemorar la Muerte del Señor General Felipe Angeles," *El Demócrata*, 27 de noviembre de 1922.

22. Juan B. Cervantes, "Obregón Ante la Historia," *El Demócrata*, 7 de febrero de 1924; J. A. Tamayo, *El Gral. Obregón y la Guerra* (México, 1922).

23. C. Gutiérrez Cruz, *El Brazo de Obregón* (Mexico: La Liga de Escritores revolucionarios, 1924), pp. 24–25.

24. "Discurso Pronunciado el Día 24 de Julio de 1927," in *Discursos del General Obregón* (México: Biblioteca de la Dirección General de Educación Militar, 1932), pp. 138–39.

25. Simmons, *The Mexican Corrido*, p. 269.

26. "En la Convención Cooperistista se Siguen Lanzando Formidables Acusaciones Contra el C. Presidente y el General Calles," *El Demócrata*, 22 de noviembre de 1923.

27. Ygnacio Urquijo, *Apuntes para la Historia de México (1910–1924)* (México: N.p., 1925), p. 95. Also see Blas Urrea [Luis Cabrera], *La Herencia de Carranza* (Mexico: N.p., 1920).

28. Islas Bravo, *La Sucesión Presidencial de 1928*, pp. 40–41.

29. "El Gobierno emanado de la revolución," was a phrase used by Carranza to describe his government at the constitutional convention at Querétaro in 1916.

30. Elaine C. Lacy, "The 1921 Centennial Celebration of Mexican Independence: Contested Meaning, Memory, and National Identity," unpublished paper presented at the 1995 meeting of the Latin American Studies Association, Washington, DC, September 28–30, 1995. When the remains of the Insurgents were

transferred to the Column of Independence in 1925, the Calles government did not include Iturbide.

31. The Agrupación Pro-Madero was founded in January 1920 for the purpose "crear un culto sentimental y patriótico a la vez, de la memoria del señor Madero." From "Manifiesto a la Nación," México, DF, Enero 18 de 1920, AGN, Colección INEHRM, C. 11, Exp. 6. Fs. 24. It also lobbied the government to seek extradition of Madero's assassin, Francisco Cárdenas, from Guatemala and his prosecution for the murder. Cárdenas committed suicide before he could be returned to Mexico.

32. "El XII Aniversario de la Revolución Mexicana fue Conmemorado Ayer," *El Demócrata*, 21 de noviembre de 1922.

33. Berger and Luckmann, *The Social Construction of Reality*, p. 93.

34. Ramón Eduardo Ruíz, *Triumphs and Tragedy: A History of the Mexican People* (New York: W. W. Norton, 1992), p. 144.

35. Plutarco Elías Calles, "Eulogy of the Youth of the Revolution" [1924], in Robert Hammond Murray, trans. and ed., *Mexico Before the World: Public Documents and Addresses of Plutarco Elías Calles* (New York: The Academy Press, 1927), pp. 58, 65.

36. Calles at first adopted Carranza's phrase, "el gobierno emanado de la Revolución," as is seen in a 1923 speech. Calles, "El Marco Legal de la Revolución," in Macías, ed., *Plutarco Elías Calles*, p. 70.

37. Obregón, quoted in Bailey, "Álvaro Obregón and Anticlericalism in the 1910 Revolution," p. 191.

38. "Manana Se Conmemorará el Asesinato de los Señores Madero y Pino Suárez," *El Demócrata*, 21 de febrero de 1925.

39. *Celebración del 20 de Noviembre, 1910–1985* (México: INEHRM, 1985), pp. 104–05.

40. Miguel Yépez Solórzano, *Mensaje al Grupo Revolucionario de México: Programa de táctica revolucionaria para obtener su solidaridad y cohesión* (México: N.p., 1924), pp. 9, 28.

41. "New Year Message to the Mexican People, January 1, 1927," in Murray, ed. and trans., *Mexico Before the World*, p. 159.

42. Luis L. León, Centro Director de la Campaña Pro-Calles, to Ing. Miguel Yépez Solórzano, 6 de marzo de 1924, reprinted in Yépez Solórzano, *Mensaje al Grupo Revolucionario*, p. 5.

43. Anita Brenner, *Idols Behind Altars: The Story of the Mexican Spirit* [1929] (Reprint, New York: Beacon Press, 1970), p. 286.

44. The manifesto was published in 1924 in the seventh issue of *El Machete*. This translation by Guillermo Rivas appeared in *Mexican Life*, December 1935. It was signed by Diego Rivera, José Clemente Orozco, and others.

45. This judgment is by the art historian Dawn Ades, given in *Art in Latin America: The Modern Era, 1820–1980* (New Haven: Yale University Press, 1989), p. 151.

46. Leonard Folgarait, *Mural Painting and Social Revolution in Mexico, 1920–1940: Art of the New Order* (Cambridge: Cambridge University Press, 1998), p. 85.

47. Octavio Paz, "Re/Visions: Mural Painting," in Paz, *Essays on Mexican Art* (New York: Harcourt Brace and Co., 1993), p. 149.

48. Bertram Wolfe, "Art and Revolution in Mexico," *The Nation*, August 27, 1924: 207–8.

49. Folgarait, *Mural Painting and Social Revolution in Mexico*, p. 65.

50. *Los Zapatas de Diego Rivera* (México and Cuernavaca: Consejo Nacional para la Cultura y las Artes, Instituto Nacional de Bellas Artes, Gobierno Constitucional del Estado de Morelos, abril de 1989), pp. 70–71.

51. Jean Charlot, *Art Making from Mexico to China* (New York: Sheed and Ward, 1950), p. 129.

52. MacKinley Helm, *Man of Fire. J. C. Orozco: An Interpretative Memoir* (New York: Harcourt, Brace, 1953), pp. 35–43.

53. Folgarait, *Mural Painting and Social Revolution*, p. 68.

54. Yépez Solórzano, *Mensaje al Grupo Revolucionario de México*, p. 19.

55. Ibid., p. 10.

56. Víctor Díaz Arciniega, *Querella Por la Cultura "Revolucionaria," 1925* (México: Fondo de Cultura Económica, 1989), p. 160, n. 26.

57. Calles, "A Hundred Years of Revolution," *The Survey* 52:3 (May 1, 1924): p. 134. Calles explained that an important element of the Reaction was "foreign or native Catholic priests of evil intention." See "The Church Controversy," in Murray, ed. and trans., *Mexico Before the World*, p. 158.

58. The compulsory history textbooks of the 1960s and 1970s had "nothing to say about the Cristero War or related Church-state conflicts in the 1920s." See Dennis Gilbert, "Rewriting History: Salinas, Zedillo and the 1992 Textbook Controversy," *Mexican Studies/Estudios Mexicanos* 12:2 (Summer 1997): 282.

59. Federico Cervantes, "Gravisimós cargos al poder legislativa," *El Demócrata*, 23 de febrero de 1926.

60. "En Veracruz se ha Inciado una Transcendental Campaña Política en Contra de la Reelección," *Excelsior*, 29 de noviembre de 1926.

61. Islas Bravo, *La Sucesión Presidencial de 1928*, pp. 55–56.

62. "Los Mártires de la Revolución," *Excelsior*, 27 de junio de 1927.

63. Hector Aguilar Camin and Lorenzo Meyer, *In the Shadow of the Mexican Revolution: Contemporary Mexican History, 1910–1989* (Austin: University of Texas Press, 1993), p. 91. Luis Medina Peña writes, "El año de 1927 fue el caos total." See Medina Peña, *Hacia el nuevo Estado: México, 1920–1993* (Mexico: Fondo de Cultura Económica, 1994), p. 67.

64. Hans Werner Tobler, *La Revolución Mexicana: Transformación social y cambio político, 1876–1940* (México: Alianza Editorial, 1994), pp. 447–48.

65. Medina Peña, *Hacia el nuevo Estado*, pp. 68–69.

1. "El Camino Hacia la Más Alta y Respetada Nación de Instituciones y Leyes," in Macías, ed., *Plutarco Elías Calles*, p. 249.

2. Thomas Benjamin, "The Leviathan on the Zócalo: Recent Historiography of the Postrevolutionary State," *Latin American Research Review* 20:3 (1985): 195–217.

3. Lloyd H. Hughes, *The Mexican Cultural Mission Programme* (Paris: N.p., 1950). These missions continued in the 1930s as well as today.

4. Jesús Guisa y Azevedo, "Un revolucionario que nos da la Razón," *Excelsior*, 27 de julio de 1927.

5. Elizabeth Fox, "Latin American Broadcasting," in Leslie Bethell, ed., *The Cambridge History of Latin America. Volume X. Latin America Since 1930: Ideas, Culture, and Society* (Cambridge: Cambridge University Press, 1995), p. 523.

6. "Programa de la Dirección Portegilista," in Miguel Osorio Marban, ed., *El Partido de la Revolución Mexicana*, Tomo I (México: Impresora del Centro, 1970), pp. 206–10.

7. Mary Kay Vaughan, "The Construction of the Patriotic Festival in Tecamachalco, Puebla, 1900–1946," in William H. Beezley, Cheryl English Martin, and William E. French, eds., *Rituals of Rule, Rituals of Resistance: Public Celebrations and Popular Culture in Mexico* (Wilmington, DE: SR Books, 1994), p. 225. Also see Vaughan, *Cultural Politics in Revolution: Teachers, Peasants, and Schools in Mexico, 1930–1940* (Tucson: University of Arizona Press, 1997).

8. Calles, quoted in *El Nacional*, 21 de julio de 1934.

9. Adrian A. Bantjes, "Idolatry and Iconoclasm in Revolutionary Mexico: The De-Christianization Campaigns, 1929–1940," *Mexican Studies/Estudios Mexicanos* 13:1 (Winter 1997): 88.

10. Engracia Loyo, "Popular Reactions to the Educational Reforms of Cardenismo," in Beezley, Martin, and French, eds., *Rituals of Rule, Rituals of Resistance*, p. 253.

11. *Calendario Nacionalista y Enciclopedia Popular* (México, DF: Partido Nacional Revolucionario, 1934); *Calendario Nacionalista y Enciclopedia Popular* (México, DF: PNR, 1935); and Jacqueline Covo, "El Periódico al Servicio del Cardenismo: El Nacional, 1935," *Historia Mexicana* 46:1 (julio–septiembre de 1996): 145.

12. Angelika Rauch, "The Broken Vessel of Tradition," *Representations* 53 (Winter 1996): 82.

13. Murray Edelman, *The Symbolic Uses of Politics* (Urbana: University of Illinois Press, 1985), p. 130.

4. FESTIVAL

1. *Anuario Cívico de la Ciudad de México 1967* (México: Departamento del Distrito Federal, 1967), p. 6.

2. Paul Connerton writes, "if there is such a thing as social memory, we are likely to find it in commemorative ceremonies." Connerton, *How Societies Remember*, p. 71. This is the analytic approach of Emile Durkheim and Edward Shils. See Steven Lukes, "Political Ritual and Social Integration," *Sociology* 9:2 (May 1975): 292–93.

3. Elizabeth Barkeley Wilson, "Jacques-Louis David: Stage Manager of the Revolution," *Smithsonian*, August 1998: 85.

4. This is the analytic approach to tradition (and its rituals) of George Herbert Mead and Maurice Halbwachs. See Barry Schwartz, "The Reconstruction of Abraham Lincoln," in David Middleton and Derek Edwards, eds., *Collective Remembering* (London: Sage, 1990), p. 81–82; Eric Hobsbawm, "Mass-Producing Traditions," pp. 270–71.

5. Middleton and Edwards, "Introduction," *Collective Remembering*, p. 8.

6. Victor Turner, "Liminality and the Performative Genres," in John J. MacAloon, ed., *Rite, Drama, Festival, Spectacle: Rehearsals Toward a Theory of Cultural Performance* (Philadelphia: Institute for the Study of Human Issues, 1984), pp. 21–22.

7. Evitar Zerubavel, *Hidden Rhythms: Schedules and Calendars in Social Life* (Chicago: The University of Chicago Press, 1981), p. 45.

8. Examples would include the commemoration of the Beer Hall Putsch, November 9, in Nazi Germany, commemoration of the October Revolution, November 7, in the Soviet Union, and the commemoration of the founding of the Communist regime, October 1, in the People's Republic of China.

9. John J. MacAloon, "Olympic Games and the Theory of Spectacle in Modern Societies," in MacAloon, ed., *Rite, Drama, Festival, Spectacle*, pp. 243–257.

10. Alessandro Falassi, "Festival: Definition and Morphology," in Falassi, ed., *Time Out of Time: Essays on the Festival* (Albuquerque: University of New Mexico Press, 1987), pp. 1–7; Moyra Byrne, "Nazi Festival: The 1936 Berlin Olympics," in Falassi, ed., *Time Out of Time*, pp. 117–18; Robert E. Goodin, "Rites of Rulers," *British Journal of Sociology* 29:3 (September 1978): 281–99.

11. Sean Wilentz, "Introduction," in Wilentz, ed., *Rites of Power: Symbolism, Ritual, and Politics Since the Middle Ages* (Philadelphia: University of Pennsylvania Press, 1985), pp. 1–9.

12. "Fue grandiozo el desfile de ayer por las principales calles de la capital," *La Prensa*, 22 de noviembre de 1937.

13. Linda A. Curcio-Nagy, "Giants and Gypsies: Corpus Christi in Colonial Mexico City," in Beezley, Martin, and French, eds., *Rituals of Rule, Rituals of Resistance*, pp. 1–2.

14. Plasencia de la Parra, pp. 9–15, 116.

15. Matthew D. Esposito, "From Cuauhtémoc to Juárez: Monuments, Myth, and Culture in Porfirian Mexico, 1876–1900," Master's thesis, Arizona State University, 1993; see Chapter 8, "Past and Present during National Holidays," pp. 93–107.

16. Begoñia Hernández y Lazo, ed., *Celebración del Grito de Independencia: Recopilación Hemerográfica, 1810–1985* (Mexico: INEHRM, 1985), pp. 80–84.

17. The Díaz regime led a movement to establish a Juárez myth through commemorations and monuments to unify the liberal party and enhance the legitimacy of President Díaz, Juárez's most important general and genuine successor. See Charles A. Weeks, *The Juárez Myth in Mexico* (Tuscaloosa: University of Alabama Press, 1987), and Daniel J. O'Neil, "The Cult of Juárez," *Journal of Latin American Lore* 4:1 (1978): 49–60.

18. Sierra, quoted in Enrique Krauze, *Mexico: Biography of Power* (New York: Harper Collins, 1997), p. 31. The regime documented the affair in Genaro García, ed., *Crónica oficial de las fiestas del primer centenario de la independencia de México* (México: Secretaría de Gobernación, Talleres del Museo Nacional, 1911).

19. Francisco I. Madero, "Plan de San Luis," 5 de octubre de 1910, from DHRM:RRM, I, 1964, p. 72.

20. Cumberland, *Mexican Revolution*, p. 127.

21. Paul Vanderwood, *Disorder and Progress: Bandits, Police and Mexican Development* (Lincoln: University of Nebraska Press, 1981), p. 159.

22. Zdzislaw Mach, *Symbols, Conflict, and Identity: Essays in Political Anthropology* (Albany: State University of New York Press, 1993), p. 106.

23. Chapter Five considers this topic in more detail.

24. *El Tiempo*, 20 y 21 de noviembre de 1911.

25. *Nueva Era*, 20 de noviembre de 1911.

26. "Excitativa," *Puebla*, Diciembre de 1911, Archivo General de la Nación, Colección Documental del Instituto Nacional de Estudios Históricos de la Revolución Mexicana, Caja 11, Expediente 2, Folio 15 (Hereafter cited as AGN, Colección Documental del INEHRM).

27. *El Día*, 21 de noviembre de 1912.

28. Lic. Blas Urrea, "La Sombra de Aquiles Serdán," in Urrea, *Obras políticas*, pp. 359–60.

29. The Epiphany in the Christian calendar refers to the coming of the Magi to Jesus at Bethlehem. The quotation is from *El Pueblo*, 21 de noviembre de 1916, reprinted in full in *Celebración del 20 de Noviembre, 1910–1985*, p. 59.

30. See, for example, "Solemne Manifestación en Honor del Sr. Madero," *El Demócrata*, 18 de septiembre de 1914; and "Una Grandiosa Manifestación se Llevará Mañana a Cabo en Memoria del Sr. Madero, para Celebrar su Natalico," *El Demócrata*, 29 de octubre de 1914. The Constitutionalist government also named one of the central avenues in the center of Mexico City after Madero.

31. *El Pueblo*, 21 de noviembre de 1916, quoted in *Celebración del 20 de Noviembre*, p. 60.

32. "Todas las oficinas públicas deberán trabajar hoy," *El Nacional*, 20 de noviembre de 1917, quoted in *Celebración del 20 de Noviembre*, p. 68.

33. "El Plan de Guadalupe, Firmado Hoy Hace Cuatro Anos," *El Demócrata*,

26 de marzo de 1917; and "Conmemoración del 5° Aniversario de la Firma del Plan de Guadalupe," *El Demócrata*, 26 de marzo de 1918.

34. "Sencilla fue la celebración del 20 de noviembre," *Excelsior*, 21 de noviembre de 1917; "El aniversario de la Revolución," *Excelsior*, 21 de noviembre de 1919, both reprinted in *Celebración del 20 de Noviembre*, pp. 70–71.

35. "El Veinte de Noviembre," *El Demócrata*, 20 de noviembre de 1920.

36. "Se Declara Día de Fiesta Nacional el Decimo Aniversario de la Revolución," *El Demócrata*, 12 de noviembre de 1920; "Solamente Fueron Recordados y Venerados los Mártires de la Revolución de 1910," *El Demócrata*, 21 de noviembre de 1920; "Fue Glorifiada Ayer la Memoria de los Mártires de la Democracia," *El Demócrata*, 23 de febrero de 1921.

37. During the 1920s, the *agrupación* was headed by Alfredo Álvarez and Calixto Maldonado R., president and vice-president, respectively, of the Antireelectionist Party in 1910. See, *Diccionario Porrúa de historia, biografía y geografía de México*, quinta edición (Mexico: Editorial Porrúa, 1986), pp. 115, 1743.

38. "La Revolución de 1910 fue conmemorada ayer," *Excelsior*, 21 de noviembre de 1924, reprinted in *Celebración del 20 de Noviembre*, pp. 99–100.

39. *Excelsior*, for example, refers to various "*verbenas populares*" (evening celebrations) that would take place in Mexico City. See, "Velada en memoria de la Revolución y del C. Francisco I. Madero," *Excelsior*, 18 de noviembre de 1928, reprinted in *Celebración del 20 de Noviembre*, p. 106.

40. "Mañana Se Conmemorará el Asesinato de los Señores Madero y Pino Suárez," *El Demócrata*, 21 de febrero de 1925.

41. "Con una Sugestiva Velada se Conmemoro la Iniciación de la Revolución de 1910," *El Demócrata*, 21 de noviembre de 1925; "Fue inaugurado el monumento a Carrillo Puerto en Tacuba," *Excelsior*, 21 de noviembre de 1925, reprinted in *Celebración del 20 de Noviembre*, pp. 101–03.

42. "Solemne Ceremonia para Conmemorar el XIII Aniversario del Asesinato de los Apostoles de la Revolución," *El Demócrata*, 21 de febrero de 1926; "Resultó muy hermoso la velada de la Revolución," *Excelsior*, 21 de noviembre de 1926.

43. By 1942, for example, the government of the Federal District organized 121 "civic festivals and ceremonies" during the year. *Memoria del Departamento del Distrito Federal, 1941–1942* (México: N.p., 1942), p. 187.

44. Eric J. Hobsbawm, *Nations and Nationalism Since 1780: Programme, Myth, Reality* (Cambridge: Cambridge University Press, 1990), p. 143.

45. *Memoria del Departamento del Distrito Federal, 1941–1942*, p. 187.

46. Joseph L. Arbena, "Sport, Development, and Mexican Nationalism, 1920–1970," *Journal of Sport History* 18:3 (Winter 1991): 354–55.

47. Mary Kay Vaughan, "The Construction of the Patriotic Festival in Tecamachalco," p. 225.

48. "El aniversario de la Revolución, conmemorado de manera solemne en la Capital de la Nación," *Excelsior*, 21 de noviembre de 1929, reprinted in *Celebración del 20 de Noviembre*, pp. 107–09.

49. "Grandiosamente se conmemoró el Aniversario de la Revolución," *El Nacional Revolucionario*, 21 de noviembre de 1929.

50. David E. Lorey, "The Revolutionary Festival in Mexico: November 20 Celebrations in the 1920s and 1930s," *The Americas* 54:1 (July 1997): 63.

51. "Treinta mil atletas desfilaron en una gran fiesta de juventud," *Excelsior*, 21 de noviembre de 1930, reprinted in *Celebración del 20 de Noviembre*, p. 115; "La conmemoración del día de la Revolución," *El Nacional Revolucionario*, 21 de noviembre de 1930.

52. "El Presidente Cárdenas fue ovacionado ayer en forma amplia y calurosa," *Excelsior*, 21 de noviembre de 1935; "Brillante e imponente fue el desfile deportivo efectuado la mañana de ayer en la metrópoli," *La Prensa*, 20 de noviembre de 1939, both reprinted in *Celebración del 20 de Noviembre*, pp. 150, 203.

53. "Establecimientos que cerrarán de día 20," *El Universal*, 16 de noviembre de 1949; "Desfile de veinte mil auténticos deportistas," *El Nacional*, 21 de noviembre de 1955, both reprinted in *Celebración del 20 de Noviembre*, pp. 309, 389.

54. Max and Mary Gluckman, "On Drama, Games, and Athletic Contests," in Sally F. Moore and Barbara G. Myerhoff, eds., *Secular Ritual* (Amsterdam: Van Gorcum, 1977).

55. "Solemne juramento de 8,000 atletas ante el C. Presidente," *La Prensa*, 21 de noviembre de 1930.

56. Arbena, "Sport, Development, and Mexican Nationalism," p. 56.

57. "El público que llenaba las graderías del parque Presidente Calles, aplaudió con entusiasmo a los jóvenes competidores que desfilaron," *El Nacional*, 21 de noviembre de 1951; "Cuatro premios especiales serán otorgados en los II Juegos Juveniles de la Revolución," *El Nacional*, 16 de noviembre de 1952, reprinted in *Celebración del 20 de Noviembre*, pp. 335–38.

58. "LXV Aniversario de la Revolución Mexicana," *El Gobierno Mexicana*, noviembre de 1975: 246; José Luis López, "20 de Noviembre, exhibición masiva de miseria deportiva," *Proceso* 525 (24 de noviembre de 1986): 62–63.

59. "Juegos Deportivos de la Revolución," *El Gobierno Mexicano*, noviembre de 1979: 119.

60. "Alcanzó brillantez el gran desfile de la Revolución," *El Nacional*, 20 de noviembre de 1944; "El Desfile Deportivo," *El Nacional*, 22 de noviembre de 1956.

61. "Athletes of Mexico Parade on Holiday," *The New York Times*, November 21, 1931.

62. *Calendario Nacionalista y Enciclopedia Nacional Popular*, 1935, p. 470.

63. "Alemán satisfecho por el grandioso suceso deportivo," *El Nacional*, 21 de noviembre de 1950, reprinted in *Celebración del 20 de Noviembre*, p. 319.

64. "Vibrante arenga en nombre del Presidente Cárdenas a los deportista mexicanos," *Excelsior*, 18 de noviembre de 1935, reprinted in *Celebración del 20 de Noviembre*, p. 146–47.

65. Roger Bousseau, President of the Mexican Olympic Committee, noted in 1973: "Mientras en todos los paises el Día de la Revolución se conmemora con

un desfile militar, aquí es deportivo. Eso para mi, es una cosa extraordinaria." From "El 20 de noviembre pueblo y gobierno recordaron a Madero, Zapata, Villa, y Carranza," *El Gobierno Mexicana*, 1–30 noviembre de 1973: 213.

66. López, "20 de Noviembre, exhibición masiva de miseria deportiva," p. 62.

67. "Alemán satisfecho por el grandioso suceso deportivo," *El Nacional*, 21 de noviembre de 1950, reprinted in *Celebración del 20 de Noviembre*, pp. 316–17.

68. "Ceremonia en el Monumento," *El Universal*, 21 de noviembre de 1957.

69. A. Berdejo y Roberto Villarreal, "52,600 atletas de luto conmemoraron el LXXIV aniversario de la Revolución," *Excelsior*, 21 de noviembre de 1984.

70. "Calido mensaje del Presidente a los mexicanos," *El Nacional*, 24 de noviembre de 1942.

71. López, "20 de Noviembre, exhibición masiva de miseria deportiva," *Proceso* 525 (24 de noviembre de 1986): 62.

72. Geertz, quoted in Mary Ryan, "The American Parade: Representations of the Nineteenth-Century Social Order," in Lynn Hunt, ed., *The New Cultural History* (Berkeley: University of California Press, 1989), p. 132.

73. Louis Marin, "Notes on a Semiotic Approach to Parade, Cortege, and Procession," in Falassi, ed., *Time Out of Time: Essays on the Festival* (Albuquerque: University of New Mexico Press, 1987), p. 227.

74. Vicente Urquiaga y Rivas, "La Avenida 20 de Noviembre," *Arquitectura y Decoración* 2:7 (mayo 1938): 35–48.

75. "Descollaron los conjuntos militares," *Excelsior*, 23 de noviembre de 1947; "El homenaje a la Revolución Mexicana, ayer," *El Nacional*, 21 de noviembre de 1951; "La gesta popular de 1910 fue exaltada en el acto del Monumento de la Revolución," *El Nacional*, 21 de noviembre de 1955; and "Ceremonia en el Monumento," *El Universal*, 21 de noviembre de 1957; all reprinted in *Celebración del 20 de Noviembre*, pp. 291, 331, 378, 401.

76. Alejandro Campos Bravo, "En una reverente ceremonia la Nación recibió ayer los restos del Apóstol de la Democracia," *El Nacional*, 21 de noviembre de 1960.

77. This conclusion was inspired by another conclusion. See Eric Van Young, "Conclusion: The State as Vampire—Hegemonic Projects, Public Ritual, and Popular Culture in Mexico, 1600–1990," in Beezley, Martin, and French, eds., *Rituals of Rule, Rituals of Resistance: Public Celebrations and Popular Culture in Mexico* (Wilmington, DE: SR Books, 1994), pp. 343–74.

5. MONUMENT

1. Françoise Choay, "Alberti: The Invention of Monumentality and Memory," *The Harvard Architecture Review* 4 (1984): 99–105; Gerald A. Danzer, "Monuments," in *Public Places: Exploring Their History* (Nashville: The American Association for State and Local History, 1987), pp. 1–16; Jean LaBatut, "Monuments and Memorials," in Talbot Hamlin, ed., *Forms and Functions of Twentieth-Century Architecture* (New York: Columbia University Press, 1952), Vol. III, pp. 521–33.

2. Edelman, *The Symbolic Uses of Politics*, pp. 95–113; David Lowenthal, *The Past is a Foreign Country* (Cambridge: Cambridge University Press, 1985), pp. 321–24.

3. William H. Gass, "Monumentality/Mentality," *Oppositions* 25 (Fall 1982): 130.

4. Mircea Eliade, *Symbolism, the Sacred, and the Arts* (New York: Crossroad, 1985), pp. 107, 115, and 120; George L. Mosse, *Fallen Soldiers: Reshaping the Memory of the World Wars* (New York: Oxford University Press, 1990), pp. 32–33, 100–04; and Hobsbawm, *Nations and Nationalism Since 1780*, pp. 80–85.

5. James E. Young, "The Biography of a Memorial Icon: Nathan Rapoport's Warsaw Ghetto Monument," *Representations* 26 (Spring 1989): 99; David Glassberg, "Monuments and Memories," *American Quarterly* 43:1 (March 1991): 143–56.

6. Jacobo Dale Vuelta, "Está concluido el Monumento a la Revolución," *El Universal*, 12 de septiembre de 1937.

7. Graciela de Garay, "La Ciudad de la Andamios," in *Asamblea de Ciudades: Años 20s/50s, Ciudad de México* (México: Museo del Palacio de Bellas Artes and CNCA, 1991), p. 68.

8. Neil Asher Silberman, "Fallen Idols," *Archaeology*, January–February 1992: 88.

9. This phrase is from Luis González y González, *Todo es historia* (México: Aguilar, 1989), pp. 20–21.

10. Hale, *The Transformation of Liberalism*, pp. 104–06, 245.

11. Quoted in Carlos Monsiváis, "On Civic Monuments and Their Spectators," in Helen Escobedo, ed., *Mexican Monuments: Strange Encounters* (New York: Abbeville Press, 1989), p. 110.

12. Monsiváis, "On Civic Monuments," p. 118. Ida Rodríguez Prampolini writes, "a partir de 1880, aproximadamente, se despierta al clamor de un exaltado nacionalismo patriótico, un afan de levantar monumentos públicos, estatuas de nuestros hombres celebres." Rodríguez Prampolini, *La Crítica de Arte en México en el Siglo XIX* (México: Imprenta Universitaria, 1964), Tomo I, p. 127.

13. In 1877 a private donor erected a monument to Christopher Columbus in one of the *glorietas*. The proposed Reforma monument was never constructed on the Paseo.

14. See Esposito, "From Cuauhtémoc to Juárez," Chap. 6.

15. Francisco Sosa, *Las Estatuas de la Reforma* (México: Colección Metropolitana, 1974), Tomo I, pp. 11–18; Barbara A. Tenenbaum, "Streetwise History: The Paseo de la Reforma and the Porfirian State, 1876–1910," in Beezley, Martin, and French, eds., *Rituals of Rule, Rituals of Resistance: Public Celebrations and Popular Culture in Mexico* (Wilmington: SR Books, 1994), pp. 127–150.

16. *El Universal*, 6 de agosto de 1892, p. 2.

17. Patricia Pérez Walters, "Jesús F. Contreras," in *Jesús F. Contreras, 1866–1902: Escultor finisecular* (México: CNCA, INBA, Museo Nacional de Arte, 1990), pp. 23–26.

18. Hobsbawm, "Mass-Producing Traditions," p. 271.

19. Mario Monteforte Toledo, *Las piedras vivas: Escultura y sociedad en México* (Mexico: UNAM, 1979), pp. 161–63.

20. "Restauración del 'Angel,'" *El Nacional*, 11 de junio de 1958.

21. *Altares de la Patria* (México: Departamento del Distrito Federal, 1956), pp. 16–19.

22. Ámparo Gómez Tepexicuapan, "El Paseo de la Reforma, 1864–1910," in B. Wendy Coss y Léon, ed., *Historia del Paseo de la Reforma* (Mexico: INBA, 1994), pp. 47–52.

23. City officials throughout the country, however, honored the president by naming streets, parks, bridges, and other public spaces after him. Esposito, "From Cuauhtémoc to Juárez," p. 12.

24. A drawing of the proposed monument is found in Justino Fernández, *El Arte Moderno en México. Breve Historia—Siglos XIX y XX* (México: Antigua Liberia Robredo, José Porrua e Hijos, 1937), Fig. 103. It is discussed in Fernández, "El Monumento a Porfirio Díaz," in Daniel Schavelzon, ed., *La polémica del arte nacional en México, 1850–1910* (México: Fondo de Cultura Económica, 1988), p. 249.

25. Miranda Valtierra Moisés, "Historia de un Símbolo: El Monumento a la Revolución," unpublished paper (México: Museo Nacional de la Revolución, 1989), pp. 2–3.

26. Francisco Ortiz Pinchetti, "La Revolución descuidó su monumento, que ahora amenaza todo lo que lo rodea," *Proceso* 349 (11 de julio de 1983): 24.

27. "Juarez Sigue Siendo la Cabeza del Partido Liberal," *El Demócrata*, 22 de marzo de 1917.

28. "El Aniversario de la Constitución, se Conmemoró con un Acto Cívico en el Hemiciclo de Juárez," *El Demócrata*, 6 de febrero de 1925.

29. José de J. Nuñez y Dominguez, and Nicolas Rangel, *El Monumento A la Independencia: Bosquejo histórico* (México: Departamento del Distrito Federal, 1930), p. 72.

30. "¿Monumento a la Revolución?" *El Universal*, 21 de febrero de 1923.

31. "Excitativa," broadside from the Archivo General de la Nación (AGN), Colección Documental de INEHRM, Caja 11, Expediente 2.

32. See AGN, Archivo G. Narvaez, Colección Documental de INEHRM, Folio 56, Exp. 6/2, Folio 12, Exp. 6/11, both in Caja 1.

33. See, for example, "En Puebla Se Celebró el Aniversario de la Iniciación de la Revolución de 1910," *El Demócrata*, 22 de noviembre de 1915; "Conmemoración del 5° Aniversario de la Firma del Plan de Guadalupe," *El Demócrata*, 26 de marzo de 1918; "Se Declara Día de Fiesta Nacional el Décimo Aniversario de la Revolución," *El Demócrata*, 13 de noviembre de 1920; and "Un Grupo de Constituyentes Celebró Ayer el Aniversario de la Constitución," *El Demócrata*, 6 de febrero de 1923.

34. "Vaya a Erigirse Primer Monumento a Madero," *El Demócrata*, 18 de marzo de 1917.

35. "Manifiesto a la Nación," México, 18 de enero de 1920, AGN, Colección Documental de INEHRM, Caja 11, Exp. 6, Fs. 24.

36. "La Primera Piedra," *El Universal*, 24 de febrero de 1923; "A la Revolución," *El Universal*, 20 de febrero de 1923.

37. "Una Estatua del Apóstol F. I. Madero," *El Nacional*, 18 de noviembre de 1956. This statue was later moved to the grounds of Los Pinos, the presidential mansion.

38. Juan Sánchez Azcona, "Bifurcaciones de la Revolución," *El Universal*, 22 de junio de 1925.

39. Juan Barragán, San Antonio, TX, to Pascual Ortiz Rubio, México, 19 de agosto de 1929, Archivo Juan Barragán (UNAM), Caja XVII, Exp. 18, Foja 25.

40. "La Memoria de Felipe Carrillo Puerto Fue Solemnemente Honrada Ayer en Tacuba," *El Demócrata*, 21 de noviembre de 1925.

41. Palabras del Señor General Álvaro Obregón, Pronunciadas el Día 30 de Abril de 1928, *Discursos del Gral. Obregón. Segunda Parte, de 1924 a 1928* (México: Tallares Gráficos de la Nación, 1928), p. 408.

42. "Un Monumento, Homenaje de los Socialistas de Yucatán, Para Felipe Carrillo Puerto," *El Nacional*, 3 de noviembre de 1932; "Perpetuación Ideológica y Material de la Memorial de F. Carrillo Puerto," *El Nacional*, 9 de noviembre de 1932.

43. *Primer Congreso de Unificación de las Organizaciones Campesinas de la República. Celebrado en la Ciudad de México, D. F., del 15 al 20 Noviembre de 1926* (Puebla, 1927), p. 72.

44. "Homenaje a la Memoria de E. Zapata," *El Nacional Revolucionario*, 10 de abril de 1930.

45. José Córdova, "La Glorificación de Zapata," *El Nacional*, 14 de abril de 1932. The first monument to Zapata, also an equestrian statue, in the Federal District was erected in Huipulco in 1958. This statue was later transferred to a park off Calle Miramontes. Samuel Brunk, personal communication, 1998.

46. Critics of the monument said it looked more like an ancient Egyptian temple than a Mexican pyramid, while Ignacio Asúnsolo defended it as "completely Mexican." See "Obra Netamente Mexicana es el Monumento al Gral. Obregón," *El Universal*, 5 de febrero de 1958.

47. *Monumento al General Álvaro Obregón. Homenaje nacional en el lugar de su sacrificio* (México: Departamento del Distrito Federal, 1934).

48. Aarón Sáenz, "Discurso de 17 de julio de 1935," in Sáenz, *Obregón, aspectos de su vida* (México: Editorial "Cvltvra," 1935), p. 210.

49. "Los Restos de D. Venustiano," *El Nacional*, 9 de noviembre de 1932.

50. Ignacio Suárez, El Organizador de la Estela Conmemorativa, to General Don Juan Barragán, México, D. F., febrero de 1936, Archivo Barragán, Caja XVII, Exp. 30. The first monument to Carranza in Mexico City was sculpted in bronze by Ignacio Asúnsolo and erected by the city on December 2, 1960.

51. Federico Medrano, head of the Bloc Obregonista of the Chamber of Depu-

ties, quoted in "Consolidación de la Unidad Revolucionaria," *El Nacional Revolucionario*, 27 de septiembre de 1929.

52. Juan Sánchez Azcona, "Bifurcaciones de la Revolución," *El Universal*, 22 de junio de 1925.

53. Moisés Sáenz, *Mexico: An Appraisal and a Forecast* (New York: The Committee on Cultural Relations with Latin America, 1929), p. 12.

54. Carlos Obregón Santacilia, *El Monumento a la Revolución: Simbolismo e historia* (México: Secretaría de Educación Pública, 1960); Enrique X. de Anda Alanis, *La Arquitectura de la Revolución Mexicana: Corrientes estilos de la década de los veintes* (México: UNAM, 1990), pp. 102–06.

55. "El Monumento a Zapata," *El Nacional Revolucionario*, 2 de enero de 1930.

56. Luis Ortiz Monasterio, "La disputa de la escultura," *Revista de Revistas* 22:1135 (14 de febrero de 1932): 23; Guadalupe Tolosa Sánchez, "Luis Ortiz Monasterio," in *La escuela mexicana de escultura. Maestros fundadores* (Mexico: INBA, 1990), pp. 113–25.

57. "Monumento a la Revolución," *El Nacional*, 15 de Abril de 1932.

58. In his memoirs, Pani claims that the idea for the Monument to the Revolution was his originally and that he approached the architect Obregón Santacilia. See Alberto J. Pani, *Apuntes autobiográficos* (México: Librería de Manuel Porrua, 1950), Tomo II, pp. 180–81.

59. *El Monumento de la Revolución. Texto de la Iniciativa Presentada al Ciudadano Presidente de la República por los Ciudadanos Gral. Plutarco Elías Calles e Ing. Alberto J. Pani y del Acuerdo Presidencial Recaido sobre la Misma* (México: Editorial "Cvltvra," 1933), pp. 7, 11–13.

60. Graciela de Garay Arellano, *La Obra de Carlos Obregón Santacilia, Arquitecto* (Mexico: SEP/INBA, 1979), p. 54; Carlos Obregón Santacilia, *50 Años de Arquitectura Mexicana* (México: Patria, 1952), pp. 84–87; and Obregón Santacilia, *El Monumento de la Revolución*, pp. 42–43.

61. Marte R. Gómez to Oliverio Martínez, México, D.F., 22 de marzo de 1933, Archivo del Centro Nacional de Investigación, Documentación, e Información de Artes Plásticas—Instituto Nacional de Bellas Artes (CENIDIAP-INBA), Mexico City.

62. "Se han Instalado ya las Esculturas cn el Grandioso Monumento," *Excelsior*, 23 de agosto de 1934; *Oliverio Martínez, 1901–1938*, Catálogo, julio-agosto, 1991, Rafael Matos Galeria de Arte, Mexico City, in the archive of the CENIDIAP-INBA.

63. Agustín Arteaga, "Oliverio Martínez," in *Escuela mexicana de escultura. Maestros fundadores* (Mexico: INBA, 1990), p. 104.

64. Obregón Santacilia, *El Monumento a la Revolución*, p. 8.

65. Ibid., p. 73.

66. Ibid., pp. 7–8.

67. A. J. Pani to the Gobernador del Estado de Oaxaca, 20 de septiembre de 1933, Expediente "Monumento a la Revolución," Gaveta 54, Archivo Plutarco Elías Calles (APEC), Mexico City.

68. Letters and telegrams regarding the funding of the monument are found in the file titled "Monumento a la Revolución," Gaveta 54, APEC.

69. Gustavo de Anda, "La Tumba de la Revolución," *Impacto*, 1 de Febrero de 1967.

70. Ibid., p. 9. This inscription, however, was never made.

71. J. H. Plenn, *Mexico Marches* (Indianapolis: The Bobbs-Merrill Co., 1939), p. 142.

72. Pani to los Gobernadores estatales, 20 de septiembre de 1933, APEC.

73. Obregón Santacilia's architectural plans are reprinted in Garay Arellano, *La obra de Carlos Obregón Santacilia*, p. 89.

74. Obregón Santacilia obliquely referred to the Cárdenas administration's reluctance to fund the monument in a letter to Calles, 13 de mayo de 1935, Gav. 56, Inv. 4051. For discussion on funding problems, see the expediente "Monument a la Revolución," Gav. 54, APEC. Also see "Para Acabar el Monumento," *El Nacional*, 13 de enero de 1935.

75. Pani, *Apuntes autobiográficos*, Tomo II, pp. 183–84.

76. Marianne Doezema, "The Public Monument in Tradition and Transition," in *The Public Monument and its Audience* (Cleveland: The Cleveland Museum of Art, 1977), p. 14.

77. Obregón Santacilia, *El Monumento a la Revolución*, p. 62.

78. Balmori's woodcut was the cover illustration of *Cárdenas Habla!* (México: Partido de la Revolución Mexicana, 1940).

79. "Los Homenajes a Madero y Pino Suárez," *El Nacional*, 21 de noviembre de 1960.

80. Jesús Silva Herzog, "Estadista visionario," *El Gobierno Mexicano* 35 (octubre de 1979): 89.

81. Gass, "Monumentality/Mentality," p. 137.

82. Garay Arellano, *La obra de Carlos Obregón Santacilia*, p. 95.

83. "Reposan en el monumento a la Revolución sus adalides," *El Nacional*, 10 de enero de 1942.

84. Mosse, *Fallen Soldiers*, p. 99; *Catálogo de Monumentos Escultóricos y Conmemorativos* (México: Oficina de Conservación de Edificios Públicos y Monumentos, 1976), p. 281; "México despide a Cárdenas," *Siempre* 907 (11 de noviembre de 1970), pp. 40–2. The government has attempted to obtain the remains of Emiliano Zapata for the monument, but the family has resisted the transfer. See Ilene V. O'Malley, *The Myth of the Mexican Revolution: Hero Cults and the Institutionalization of the Mexican State, 1920–1940* (New York: Greenwood Press, 1986), pp. 69–70.

85. "Severa Recordación de la Muerte de Carranza," *El Nacional*, 22 de mayo de 1945.

86. "Plutarco Elías Calles y Lázaro Cárdenas," in *El Gobierno Mexicano*, segunda época 11 (1/31 de octubre de 1971): 166, 180.

87. Avner Ben-Amos writes that "ancestors' shrines are sacred sites in most human societies. They are the places where communities get together to commu-

nicate with their founding fathers and to celebrate their shared values." See Ben-Amos, "The Sacred Center of Power: Paris and Republican State Funerals," *Journal of Interdisciplinary History* 22:1 (Summer 1991): 37.

88. "Sobria Sencillez para Honrar a D. Venustiano," *El Universal,* 27 de mayo de 1951.

89. "Reflexión y a la Historia," *Siempre* 1953 (28 de noviembre de 1990); the brief history of the Revolution that is sold at the Museum is . . . *y nos fuimos a la Revolución* (México: Museo del Monumento a la Revolución, 1987).

90. Young, "The Biography of a Memorial Icon," p. 99.

91. There is, as well, an unofficial, dissident "text" of the monument invented by critics of the regime and system. This is discussed in the conclusion of this book.

6. HISTORY

1. "Impresionante Acto de Unidad Revolucionaria," *El Nacional,* 27 de agosto de 1966.

2. D. Rafael Nieto, "El México de Ayer y el de Hoy," *El Universal,* 9 de junio and 10 de junio de 1925.

3. Vaughan, *Cultural Politics in Revolution,* p. 37.

4. "Cual es el Mejor Tratado sobre la Historia General de México." *Excelsior,* 21 de julio de 1927.

5. Juan Sanchez Azcona, "Bifurcaciones de la Revolución," *El Universal,* 22 de junio de 1925.

6. Draft of a letter, recipient unknown, 1928, from Archivo Juan Barragán, UNAM, Caja XVII, Exp. 19.

7. Castillo, *Bibliografía de la Revolución Mexicana de 1910–1966.*

8. Roberto Ramos, *Bibliografía de la Revolución Mexicana (Hasta Mayo de 1931)* (México: Monografías Bibliográficas Mexicanas, Imprenta de la Secretaría de Relaciones Exteriores, 1931).

9. Judge Ramón Prida, *From Despotism to Anarchy: Facts and Commentaries about the Mexican Revolutions at the Beginning of the Twentieth Century* (New York: N.p., 1914), pp. 3, 9; Prida, *De la dictadura a la anarquía* (San Antonio, TX: N.p., 1914).

10. Prida, *From Despotism to Anarchy,* p. 255.

11. Francisco Bulnes, *El veradero Díaz y la revolución* (Mexico: N.p., 1920); Manuel Calero y Sierra, *Un decenio de política mexicana* (New York: N.p., 1920); Emilio Rabasa, *La evolución histórica de México* (México: N.p., 1920); and José López-Portillo y Rojas, *Elevación y caida de Porfirio Díaz* (México: N.p., 1921).

12. Gloria Villegas, "El Viraje de la Historiografía Mexicana Frente a la Crisis Revolucionaria, 1914–1916," *Anuario de Historia* 11 (1983): 216–17.

13. Acuña, *Memoria de la Secretaría de Gobernación.*

14. T. Esquivel Obregón, "Factors in the Historical Evolution of Mexico," *Hispanic American Historical Review* 2 (May 1919): 136.

15. Rosendo Salazar and José G. Escobedo, *Las pugnas de la gleba, 1907–1922* (México: N.p., 1923).

16. For a full bibliography, see James D. Cockcroft, *Intellectual Precursors of the Mexican Revolution, 1900–1913* (Austin: University of Texas Press, 1968).

17. Aurelio Palacios, *Historia Verídica del célebre guerrillo del Sur, Emiliano Zapata* (Orizaba: N.p., 1924); Germán List Arzubide, *Emiliano Zapata. Exaltación* (Jalapa: N.p., 1927); and Carlos Reyes Aviles, *Cartones Zapatistas* (México: N.p., 1928).

18. "Cual es el Mejor Tratado sobre la Historia General de México," *Excelsior*, 21 de julio de 1927.

19. Andrés Lira, "Justo Sierra: La Historia Como Entendimiento Responsable," in Enrique Florescano and Ricardo Pérez Montfort, eds., *Historiadores de México en la Siglo XX* (México: Fondo de Cultura Económica, 1995), p. 38.

20. Díaz Arciniega, *Querella por la Cultura "Revolucionaria," 1925*, pp. 21–22.

21. Tzvi Medin, *El minimato presidencial: historia política del maximato, 1928–1935* (México: Ediciones Era, 1982), p. 29.

22. Plutarco Elías Calles, "En pos de la unificación revolucionaria," 7 de diciembre de 1928, in Macias, ed., *Plutarco Elías Calles: Pensamiento político y social*, p. 284.

23. Comité Organizador del Partido Nacional Revolucionario, "A las Agrupaciones Revolucionarias de la República," 5 de enero de 1929, in *La Democracia Social en México. Historia de la Convención Nacional Revolucionaria. Sucesión Presidencial de 1929* (Mexico: N.p., 1929), p. 102.

24. "El Partido Nacional Revolucionario y el Partido Reaccionario," *El Nacional Revolucionario*, 5 de agosto de 1929.

25. "Va a Escribir la Historia de la Revolución," *El Nacional Revolucionario*, 20 de agosto de 1930.

26. Tomás Garza Felan, "Ideario de la Revolución," *El Nacional*, 9 de julio de 1932.

27. Gerardo Galarza, "A los héroes que la vida separó, ni tener su nombre en la Cámara los reune," *Proceso*, 7 de enero de 1985: 21–24.

28. Jesús Corral, "La Glorificación de los Héroes Revolucionarios," *El Nacional*, 8 de julio de 1931.

29. Emilio Portes Gil, *En memoria de Zapata. Un balance social político del momento actual en México* (México: PNR, Biblioteca de Cultura Social y Política, 1936), p. 5.

30. *Calendario Nacionalista y Enciclopedia Popular*, 1935, pp. 9, 443.

31. A good example would be the polemic between Alfonso Junco and Miguel Alessio Robles with regard to the reputation of Venustiano Carranza. See Junco, *Carranza y los orígenes de su rebelión* (México: N.p., 1934) and Alessio Robles, *Ideales de la Revolución* (México: Editorial "Cvltvra," 1935).

32. Luis Chávez Orozco, "Simplicidad Histórica," *El Nacional*, 17 de abril de 1933.

33. Francisco S. Mancilla, "Historiadores sin Documentación y Crítico sin Criterio," *El Universal*, 16 de marzo de 1934. Also see Juan Sánchez Azcona, "Los Historiógrafos de la Revolución," *El Universal*, 20 de enero de 1933; Luis Chávez Orozco, "Historia y Partidarismo," *El Nacional*, 3 de abril de 1933; and P. Mar-

tínez de la Rosa, "La Falsa Ciencia de Nuestros Historiógrafos," *El Universal,* 2 de noviembre de 1933.

34. Rubén Salido Orcillo, "La Historia y la Política," *El Nacional,* 1 de julio de 1933.

35. J. D. Ramírez Garrido, "El por qué de esta Revista," *La Revolución Mexicana. Revista Ilustrada de Historia y Literatura* 1 : 1 (junio 1934): 3–4.

36. Rafael Ramos Pedrueza, *Sugerencias Revolucionarias para la Enseñanza de la Historia* (México: UNAM, Sección Editorial, 1932), pp. 34–35.

37. Ramírez Garrido, "El por qué de esta Revista," p. 4.

38. "La Editorial de Escritores Revolucionarios y el Diccionario Histórico, Geográfico, Biográfico y Bibliográfico de la Revolución Mexicana," *La Revolución Mexicana* 1 : 4 (octubre 1934): 85–87.

39. Francisco Naranjo, *Diccionario Biográfico Revolucionario* (Mexico: Editorial Cosmos, 1935), p. 9.

40. Carmen Nava Nava, *Ideología del partido de la Revolución Mexicana* (México: Centro de Estudios de la Revolución Mexicana, "Lázaro Cárdenas," A. C., 1984), pp. 20–47.

41. Escobedo and Meléndez to Cárdenas, 16 de enero de 1935, AGN, Ramo Presidentes, Cárdenas del Rio, 704. 1/52, Exp. 13174.

42. Escobedo and Meléndez to Cárdenas, 2 de febrero de 1935, AGN, Cárdenas, 704. 1/52, Exp. 17549.

43. Palacios, "La idea oficial de la 'Revolución Mexicana'," p. 273.

44. Cárdenas, quoted in Adolfo Gilly, "Memoria y Olvido. Razón y Esperanza: Sugerencias para el Estudio de la Historia de las Revoluciones," *Brecha* 1 (Otoño 1986): 10.

45. Dr. Ramón Puente, "Prólogo," in José T. Meléndez, ed., *Historia de la Revolución Mexicana* (México: Talleres Gráficos de la Nación, 1936), Tomo I, p. 8.

46. Octavio Paz, "Muertes Paralelas," in *Tres revolucionarios, tres testimonios* (México: EOSA, 1986), Tomo I, pp. 11–12.

47. Sánchez Azcona, "Francisco I. Madero," in Meléndez, ed., *Historia de la Revolución Mexicana,* Tomo I, p. 51.

48. Paz, "Muertes Paralelas," Tomo I, p. 14.

49. Puente, "Francisco Villa," in Meléndez, ed., *Historia de la Revolución Mexicana,* Tomo I, p. 254.

50. Octavio Paz Solórzano, "Emiliano Zapata," in Meléndez, ed., *Historia de la Revolución Mexicana,* Tomo I, p. 378.

51. Paz, "Muertes Paralelas," Tomo I, p. 13.

52. Meléndez failed to obtain support for the publication from Cárdenas at this time as a result, most likely, of the 1938 rebellion by his sponsor, General Cedillo, against the national government. The second volume was published by a private press.

53. Vicente Peredo y Saavedra, "La Revolución as Servicio de la Patria," in José T. Meléndez, ed., *Historia de la Revolución Mexicana* (México: Ediciones Aguilas, 1940), Tomo II, p. 9.

54. Francisco L. Urquizo, "Venustiano Carranza," in Meléndez, ed., *Historia de la Revolución Mexicana,* Tomo II, p. 14. Urquizo was a loyal Carrancista from 1913 until 1920.

55. General Rubén García, "Álvaro Obregón," in Meléndez, ed., *Historia de la Revolución Mexicana,* Tomo II, p. 108. García was first a Carrancista, then an Obregonista. When he wrote the essay he was sub-jefe de la comisión de historia de la secretaría de guerra y marina.

56. Puente, "Plutarco Elías Calles," in Meléndez, ed., *Historia de la Revolución Mexicana,* Tomo II, p. 193.

57. Introduction to the 1987 reprint of Mcléndez, ed., *Historia de la Revolución Mexicana* (México: INEHRM, 1987), n. p.

58. Paz, "Muertes Paralelas," p. 9.

59. J. M. Puig Casauranc, *Galatea rebelde a varios pigmaliones* (México: N.p., 1938), p. 55. Following the historiography of the French Revolution and quoting Georges Clemenceau's famous pronouncement of 1891, he wrote that "'La Revolución es un bloque,' fallaron ya, de la de Francia, los historiadores. Y lo mismo diran de la nuestra."

60. Andrés Molina Enríquez, *Esbozo de la historia de los primeros diez años de la Revolución Agraria de México (de 1910-1920) Hecho a grandes rasgos* (México: Talleres Gráficos del Museo Nacional de Arqueología, Historia y Etnografía, 1932-36). Despite its title, this work largely focused on the social and economic history of Mexico before 1910. Only the last four chapters of the fifth volume concern the period 1910-20. Also see Agustín Basave Benítez, *México mestizo: Análisis del nacionalismo mexicano en torno a la mestizofilia de Andrés Molina Enríquez* (México: Fondo de Cultura Económica, 1992), pp. 76-77.

61. Miguel Alessio Robles, *Historia política de la Revolución* (México: Ediciones Botas, 1938); Dr. Ramón Puente, *La Dictadura, la Revolución y sus hombres* (México: N.p., 1938); Alfonso Teja Zabre, *Panorama histórico de la Revolución mexicana* (México: Ediciones Botas, 1938); Jesús Romero Flores, *Anales históricos de la Revolución Mexicana* (México: Ediciones Encuadernables de El Nacional, 1939), 4 vols.; Félix F. Palavicini, ed., *México: Historia de su evolución constructiva* (México: Editorial Libro, 1945), 4 vols.

62. Vito Alessio Robles, "Gajos de Historia," *Excelsior,* 17 de enero de 1947; Gustavo Casasola, *Historia gráfica de la revolución mexicana, 1900-1940* (México: N.p., 1945), 5 vols. Alessio Robles ignored the anti-Zapatista bias in the Casasola series.

63. "Introducción," *Documentos de la Revolución Mexicana* (México: Biblioteca Enciclopedia Popular, SEP, 1945), p. vi.

64. Teodoro Hernández, *La historia de la Revolución debe hacerse* (México: N.p., 1950), p. 3.

65. Baltasar Dromundo, "¿La Historia de la Revolución?" *Excelsior,* 24 de octubre de 1949.

66. Agustín Cue Canovas, "Notas de Historia," *El Nacional,* 27 de septiembre de 1951.

67. José López Bermúdez, "Introducción: Nuestra Historia y sus Hombres," in Alberto Morales Jiménez, *Historia de la Revolución Mexicana* (México: Instituto de Investigaciones Políticas, Económicas y Sociales del PRI, 1951), p. xv.

68. Ibid., p. xv.

69. Morales Jiménez, *Historia de la Revolución Mexicana*, pp. 175, 180, 191–92.

70. The letter of approval from the Comisión Revisora de Libros de Texto y de Consulta is printed in the third edition. See Alberto Morales Jiménez, *Historia de la Revolución Mexicana*, tercero edición (México: Editorial Morelos, 1961).

71. Lic. Manuel González Ramírez, Patronato de la Historia de Sonora to President Miguel Alemán, 23 de enero de 1952, and "Memorandum para el Señor Licenciado Miguel Alemán Valdés," AGN, Alemán Valdés, 920/25743.

72. The series was called, "Fuentes para la Historia de la Revolución Mexicana."

73. González Ramírez, "Nota," in *Manifiestos Políticos, 1892–1912* (México: Fondo de Cultura Económica, 1957), p. vi.

74. "Decreto que Crea el Instituto Nacional de Estudios Históricos de la Revolución Mexicana que Funcionará como Órgano de la Secretaría de Gobernación, *Diario Oficial*, 199: 52 (29 de agosto de 1953).

75. Javier Garciadiego Dantan, "Salvador Azuela: aproximación biográfica," in Azuela, *La Revolución Mexicana: Estudios Históricos*, selección de Garciadiego Dantan (México: INEHRM, 1988), p. xxvii.

76. *Catálogo de Publicaciones del Instituto Nacional de Estudios Históricos de la Revolución Mexicana, 1953–1993* (México: INEHRM, 1993), pp. 39, 86. I wish to thank Clemente Martínez for giving me this catalogue.

77. Thomas Benjamin, "Regionalizing the Revolution: The Many Mexicos in Revolutionary Historiography," in Benjamin and Mark Wasserman, eds., *Provinces of the Revolution: Essays on Regional Mexican History, 1910–1929* (Albuquerque: University of New Mexico Press, 1999), pp. 330–31.

78. Allen Wells, "Oaxtepec Revisited: The Politics of Mexican Historiography, 1968–1988," *Mexican Studies/Estudios Mexicanos* 7:2 (Summer 1991): 333.

79. Álvaro Matute, "La Revolución recordada, inventada, rescatada," in Monroy de Martí, ed., *Memoria del Congreso Internacional sobre la Revolución Mexicana* (México: INEHRM, 1991), Tomo II, p. 444.

CONCLUSION

1. An anonymous contributor to "Adelita," quoted in Downing, *The Mexican Earth*, pp. 247–48.

2. José Iturriaga, "México y su Crisis Histórica," *Cuadernos Americanos*, May–June 1947: 21–37; and Jesús Silva Herzog, "La Revolución Mexicana es ya un Hecho Histórico," *Cuadernos Americanos*, September–October, 1949: 7–16; both translated by Stanley R. Ross and reprinted in Ross, ed., *Is the Mexican Revolution Dead?* Second edition (Philadelphia: Temple University Press, 1975), pp. 92, 107.

3. Charles Henry Haight, "The Contemporary Mexican Revolution as Viewed

by Mexican Intellectuals" (unpublished Ph.D. Dissertation, Department of History, Stanford University, 1956), p. 12.

4. Manuel Germán Parra, quoted in an interview with Ernesto Álvarez Nolasco originally published in *Mañana*, August 30, 1952 and reprinted in Ross, ed., *Is the Mexican Revolution Dead?*, p. 157.

5. Haight, "The Contemporary Mexican Revolution," p. 307.

6. Ross, ed., *Is the Mexican Revolution Dead?*, p. 24.

7. *México, la revolución congelada* ("The Frozen Revolution") is the title of a documentary film released in 1971.

8. Pablo González Casanova, *La democracia en México* (México: Ediciones ERA, 1965).

9. Stanley R. Ross, "La protesta de los intelectuales ante México y su revolución," *Historia Mexicana* 26 (enero–marzo 1977): 412–20.

10. Lorenzo Meyer and Manuel Camacho, "La ciencia política en México: Su desarrollo y estado actual," in *Ciencias sociales en México: Desarrollo y perspectiva* (Mexico City: El Colegio de México, 1979), p. 20.

11. David C. Bailey, "Revisionism and the Recent Historiography of the Mexican Revolution," *Hispanic American Historical Review* 58:1 (1978): 63.

12. Luis González y González, *Pueblo en vilo. Microhistoria de San José de Garcia* (México: El Colegio de México, 1968); John Womack, *Zapata and the Mexican Revolution*; James D. Cockcroft did the same for Magonismo in *Intellectual Precursors of the Mexican Revolution, 1900–1913*; Adolfo Gilly, *La revolución interrumpida: México (1910–1920), una guerra campesina por la tierra y el poder* (México: Ediciones "El Caballito," 1971).

13. Donald Keesing, "Structural Change Early in Development: Mexico's Changing Industrial and Occupational Structure from 1895 to 1950," *Journal of Economic History* 29 (December 1969): 716–38; Arnaldo Córdova, *La ideología de la Revolución Mexicana*; Córdova, *La política de masas del cardenismo* (México: Serie Popular Era, 1974); Peter H. Smith, *Labyrinths of Power: Political Recruitment in Twentieth-Century Mexico* (Princeton: Princeton University Press, 1979). Also see Thomas Benjamin and Marcial Ocasio-Meléndez, "Organizing the Memory of Modern Mexico: Porfirian Historiography in Perspective, 1880s–1980s, *Hispanic American Historical Review* 64:2 (1984): 323–64.

14. See Benjamin, "Regionalizing the Revolution," pp. 319–57.

15. Thomas Benjamin, "The Leviathan on the Zócalo," p. 196.

16. Alan Knight, *The Mexican Revolution*; and John Mason Hart, *Revolutionary Mexico*.

17. Rius, "Aniversario," *Rius en Proceso* (Mexico: Revista Proceso, 1983), p. 80; Rocha, "Años Despues," *La Jornada*, 19 de noviembre de 1990; Naranjo, "Los festejos," *Proceso*, 18 de noviembre de 1985, p. 5, and "Recogido," *Proceso*, 21 de noviembre de 1988.

18. Anda, "La Tumba de la Revolución."

19. James E. Young, *The Texture of Memory: Holocaust Memorials and Meaning* (New Haven: Yale University Press, 1993), p. 3.

20. Daniel Esparza Hernández, "Las diversas facetas del México moderno y revolucionario, presentes en el desfile," *El Universal,* 21 de noviembre de 1993.

21. "La Revolución Mexicana," *Excelsior,* 21 de noviembre de 1950.

22. Aurora Serrano González, "La fiesta institucional que no cambia," *Unomásuno,* 21 de noviembre de 1993.

23. Alfonso Martínez Domínguez, "En el Monumento a la Revolución. El 20 de noviembre de 1968," in *Anuario Cívico de la Ciudad de México 1968* (México: Departamento del Distrito Federal, 1968), p. 193.

24. Rius, "Los dos Méxicos," *Proceso* 236, 11 de mayo de 1981: 31; and Rius, "Avanzando," *Proceso,* 19 de noviembre de 1984.

25. *Siempre! Presencia de Mexico,* 25 de noviembre de 1992.

26. *Unomásuno,* 21 de noviembre de 1978; Alejandro Gómez Arias, "El Festín de Los Enanos," *Siempre!,* Diciembre 6 de 1978: 20.

27. ". . . Y ¿dónde quedó el desfile?" *Reforma,* 21 de noviembre de 1993.

28. Manuel Moreno Sánchez, "¿Cuál Revolución Conmemoramos?" *Siempre!,* 8 de diciembre de 1982: 24.

29. Martin Chacon Albarran, "Marcharon campesinos al Zócalo," *El Nacional,* 21 de noviembre de 1993.

30. Miguel Pérez, "Pide Cárdenas debate con CSG," *Reforma,* 21 de noviembre de 1993.

31. Day after tomorrow, noted Samuel Máynez Puente on the eve of the seventy-fifth anniversary of the Revolution, "we will commemorate a falsified Revolution, one betrayed daily." See "Siniestro aniversario," *Proceso* 472 (18 de noviembre de 1985): 38.

32. President Lázaro Cárdenas, November 30, 1938, quoted in Ross, ed., *Is the Mexican Revolution Dead?,* p. 183.

33. José Revueltas in an article published in *Excelsior,* April 18, 1947 and reprinted in Ross, ed., *Is the Mexican Revolution Dead?,* p. 143.

Sources

ARCHIVES AND LIBRARIES:

Archivo Juan Barragán, Biblioteca Nacional, Universidad Nacional Autónoma de México, Mexico City.

Archivo del Centro Nacional de Investigación, Documentación, e Información de Artes Plásticas, Instituto de Bellas Artes, Mexico City.

Archivo General de la Nación, Colección Documental del Instituto Nacional de Estudios Históricos de la Revolución Mexicana, and Ramo de Presidentes: Cárdenas del Rio and Alemán Valdés, Mexico City.

Archivo Plutarco Elías Calles, Fideicomiso Archivos Elías Calles y Fernando Torreblanca, Mexico City.

Clements Library, University of Michigan, Ann Arbor, Michigan.

Biblioteca Nacional, Universidad Nacional Autónoma de México, Mexico City.

Colección Basave, Biblioteca de México, Mexico City.

Colección de Folletos de la Revolución Mexicana, Biblioteca Lerdo de Tejeda, Mexico City.

Hemeroteca Nacional, Universidad Nacional Autónoma de México, Mexico City.

Library of Congress, Manuscript Division, Washington, DC.

Lilly Library, Indiana University, Bloomington, IN.

University Library, University of Groningen, Groningen, The Netherlands.

NEWSPAPERS AND MAGAZINES:

El Demócrata, 1914–26.
El Día, 1912.
Diario Oficial, 1953.
Excelsior, 1917–present.
El Gobierno Mexicana, 1971–79.
La Jornada, 1983–present.
México Nuevo, 1911–13.
El Nacional Revolucionario, 1929–30.
El Nacional, 1931–present.
Nueva Era, 1911.
El País, 1914.

La Prensa, 1930–39.
Proceso, 1977–present.
Reforma, 1993–present.
El Renovador, 1914.
Revista de Revistas, 1932.
Revolución, 1938.
La Revolución Mexicana, 1934.
Siempre, 1953–present.
El Tiempo, 1911.
El Universal, 1892, 1920–present.
Unomásuno, 1977–present.
La Voz de Sonora, 1913.

Bibliography

Abad Santillán, Diego. *Ricardo Flores Magón. El Apóstol de la Revolución Social Mexicana*. México: Grupo Cultural 'Ricardo Flores Magón,' 1925.

Acevedo, Esther. "Las decoraciones que pasaron a ser revolucionarias." In Acevedo, ed., *El nacionalismo y el arte mexicano*. México: Universidad Nacional Autónoma de México, 1986.

Acton, Lord. "Nationality." *The Home and Foreign Review* 1 (July 1862).

Acuña, Jesús. *Memoria de la Secretaría de Gobernación correspondiente al período revolucionario comprendido entre el 19 de febrero de 1913 y al 30 de noviembre de 1916*. México: Revista de Revistas, 1916.

Ades, Dawn. *Art in Latin America: The Modern Era, 1820–1980*. New Haven: Yale University Press, 1989.

Aguilar, Rafael. *Madero sin máscra*. México: Imprenta Popular, 1911.

Aguilar Camín, Héctor. "La invención de México. Notas sobre nacionalismo e identidad nacional." In Aguilar Camín, *Subversiones Silenciosas: Ensayos de historia y política de México*, pp. 19–56. México: Nuevo Siglo, 1993.

Aguilar Camin, Héctor, and Lorenzo Mcyer. *In the Shadow of the Mexican Revolution: Contemporary Mexican History, 1910–1989*. Austin: University of Texas Press, 1993.

Alcerreca, Félix M. *Crónica Histórica de los Acontecimientos trágicos y políticos que tuvieron lugar en la ciudad de México del 9 al 29 de febrero de 1913*. México: Imprenta Mixta Avenida de la Paz, 1913.

Alessio Robles, Miguel. *Historia política de la Revolución*. México: Ediciones Botas, 1938.

Alessio Robles, Miguel. *Ideales de la Revolución*. México: Editorial "Cvltvra," 1935.

Alessio Robles, Miguel. *Idolos Caídos*. México: Imprenta Manuel León Sánchez, 1931.

Alessio Robles, Miguel. *Obregón como militar*. México: Editorial "Cvltvra," 1935.

Altares de la Patria. México: Departamento del Distrito Federal, 1956.

Alvarado, Salvador. *Cartilla Revolucionaria para los Agentes de Propaganda de la Causa Constitucionalista*. Mérida de Yucatán: N.p., 1915.

Amado, Enrique. *La Revolución mexicana de 1913*. Valencia: Prometeo, 1914.

Análisis Ideológico de la Revolución Mexicana, 1910-1971. México: CEN del Partido Revolucionario Institucional, 1972.

Anaya Merchant, Luis. "La Construcción de la Memoria y la Revisión de la Revolución." *Historia Mexicana* 54:4 (abril–junio 1995).

Anda, Gustavo de. "La Tumba de la Revolución." *Impacto*, 1 de febrero de 1967.
Anda Alanis, Enrique X. de. *La Arquitectura de la Revolución Mexicana: Corrientes estilos de la década de los veintes*. México: Universidad Nacional Autónoma de México, 1990.
Anderson, Benedict. *Imagined Communities: Reflections on the Origin and Spread of Nationalism*. Revised edition. London: Verso, 1991.
Anuario Cívico de la Ciudad de México 1967. México: Departamento del Distrito Federal, 1967.
Anuario Cívico de la Ciudad de México 1968. México: Departamento del Distrito Federal, 1968.
Anuario Constitucionalista. Puebla: La Nacional, 1916.
Aragón, Alfredo. *¡A Las Armas!* México: N.p., 1916.
Aragón, Alfredo. *El desarme del Ejército Federal por la Revolución de 1913*. Paris: N.p., 1915.
Araquistain, Luis. *La Revolución Mejicana. Sus Origenes, Sus Hombres, Su Obra*. Madrid: Biblioteca del Hombre Moderno, 1929.
Arbena, Joseph L. "Sport, Development, and Mexican Nationalism, 1920–1970." *Journal of Sport History* 18:3 (Winter 1991): 350–64.
Arteaga, Agustín. "Oliverio Martínez." In *Escuela mexicana de escultura. Maestros fundadores*, pp. 103–09. Mexico: Instituto Nacional de Bellas Artes, 1990.
Asi fué la revolución mexicana. 8 vols. México: Consejo Nacional de Fomento Educativo Comisión Nacional para las Celebraciones del 175 Aniversario de la Independencia Nacional y 75 Aniversario de la Revolución Mexicana, 1985–.
Atl, Dr. [Geraldo Murillo]. *Confederación Revolucionaria: Conferencias Públicas. El País y los partidos. El momento decisivo de la acción*. México: N.p., 2 de Febrero de 1915.
Aub, Max. "De algunas aspectos de la novela de la Revolución mexicana." *Dialogos* 7:37 (enero–febrero 1971).
Ausband, Stephen C. *Myth and Meaning, Myth and Order*. Macon, GA: Mercer University Press, 1983.
Azcona B., Francisco. *Luz y Verdad: "Pancho" Villa, el Cientificismo y la Intervención*. New Orleans: Coste and Frichter, 1914.
Azuela, Mariano. *The Underdogs*. 1915. Reprint. New York: Signet Classic, 1996.
Bailey, David C. "Álvaro Obregón and Anticlericalism in the 1910 Revolution." *The Americas* 26:2 (October 1969): 183–98.
Bailey, David C. "Obregón: Mexico's Accommodating President." In George Wolfskill and Douglas Richmond, eds., *Essays on the Mexican Revolution: Revisionist Views of the Leaders*, pp. 52–99. Austin: University of Texas Press, 1979.
Bailey, David C. "Revisionism and the Recent Historiography of the Mexican Revolution." *Hispanic American Historical Review* 58:1 (February 1978): 62–79.
Bailey, David C. "El revisionismo y la historiografía reciente de la revolu-

ción mexicana." *La Cultura en México*, suplemento de *Siempre!*, 4 de mayo 1979: 2–8.

Bantjes, Adrian A. "Idolatry and Iconoclasm in Revolutionary Mexico: The De-Christianization Campaigns, 1929-1940." *Mexican Studies/Estudios Mexicanos* 13:1 (Winter 1997).

Basave del Castillo, C. *Exploraciones y anotaciones en libros y folletos que tratan de la Revolución Mexicana*. México: N.p., 1931.

Basave Benítez, Agustín. *México mestizo: Análisis del nacionalismo mexicano en torno a la mestizofilia de Andrés Molina Enríquez*. México: Fondo de Cultura Económica, 1992.

Bastian, Jean-Pierre. "El paradigma de 1789. Sociedades de ideas y revolución mexicana." *Historia Mexicana* 38:1 (julio–septiembre, 1988): 79–88.

Becker, Carl. *Everyman His Own Historian: Essays on History and Politics*. Chicago: Quadrangle Books, 1966.

Beezley, William H. *Judas at the Jockey Club and Other Episodes of Porfirian Mexico*. Lincoln: University of Nebraska Press, 1987.

Beezley, William H., Cheryl English Martin, and William E. French, eds. *Rituals of Rule, Rituals of Resistance: Public Celebrations and Popular Culture in Mexico*. Wilmington, DE: SR Books, 1994.

Ben-Amos, Avner. "The Sacred Center of Power: Paris and Republican State Funerals." *Journal of Interdisciplinary History* 22:1 (Summer 1991): 27–48.

Benjamin, Thomas. "Historiography." In Michael S. Werner, ed., *Encyclopedia of Mexico: History, Society and Culture*, Vol. 1, pp. 646–50. Chicago: Fitzroy Dearborn Publishers, 1997.

Benjamin, Thomas. "The Leviathan on the Zócalo: The Recent Historiography of the Postrevolutionary Mexican State." *Latin American Research Review* 20:3 (1985): 195–217.

Benjamin, Thomas. "The Past in the Mexican Revolution." In Hub. Hermans, Dick Papousek, and Catherine Raffi-Béroud, comps, *México en Movimiento. Concierto Mexicano, 1910–1940: Repercusión e Interpretaciones*, pp. 11–25. Groningen, The Netherlands: Centro de Estudios Mexicanos, 1997.

Benjamin, Thomas. "Rebuilding the Nation, 1920–1945." In Michael C. Meyer and William H. Beezley, eds., *The Oxford History of Mexico*. New York: Oxford University Press, forthcoming.

Benjamin, Thomas. "Regionalizing the Revolution: The Many Mexicos in Revolutionary Historiography." In Thomas Benjamin and Mark Wasserman, eds., *Provinces of the Revolution: Essays on Regional Mexican History, 1910–1929*, pp. 319–57. Albuquerque: University of New Mexico Press, 1990.

Benjamin, Thomas. "La Revolución hecha monumento: El Monumento a la Revolución." *Historia y Grafía* 6 (1996): 113–39.

Benjamin, Thomas, and Marcial Ocasio-Meléndez. "Organizing the Memory of Modern Mexico: Porfirian Historiography in Perspective, 1880s–1980s." *Hispanic American Historical Review* 64:2 (1984): 323–64.

Berger, Peter L., and Thomas Luckmann. *The Social Construction of Reality: A Treatise in the Sociology of Knowledge*. New York: Anchor Books, 1967.

Berger, Peter L., and Stanley Pullberg. "Reification and the Sociological Critique of Consciousness." *History and Theory* 4:2 (1965).

Berlanga, David G. *Pro-Patria*. Aguascalientes: N.p., 1914.

Berlanga, M. Aguirre. *Revolución y reforma. Génesis legal de la Revolución Constitucionalista*. México: Imprenta Nacional, 1918.

Berlin, Isaiah. "The Bent Twig: On the Rise of Nationalism." In Henry Hardy, ed., *The Crooked Timber of Humanity: Chapters in the History of Ideas*. New York: Vintage Books, 1992.

Beteta, Ramón. *The Mexican Revolution: A Defense*. México: DAPP, 1937.

Bhabha, Homi K. *Nation and Narration*. London: Routledge, 1990.

Bloque Nacional Revolucionario de la Cámara de Diputados: Versión Taquigráfica de las Sesiones en las cuales los Representantes de Diversos Grupos Obreros y Patronales, Expusieron sus Puntos de Vista sobre el Proyecto de Código Federal del Trabajo. México: N.p., 1929.

Bodmer, Beatriz Pastor. *The Armature of Conquest: Spanish Accounts of the Discovery of America, 1492-1589*. Stanford: Stanford University Press, 1992.

Bodnar, John. *Remaking America: Public Memory, Commemoration, and Patriotism in the Twentieth Century*. Princeton: Princeton University Press, 1992.

Bonilla, Manuel. *Díaz años de Guerra: Sinopsis de la historia verdaderamente de la Revolución mexicana. Primera Parte 1910–1913*. Mazatlan: N.p., 1922.

Bonilla, Manuel. *El Régimen maderista*. México: "El Universal," 1922.

Brading, D. A. *The First America: The Spanish Monarchy, Creole Patriots, and the Liberal State, 1492–1867*. Cambridge: Cambridge University Press, 1991.

Brading, D. A. "Liberal Patriotism and the Mexican Reforma." *Journal of Latin American Studies* 20 (1988): 27–48.

Brading, D. A. "Mexican Intellectuals and Political Legitimacy." In Roderic A. Camp, Charles A. Hale, and Josefina Zoraida Vásquez, eds., *Los intelectuales y el poder en México*. Los Angeles: El Colegio de México and UCLA Latin American Center Publications, 1991.

Brading, D. A. *Mito y profecía en la historia de México*. México: Vuelta, 1988.

Brading, D. A. *Los origines del nacionalismo mexicano*. México: SepSetentas, 1973.

Brenner, Anita. *Idols Behind Altars: The Story of the Mexican Spirit*. 1929. Reprint. New York: Beacon Press, 1970.

Brodsky, Joseph. "Profile of Clio." *The New Republic*, February 1, 1993: 60–6.

Brunk, Samuel. *¡Emiliano Zapata! Revolution and Betrayal in Mexico*. Albuquerque: University of New Mexico Press, 1995.

Brunk, Samuel. "Remembering Emiliano Zapata: Three Moments in the Posthumous Career of the Martyr of Chinameca." *Hispanic American Historical Review* 78:3 (August 1998): 457–90.

Bulnes, Francisco. *El verdadero Díaz y la revolución*. México: N.p., 1920.

Bulnes, Francisco. *The Whole Truth About Mexico*. New York: N.p., 1916.

Bustamante, Luis F. *Bajo el Terror Huertista*. San Luis Potosí: N.p., 1916.
Byrne, Moyra. "Nazi Festival: The 1936 Berlin Olympics." In Alessandro
Falassi, ed., *Time Out of Time: Essays on the Festival*. Albuquerque: University
of New Mexico Press, 1987.
Cabrera, Luis. *Discurso pronunciado ante la Soberana Convención Revolucionaria de
la Ciudad de México de 5 de octubre de 1914*. Nueva York: Edgar Printing and
Stationery Co., 1914.
Cabrera, Luis. *Obras Completas*. Vol. III, *Obra Política* (México: Ediciones Oasis,
1975).
Cabrera, Luis. *La Revolución es la Revolución. Antología*. México: Comisión Nacio-
nal Editorial del CEN. del Partido Revolucionario Institucional, 1985.
Calderón Arzamendi, Ricardo. *Síntesis de la Revolución Mexicana*. Santiago de
Chile: La Sud-America, 1929.
Calendario Nacionalista y Enciclopedia Popular. México: Partido Nacional Revolu-
cionario, 1934.
Calendario Nacionalista y Enciclopedia Popular. Rafael E. Melgar, ed. México: Par-
tido Nacional Revolucionario, 1935.
Calero y Sierra, Manuel. *Un decenio de política mexicana*. New York: N.p., 1920.
Calles, Plutarco Elías. "A Hundred Years of Revolution," *The Survey* 52:3
(May 1, 1924).
Calvert, Peter. *Mexico*. New York: Praeger, 1972.
Cárdenas Habla. México: Partido de la Revolución Mexicana, 1940.
Casasola, Gustavo, ed. *Historia gráfica de la revolución mexicana, 1900–1940*.
5 vols. México: N.p., 1945.
Casasola, Gustavo, ed. *Historia gráfica de la revolución mexicana, 1900–1970*.
10 vols. México: Editorial Trillas, 1973.
Cassirer, Ernst. *An Essay on Man*. New York: N.p., 1946.
Castillo, Ignacio B. del. *Bibliografía de la Revolución Mexicana de 1910–1916.
Historia, Legislación, Literatura, Cuestiones Sociales, Políticas y Económicas, Docu-
mentos, etc. Marzo de 1908 a Junio de 1916*. México: Talleres Gráficos de la
Secretaría de Comunicaciones y Obras Públicas, 1918.
Catálogo de Monumentos Escultóricos y Conmemorativos del Distrito Federal. México:
Oficina de Conservación de Edificios Públicos y Monumentos, 1976.
*Catálogo de Publicaciones del Instituto Nacional de Estudios Históricos de la Revolución
Mexicana, 1953–1993*. México: Instituto Nacional de Estudios Históricos de
la Revolución Mexicana, 1993.
Ceballos Dosamantes, Jesús. *La Gran Mistificación Maderista*. México: Carranza
y Hijos, 1911.
Celebración del 20 de Noviembre, 1910–1985. México: Instituto Nacional de
Estudios Históricos de la Revolución Mexicana, 1985.
Charlot, Jean. *Art Making from Mexico to China*. New York: Sheed and Ward,
1950.
Choay, Françoise. "Alberti: The Invention of Monumentality and Memory."
The Harvard Architecture Review 4 (1984): 99–105.

Cockcroft, James D. *Intellectual Precursors of the Mexican Revolution, 1900–1913.* Austin: University of Texas Press, 1968.

Colley, Linda. *Britons: Forging the Nation, 1707–1837.* New Haven: Yale University Press, 1992.

El conflicto personal de la Revolución mexicana. México: N.p., n.d. (circa early 1915).

Congreso de crítica de la revolución mexicana, 1910–1945. México: Editorial Libros de México, 1970.

Connerton, Paul. *How Societies Remember.* Cambridge: Cambridge University Press, 1989.

Conversaciones con Enrique Flores Magón. Combatimos la Tiranía. Un Pionero Revolucionario Mexicano Cuenta su Historia a Samuel Kaplan. México: Biblioteca del Instituto Nacional de Estudios Históricos de la Revolución Mexicana, 1958.

Córdova, Arnaldo. *La ideología de la Revolución Mexicana: La formación del nuevo régimen.* México: Ediciones Era, 1973.

Córdova, Arnaldo. *La política de masas del cardenismo.* México: Serie Popular Era, 1974.

Córdova, Arnaldo. "Regreso a la Revolución Mexicana." *Nexos* 3:30 (junio 1980): 3–8.

Coronado, Juan. "Revolución: metáfora y alegoría." *Unomásuno,* 22 de noviembre de 1984.

Coss y León, B. Wendy, ed. *Historia del Paseo de la Reforma.* México: Instituto Nacional de Bellas Artes, 1994.

Costeloe, Michael P. *The Central Republic in Mexico, 1835–1846: Hombres de Bien in the Age of Santa Anna.* Cambridge: Cambridge University Press, 1993.

Costeloe, Michael P. "A Pronunciamiento in Nineteenth Century Mexico: '15 de julio de 1840'." *Mexican Studies/Estudios Mexicanos* 4:2 (Summer 1988): 245–64.

Covarrubias, José. *La trascendencia política de la reforma agraria.* México: N.p., 1922.

Covo, Jacqueline. "La Idea de la Revolución Francesa en el Congreso Constituyente de 1856–1857." *Historia Mexicana* 38:1 (julio–septiembre, 1988): 69–81.

Covo, Jacqueline. "El Periódico al Servicio del Cardenismo: *El Nacional,* 1935." *Historia Mexicana* 46:1 (julio–septiembre, 1996): 133–61.

Cumberland, Charles C. "'Dr. Atl' and Venustiano Carranza." *The Americas* 13:3 (January 1957).

Cumberland, Charles C. *Mexican Revolution: Genesis under Madero.* Austin: University of Texas Press, 1952.

Cumberland, Charles C., with additional material by David C. Bailey. *Mexican Revolution: The Constitutionalist Years.* Austin: University of Texas Press, 1972.

Curcio-Nagy, Linda A. "Giants and Gypsies: Corpus Christi in Colonial Mexico City." In William H. Beezley, Cheryl English Martin, and William E.

French, eds., *Rituals of Rule, Rituals of Resistance: Public Celebrations and Popular Culture in Mexico*, pp. 1–26. Wilmington, DE: SR Books, 1994.

Curso, balance y perspectivas de la Revolución mexicana. México: Partido Revolucionario Institucional, Comisión Nacional de Ideología, 1983.

Danzer, Gerald A. "Monuments." In *Public Places: Exploring Their History*. Nashville: The American Association for State and Local History, 1987.

Davis, Natalie Zemon, and Randolph Starn. "Introduction" to the special issue on "Memory and Counter-Memory." *Representations* 16 (Spring 1989): 1–6.

de la Madrid, Miguel. "Third State of the Nation Report by the President of Mexico, Halfway Along the Road." *Mexico Today* 34 (September 1985): 1–12.

De la Pasión Sectaria a la Nación de las Instituciones. México: N.p., 1932.

La Democracia Social en México. Historia de la Convención Nacional Revolucionaria. Sucesión Presidencial de 1929. México: N.p., 1929.

Dewey, John, and Arthur F. Bentley. *Knowing and the Known*. Boston: Little, Brown, 1960.

Diario de los Debates del Congreso Constituyente 1916–1917. 2 vols. México: Instituto Nacional de Estudios Históricos de la Revolución Mexicana, 1960.

Díaz Arciniega, Víctor. *Querella Por la Cultura "Revolucionaria," 1925*. México: Fondo de Cultura Económica, 1989.

Diccionario Porrúa de historia, biografía y geografía de México. 3 vols. Quinta edición. México: Editoria Porrúa, 1986.

Diplomatic Dealings of the Constitutionalist Revolution of Mexico. Mexico: Mexican Foreign Office, n.d.

Discurso Leido por el C. Coronel Roque González Garza en la solemne apertura de la Convención Militar Revolucionaria de Aguascalientes, la noche del 14 de Octubre de 1914. Aguascalientes: N.p., 1914.

Discursos del Gral. Obregón. Segunda Parte, de 1924 a 1928. México: Talleres Gráficos de la Nación, 1928.

Discursos del General Obregón. México: Biblioteca de la Dirección General de Educación Militar, 1932.

Documentos de la Revolución Mexicana. México: Biblioteca Enciclopedia Popular, Secretaría de Educación Pública, 1945.

Doezema, Marianne. "The Public Monument in Tradition and Transition." In *The Public Monument and its Audience*. Cleveland: The Cleveland Museum of Art, 1977.

Downing, Todd. *The Mexican Earth*. 1940. Reprint. Norman: University of Oklahoma Press, 1996.

Dulles, John W. F. *Yesterday in Mexico: A Chronicle of the Revolution, 1919–1936*. Austin: University of Texas Press, 1961.

Edelman, Murray. *Constructing the Political Spectacle*. Chicago: University of Chicago Press, 1988.

Edelman, Murray. *The Symbolic Uses of Politics*. Urbana: University of Illinois Press, 1985.

Eliade, Mircea. *Symbolism, the Sacred, and the Arts*. New York: Crossroad, 1985.

Escobedo, Helen, ed. *Mexican Monuments: Strange Encounters*. New York: Abbeville Press, 1989.

Esposito, Matthew D. "From Cuauhtémoc to Juárez: Monuments, Myth, and Culture in Porfirian Mexico, 1876–1900." Master's thesis, Arizona State University, 1993.

Esquivel Obregón, T. "Factors in the Historical Evolution of Mexico." *Hispanic American Historical Review* 2 (May 1919).

Estrada, Roque. *La Revolución y Francisco I. Madero*. Guadalajara: Imprenta Americana, 1912.

Fabela, Isidro. *Arengas Revolucionaria. Discursos y Artículos Políticos*. Madrid: N.p., 1916.

Fabela, Isidro, ed. *Documentos Históricos de la Revolución Mexicana: Revolución y Régimen Maderista*. 5 vols. México: Fondo de Cultura Económica, 1964–65.

Fabela, Isidro, ed. *Documentos Históricos de la Revolución Mexicana: Revolución y Régimen Constitucionalista*. 5 vols. México: Fondo de Cultura Económica, 1960–70.

Falassi, Alessandro, ed. *Time Out of Time: Essays on the Festival*. Albuquerque: University of New Mexico Press, 1987.

Fernández, José Diego. *Discursos en el Senado. La Revolución de 1910. Golpe de Estado en Morelos*. México: N.p., 1914.

Fernández, Justino. *El Arte Moderno en México. Breve Historia—Siglos XIX y XX*. México: Antigua Liberia Robredo, José Porrua e Hijos, 1937.

Fernández, Justino. "El Monumento a Porfirio Díaz." In Daniel Schavelzon, ed., *La polémica del arte nacional en México, 1850–1910*, pp. 249–50. México: Fondo de Cultura Económica, 1988.

Fernández Güell, Rogelio. *El moderno Juárez. Estudio sobre la personalidad de Don Francisco I. Madero*. México: Tipografia Artística, 1911.

Fernández Rojas, José. *La Revolución Mexicana de Porfirio Díaz a Victoriano Huerta, 1910–1913*. México: N.p., 1913.

Figuroa Domenech, J. *Veinte Meses de Anarquía. Segunda Parte de la Revolución y sus Heroes*. México: N.p., 1918.

Florescano, Enrique. *Memory, Myth and Time in Mexico: From the Aztecs to Independence*. Austin: University of Texas Press, 1994.

Florescano, Enrique. *El nuevo pasado mexicano*. México: Cal y Arena, 1991.

Florescano, Enrique. "La Revolución mexicana en la mira." *La Jornada Semanal*, 15 de julio de 1990: 23–31.

Florescano, Enrique, ed. *Mitos Mexicanos*. México: Nuevo Siglo, 1995.

Fogelquist, Donald. "The Figure of Pancho Villa in the Corridos of the Mexican Revolution." *Hispanic-American Studies* 3 (1942): 11–12.

Folgarait, Leonard. *Mural Painting and Social Revolution in Mexico, 1920–1940: Art of the New Order*. Cambridge: Cambridge University Press, 1998.

Fornaro, Carlo de. "The Great Mexican Revolution: An Analysis." *The Forum* 59 (November 1915).

Foucault, Michel. *Language, Counter-memory, Practice: Selected Essays and Interviews*, Donald F. Bouchard, trans. and ed. Ithaca: Cornell University Press, 1977.

Fox, Elizabeth. "Latin American Broadcasting." In Leslie Bethell, ed., *The Cambridge History of Latin America*. Vol. X: *Latin America Since 1930: Ideas, Culture, and Society*, 519–68. Cambridge: Cambridge University Press, 1995.

Furman, Necah S. "Vida Nueva: A Reflection of Villista Diplomacy, 1914–1915." *New Mexico Historical Review* 53 : 3 (April 1978): 171–92.

Galarza, Geraldo. "A los héroes que la vida separó, ni tener su nombre en la Cámara los reune." *Proceso*, 7 de enero de 1985: 21–24.

Gamio, Manuel. *Forjando Patria (Pro-Nacionalismo)*. México: Ediciones Porrua, 1916.

Garay, Graciela de. "La Ciudad de la Andamios." In *Asamblea de Ciudades: Años 20s/50s, Ciudad de México*. México: Museo del Palacio de Bellas Artes and CNCA, 1991.

Garay Arellano, Graciela de. *La Obra de Carlos Obregón Santacilia, Arquitecto.* México: Secretaría de Educación Pública/Instituto Nacional de Bellas Artes, 1979.

García, Genaro, ed. *Crónica oficial de las fiestas del primer centenario de la independencia de México*. México: Secretaría de Gobernación, Talleres del Museo Nacional, 1911.

García, General Silvino. *Vibraciones Revolucionarios (Prensa y Tribuna)*. México: N.p., 1916.

García, Telesforo. *Sobre el problema agrario en México*. México: Secretaría de Fomento, Comisión Agraria Ejecutiva, 1913.

Garciadiego Dantan, Javier. "Salvador Azuela: aproximación biográfica." In Salvador Azuela, *La Revolución Mexicana: Estudios Históricos*. Selección de Garciadiego Dantan. México: Instituto Nacional de Estudios Históricos de la Revolución Mexicana, 1988.

Gass, William H. "Monumentality/Mentality." *Oppositions* 25 (Fall 1982): 23–9.

Geertz, Clifford. *The Interpretation of Cultures*. New York: Basic Books, 1973.

Geertz, Clifford. "Learning with Bruner." *The New York Review of Books*, April 10, 1997.

Gil, Feliciano. *Biografía y Vida Militar del General Álvaro Obregón*. Hermosillo: N.p., 1914.

Gilbert, Dennis. "Rewriting History: Salinas, Zedillo and the 1992 Textbook Controversy." *Mexican Studies/Estudios Mexicanos* 12 : 2 (Summer 1997): 271–98.

Gildea, Robert. *The Past in French History*. New Haven: Yale University Press, 1994.

Gillis, John R., ed. *Commemorations: The Politics of National Memory*. Princeton: Princeton University Press, 1994.

Gilly, Adolfo. "Memoria y Olvido. Rezón y Esperanza: Sugerencias para el Estudio de la Historia de las Revoluciones." *Brecha* 1 (Otoño 1986): 7–15.

Gilly, Adolfo. *The Mexican Revolution.* London: Verso, 1983.

Gilly, Adolfo. *La revolución interrumpida: México (1910–1920), una guerra campesina por la tierra y el poder.* México: Ediciones "El Caballito," 1971.

Gimeno, Conrado. *La Canalla Rojas. Notas acerca del movimiento sedicioso.* El Paso, TX: N.p., 1912.

Giron, Nicole. "Ignacio M. Altamirano y la Revolución francesa: una recuperación liberal." In Solange Alberro, Alicia Hernandez Chavez, and Elías Trabulse, eds., *La Revolución Francesa en México,* 201–14. México: El Colegio de México, 1992.

Glassberg, David. "Monuments and Memories." *American Quarterly* 43:1 (March 1991): 143–56.

Gluckman, Max, and Mary Gluckman. "On Drama, Games, and Athletic Contests." In Sally F. Moore and Barbara G. Myerhoff, eds., *Secular Ritual.* Amsterdam: Van Gorcum, 1977.

Gómez Morin, Manuel. *1915.* México: Editorial "Cvltvra," 1927.

Gómez Tepexicuapan, Ámparo. "El Paseo de la Reforma, 1864–1910." In B. Wendy Coss y León, ed., *Historia del Paseo de la Reforma,* pp. 47–52. Mexico: Instituto Nacional de Bellas Artes, 1994.

González, Antonio P. (Kanta Klaro), and J. Figueroa Domenech. *La Revolución y sus Heroes. Crónica de los sucesos políticos ocurridos en México desde Octubre de 1910 á Mayo de 1911.* Quinta edición. México: Herrero Hermanos, 1912.

González Casanova, Pablo. *La democracia en México.* México: Ediciones Era, 1965.

González Garza, Roque. *Memorandum que en el tercer aniversario de la muerte del Presidente de la República Mexicana Francisco I. Madero dirigen al C. Venustiano Carranza y personas que integran los elementos civil y militar de su gobierno de facto.* New York: N.p., 1916.

González y González, Luis, ed. *Fuentes de la historia contemporánea en México: Libros y folletos.* 3 vols. México: El Colegio de México, 1962–63.

González y González, Luis. "La pesada herencia del pasado." *Dialogos* 17:100 (julio–agosto 1981): 31–36.

González y González, Luis. *Pueblo en vilo. Microhistoria de San José de Garcia.* México: El Colegio de México, 1968.

González y González, Luis. "La Revolución Mexicana desde el punto de vista de los revolucionados." *Historias* 8–9 (enero–junio 1985): 5–13.

González y González, Luis. "La Revolución Mexicana y los Revolucionados." *Nexos* 104 (agosto de 1986): 9–13.

González y González, Luis. *Todo es historia.* México: Aguilar, 1989.

González-Blanco, Edmundo. *Carranza y la Revolución de México.* Segunda edición. Madrid: Imprenta Helénica, 1916.

Goodin, Robert E. "Rites of Rulers." *British Journal of Sociology* 29:3 (September 1978): 281–99.

Goodman, Nelson. *Ways of Worldmaking.* Indianapolis: Hackett Publishing Company, 1978.

Greenfield, Liah. "The Modern Religion?" *Critical Review* 10:2 (Spring 1996): 169–92.

Grimaldo, Issac. *Apuntes para la historia. Contiene la vida, muerte y funerales del General Maclovio Herrera.* San Luis Potosí: N.p., 1916.

Gruening, Ernest. *Mexico and Its Heritage.* New York: The Century Co., 1928.

Guerra, Francois-Xavier. *México: del Antiguo Régimen a la Revolución.* México: Fondo de Cultura Económica, 1988.

Guilpain Peuliard, Odile. *Felipe Angeles y los destinos de la Revolución mexicana.* México: Fondo de Cultura Económica, 1991.

Gunther, John. *Inside Latin America.* New York: Harper and Brothers, 1940.

Gutiérrez Cruz, C. *El Brazo de Obregón.* México: La Liga de Escritores revolucionarios, 1924.

Haight, Charles Henry. "The Contemporary Mexican Revolution as Viewed by Mexican Intellectuals," Ph.D. Dissertation, Department of History, Stanford University, 1956.

Halbwachs, Maurice. *On Collective Memory,* Lewis A. Coser, trans. and ed. Chicago: University of Chicago Press, 1992.

Halbwachs, Maurice. *La Mémoire collective.* Paris: Presses Universitaires de France, 1950.

Hale, Charles A. "Continuidad, Ruptura y Transformaciones en el Liberalismo Mexicano." Entrevista con Rubén Gallo. *Vuelta* 19 (agosto de 1995): 31–35.

Hale, Charles A. *Mexican Liberalism in the Age of Mora, 1821–1853.* New Haven: Yale University Press, 1968.

Hale, Charles A. "Los Mitos Políticos de la Nación Mexicana: El Liberalismo y la Revolución." *Historia Mexicana* 46:4 (abril–junio 1997): 821–37.

Hale, Charles A. "The Revival of Political History and the French Revolution in Mexico." In Joseph Klaits and Michael H. Haltzel, eds., *The Global Ramifications of the French Revolution.* Cambridge: Cambridge University Press and the Woodrow Wilson Center Press, 1994.

Hale, Charles A. *The Transformation of Liberalism in Late Nineteenth-Century Mexico.* Princeton: Princeton University Press, 1989.

Hall, Linda B. *Álvaro Obregón: Power and Revolution in Mexico, 1911–1920.* College Station: Texas A & M University Press, 1981.

Hamnett, Brian. *Juárez.* London: Longman, 1994.

Hart, John Mason. *Anarchism and the Mexican Working Class, 1860–1931.* Austin: University of Texas Press, 1978.

Hart, John Mason. *Revolutionary Mexico: The Coming and Process of the Mexican Revolution.* Berkeley: University of California Press, 1987.

Hartog, Francois. "Memory and Time." *The UNESCO Courier,* March 1990.

Helm, MacKinley. *Man of Fire. J. C. Orozco: An Interpretative Memoir.* New York: Harcourt, Brace, 1953.

Helm, MacKinley. *Modern Mexican Painters: Rivera, Orozco, Siqueiros and Other Artists of the Social Realist School.* Reprint, New York: Dover Publications, 1989.

Hernández, Teodoro. *La historia de la Revolución debe hacerse*. México: N.p., 1950.

Hernández y Lazo, Begoñia, ed. *Celebración del Grito de Independencia: Recopilación Hemerográfica, 1810–1985*. México: Instituto Nacional de Estudios Históricos de la Revolución Mexicana, 1985.

Hobsbawm, E. J. *Echoes of the Marseillaise: Two Centuries Look Back on the French Revolution*. London: Verso, 1990.

Hobsbawm, E. J. "Mass-Producing Traditions: Europe, 1870–1914." In E. J. Hobsbawm and Terence Ranger, eds., *The Invention of Tradition*, pp. 263–308. Cambridge: Cambridge University Press, Canto edition, 1992.

Hobsbawm, E. J. *Nations and Nationalism Since 1780: Programme, Myth, Reality*. Cambridge: Cambridge University Press, 1990.

Hobsbawm, E. J., and Terence Ranger, eds., *The Invention of Tradition*. Cambridge: Cambridge University Press, Canto Edition, 1992.

Hodges, Donald C. *Mexican Anarchism after the Revolution*. Austin: University of Texas Press, 1995.

Hughes, Lloyd H. *The Mexican Cultural Mission Programme*. Paris: UNESCO, 1950.

Hunt, Lynn, ed. *The New Cultural History*. Berkeley: University of California Press, 1989.

Hutton, Patrick H. "Collective Memory and Collective Mentalities: The Halbwachs–Ariès Connection." *Historical Reflections/Reflexions Historiques* 15:2 (Summer 1988): 311–22.

Hutton, Patrick H. *The Cult of the Revolutionary Tradition: The Blanquists in French Politics, 1864–1893*. Berkeley: University of California Press, 1981.

Hutton, Patrick H. *History as an Art of Memory*. Hanover: University of Vermont, 1993.

Hutton, Patrick H. "The Role of Memory in the Historiography of the French Revolution." *History and Theory* 30 (1991): 56–69.

Inman, Samuel G. "The Mexican Revolution." *Southwest Review* 23:3 (April 1938).

Islas Bravo, Antonio. *La Sucesión Presidencial de 1928*. México: Imprenta Manuel Léon Sánche, 1927.

Jara, René. "The Inscription of Creole Consciousness: Fray Servando de Mier." In Jara and Nicolas Spadaccini, *1492–1992: Re/Discovering Colonial Writing*, pp. 349–82. Minneapolis: University of Minnesota Press, 1989.

Judt, Tony. "A la Recherche du Temps Perdu." *The New York Review of Books*, December 3, 1998: 51–8.

Junco, Alfonso. *Carranza y los orígenes de su rebelión*. México: N.p., 1934.

Kammen, Michael. *Mystic Cords of Memory: The Transformation of Tradition in American Culture*. New York: Vintage Books, 1991.

Katz, Friedrich. *The Life and Times of Pancho Villa*. Stanford: Stanford University Press, 1998.

Katz, Friedrich. "Mexico: Restored Republic and Porfiriato, 1867–1910." In

Leslie Bethell, ed., *The Cambridge History of Latin America. Volume V: c. 1870–1930*, pp. 3–78. Cambridge: Cambridge University Press, 1986.

Keesing, Donald. "Structural Change Early in Development: Mexico's Changing Industrial and Occupational Structure from 1895 to 1950." *Journal of Economic History* 29 (December 1969): 716–38.

Kellner, Hans. *Language and Historical Representation: Getting the Story Crooked.* Madison: University of Wisconsin Press, 1989.

Knight, Alan. "Intellectuals in the Mexican Revolution." In Roderic A. Camp, Charles A. Hale, and Josefina Zoraida Vásquez, eds., *Los intelectuales y el poder en México.* México: El Colegio de México and UCLA Latin American Center Publications, 1981.

Knight, Alan. *The Mexican Revolution.* Vol. 1: *Porfirians, Liberals and Peasants.* Cambridge: Cambridge University Press, 1986.

Knight, Alan. *The Mexican Revolution.* Vol. 2: *Counter-revolution and reconstruction.* Cambridge: Cambridge University Press, 1986.

Knight, Alan. "The Mexican Revolution: Bourgeois? Nationalist? Or Just a 'Great Rebellion?'" *Bulletin of Latin American Research* 4:2 (1985): 1037.

Knight, Alan. "Mexico, c. 1930–46." In Leslie Bethell, ed., *The Cambridge History of Latin America. Volume VII: 1930 to the Present*, pp. 3–157. Cambridge: Cambridge University Press, 1990.

Knight, Alan. "Revolutionary Project, Recalcitrant People: Mexico, 1910–1940." In Jaime E. Rodríguez O., ed., *The Revolutionary Process in Mexico: Essays on Political and Social Change*, pp. 227–64. Los Angeles: UCLA Latin American Center, 1990.

Koselleck, Reinhart. *Futures Past: On the Semantics of Historical Time.* Cambridge: The MIT Press, 1985.

Krauze, Enrique. "Founding Fathers." *The New Republic*, November 28, 1994: 58–66.

Krauze, Enrique. *Mexico: Biography of Power: A History of Modern Mexico, 1810–1996.* New York: Harper Collins, 1997.

Krauze, Enrique. "Prólogo." In Magu and Enrique Krauze, *Hidalgo y sus Gritos.* México: Sentido Contrario, 1993.

Krauze, Enrique. "Y el Mantel Olía a Pólvora." *Vuelta*, julio de 1995: 13–15.

LaBatut, Jean. "Monuments and Memorials." In Talbot Hamlin, ed., *Forms and Functions of Twentieth-Century Architecture.* Vol. III, pp. 521–33. New York: Columbia University Press, 1952.

Lacy, Elaine C. "The 1921 Centennial Celebration of Mexican Independence: Contested Meaning, Memory, and National Identity." Unpublished paper presented at the Latin American Studies Association meeting, Washington, DC, September 1995.

Langle, Arturo. *Vocabulario, Apodos, Seudónimos, Sobrenambres y Hemerografía de la Revolución.* México: Universidad Nacional Autónoma de México, 1966.

Larson, Neil. "Phenomenology and Colony: Edmundo O'Gorman's *The Inven-*

tion of America." In Larson, ed., *Reading North by South: On Latin American Literature, Culture and Politics*. Minneapolis: University of Minnesota Press, 1995.

Lerdo de Tejada, C. Trejo. *La Revolución y el Nacionalismo*. Habana: N.p., 1916.

Libro de Oro de la Revolución Mexicana: Contribución Histórica. México: N.p., 1930.

Lipsitz, George. *Time Passages: Collective Memory and American Popular Culture*. Minneapolis: University of Minnesota Press, 1989.

Lira, Andrés. "Justo Sierra: La Historia Como Entendimiento Responsable." In Enrique Florescano and Ricardo Pérez Montfort, eds., *Historiadores de México en la Siglo XX*. México: Fondo de Cultura Económica, 1995.

Lira, Andres. "La Revolución francesa en la obra de Justo Sierra." In Solange Alberro, Alicia Hernandez Chavez, and Elías Trabulse, eds., *La Revolución Francesa en México*, pp. 179–200. México: El Colegio de México, 1992.

List Arzubide, Germán. *Emiliano Zapata. Exaltación*. Jalapa: N.p., 1927.

Llorens, Antonia Pi-Suner. "La Prensa, Disfusora de los Ideales de Ayutla." In Solange Alberro, Alicia Hernandez Chavez, and Elías Trabulse, eds., *La Revolución Francesa en México*, 171–8. México: El Colegio de México, 1992.

Llorente, Enrique C. *General Francisco Villa. His Policy in Dealing with Certain of the Clergy and the Reactionary Element in Mexico—Its Justification*. Washington, DC: N.p., 1915.

Lombardo Toledano, Vicente. *Definición de la Nación Mexicana*. México: Universidad Obrera de México, 1943.

López, Alfonso E. *La Revolución de Carranza y Maytorena*. México: N.p., 1913.

López, José Luis. "20 de Noviembre, exhibición masiva de miseria deportiva." *Proceso* 525 (24 de noviembre de 1986): 60–63.

López-Portillo y Rojas, José. *Elevación y caida de Porfirio Díaz*. México: N.p., 1921.

Lorey, David E. "The Revolutionary Festival in Mexico: November 20 Celebrations in the 1920s and 1930s." *The Americas* 54:1 (July 1997): 39–82.

Lowenthal, David. *The Past is a Foreign Country*. Cambridge: Cambridge University Press, 1985.

Loyo, Engracia. "La lectura en México, 1920–1940." In *Historia de la lectura en México*. México: El Colegio de México, 1988.

Loyo, Engracia. "Popular Reactions to the Educational Reforms of Cardenismo." In William H. Beezley, Cheryl English Martin, and William E. French, eds., *Rituals of Rule, Rituals of Resistance: Public Celebrations and Popular Culture in Mexico*, pp. 247–60. Wilmington, DE: SR Books, 1994.

Lukes, Steven. "Political Ritual and Social Integration." *Sociology* 9:2 (May 1975): 289–308.

MacAloon, John J. "Olympic Games and the Theory of Spectacle in Modern Societies." In MacAloon, ed., *Rite, Drama, Festival, Spectacle: Rehearsals Toward a Theory of Cultural Performance*, pp. 243–257. Philadelphia: Institute for the Study of Human Issues, 1984.

Mach, Zdzislaw. *Symbols, Conflict, and Identity: Essays in Political Anthropology.* Albany: State University of New York Press, 1993.

Macias, Carlos, ed. *Plutarco Elías Calles. Pensamiento político y social. Antología (1913–1936).* México: Fondo de Cultura Económica, 1988.

Maciel, David R. "Los Orígenes de la Cultura Oficial en México: Los Intelectuales y el Estado en la República Restaurada." In Roderic A. Camp, Charles A. Hale, and Josefina Zoraida Vázquez, eds., *Los intelectuales y el poder en México.* Los Angeles: El Colegio de México and UCLA Latin American Center Publications, 1991.

MacLachlan, Colin M. *Anarchism and the Mexican Revolution.* Berkeley: University of California Press, 1991.

MacLachlan, Colin M., and William H. Beezley. *El Gran Pueblo: A History of Greater Mexico.* Englewood Cliffs, NJ: Prentice Hall, 1994.

Madero, por uno de sus íntimos. México: Editorial Azteca, 1916.

Manero, Antonio. *Por el honor y por la gloria. Cincuenta editoriales escritos durante la lucha revolucionaria constitucionalista en Veracruz.* México: Imprenta T. Escalante, 1916.

Manero, Antonio. *Que es la Revolución.* Veracruz: Tipografía "La Heróica," 1915.

Manifiestos Políticos, 1892–1912. México: Fondo de Cultura Económica, 1957.

Manjarrez, Froylan. *La Jornada Institucional. Parte Primera: La Crisis de la Política.* México: "Diario Oficial," 1930.

Marin, Louis. "Notes on a Semiotic Approach to Parade, Cortege, and Procession." In Alessandro Falassi, ed. *Time Out of Time: Essays on the Festival.* Albuquerque: University of New Mexico Press, 1987.

Martínez, Rafael, Carlos M. Samper, and General José P. Lomelín. *La Revolución y sus Hombres (apuntes para la Historia contemporánea).* México: "El Tiempo," 1912.

Matute, Álvaro. "La Revolución Mexicana y la Escritura de su Historia." *Revista del a Universidad de México* 36 (enero de 1982): 2–6.

Matute, Álvaro. "La Revolución recordada, inventada, rescatada." In Maria Isabel Monroy de Martí, ed., *Memoria del Congreso Internacional sobre la Revolución Mexicana.* México: Instituto Nacional de Estudios Históricos de la Revolución Mexicana, 1991.

Maytorena, José M. *Algunas verdades sobre el General Álvaro Obregón.* Los Angeles, CA: Imprenta de "El Heraldo de México," 1919.

McCaleb, Walter F. "The Press of Mexico." *Hispanic American Historical Review* 3:3 (August 1920): 443–50.

McNeill, William. "Make Mine Myth." *The New York Times,* December 28, 1981.

Medin, Tzvi. *El minimato presidencial: historia política del maximato, 1928–1935.* México: Ediciones Era, 1982.

Medina Peña, Luis. *Hacia el nuevo Estado: México, 1920–1993.* México: Fondo de Cultura Económica, 1994.

Méjico Revolucionario. A los pueblos de Europa y America. 1910–1918. Habana: N.p., n.d. (circa 1918).

Meléndez, José T., ed. *Historia de la Revolución Mexicana.* Tomo I. México: Talleres Gráficos de la Nación, 1936.

Meléndez, José T., ed. *Historia de la Revolución Mexicana.* Tomo I. Reprint. México: Instituto Nacional de Estudios Históricos de la Revolución Mexicana, 1987.

Meléndez, José T., ed. *Historia de la Revolución Mexicana.* Tomo II. México: Ediciones Aguilas, 1940.

Mellado, Guillermo. *Tres Etapas Políticas de Don Venustiano Carranza.* México: N.p., 1916.

Memoria del Departamento del Distrito Federal, del 1° de Septiembre de 1938 al 31 de Agosto de 1939. México: Talleres Gráficos de la Penitenciaria, 1939.

Memoria del Departamento del Distrito Federal, 1941–1942. México: N.p., 1942.

Mendoza, Vicente T. *El Corrido de la Revolución Mexicana.* México: Universidad Nacional Autónoma de México, 1990.

Mérito Revolucionario. Antecedentes Revolucionarios de los Militares y Civiles a quienes se les han otorgado las Condecoraciones del Mérito Revolucionario. Tomo I. México: Editorial Esparta, 1939.

The Mexican Revolution: A Defense. México: DAPP, 1937.

Mexico. An exclusive interview with Miguel de la Madrid. Mexico City: Excelsior, July 1984.

Meyer, Eugenia. "Cabrera y Carranza: Hacia la Creación de una Ideología Oficial." In Roderic A. Camp, Charles A. Hale, and Josefina Zoraida Vásquez, eds., *Los intelectuales y el poder en México.* Los Angeles: El Colegio de México and UCLA Latin American Center Publications, 1991.

Meyer, Eugenia. *Luis Cabrera: teórico y crítico de la Revolución.* México: SepSetentas, 1972.

Meyer, Jean. "History as National Identity." *Voices of Mexico,* October–December 1995: 34–7.

Meyer, Jean. "Mexico: Revolution and Reconstruction in the 1920s." In Leslie Bethell, ed., *The Cambridge History of Latin America.* Volume V: *c. 1870–1930,* pp. 155–94. Cambridge: Cambridge University Press, 1986.

Meyer, Lorenzo, and Manuel Camacho. "La ciencia política en México: Su desarrollo y estado actual." In *Ciencias sociales en México: Desarrollo y perspectiva.* México: El Colegio de México, 1979.

Middleton, David, and Derek Edwards, eds. *Collective Remembering.* London: Sage, 1990.

Molina Enríquez, Andrés. *Esbozo de la historia de los primeros díez años de la Revolución Agraria de México (de 1910–1920) Hecho a grandes rasgos.* México: Talleres Gráficos del Museo Nacional de Arqueología, Historia y Etnografía, 1932–36.

Monsiváis, Carlos. "On Civic Monuments and Their Spectators." In Helen

Escobedo, ed., *Mexican Monuments: Strange Encounters*, pp. 105–34. New York: Abbeville Press, 1989.

Monteforte Toledo, Mario. *Las piedras vivas: Escultura y sociedad en México.* México: Universidad Nacional Autónoma de México, 1979.

Monumento al General Álvaro Obregón. Homenaje nacional en el lugar de su sacrificio. México: Departamento del Distrito Federal, 1934.

El Monumento de la Revolución. Texto de la Iniciativa Presentada al Ciudadano Presidente de la República por los Ciudadanos Gral. Plutarco Elías Calles e Ing. Alberto J. Pani y del Acuerdo Presidencial Recaído sobre la Misma. México: Editorial "Cvltvra," 1933.

Moore, Sally F., and Barbara G. Myerhoff, eds. *Secular Ritual.* Amsterdam: Van Gorcum, 1977.

Mora, José María Luis. *México y sus revoluciones.* 3 vols. México: Editorial Porrua, 1950.

Morales Hesse, José. *El General Pablo González. Datos para la historia, 1910–1916.* México: N.p., 1916.

Morales Jiménez, Alberto. *Historia de la Revolución Mexicana.* México: Instituto de Investigaciones Políticas, Económicas y Sociales del Partido Revolucionario Institucional, 1951.

Morales Jiménez, Alberto. *Historia de la Revolución Mexicana.* Tercero edición. México: Editorial Morelos, 1961.

Mosse, George L. *Fallen Soldiers: Reshaping the Memory of the World Wars.* New York: Oxford University Press, 1990.

Murray, Robert Hammond, trans. and ed. *Mexico Before the World: Public Documents and Addresses of Plutarco Elías Calles.* New York: The Academy Press, 1927.

Naranjo, Francisco. *Diccionario Biográfico Revolucionario.* México: Editorial Cosmos, 1935.

Nava Nava, Carmen. *Ideología del partido de la Revolución Mexicana.* México: Centro de Estudios de la Revolución Mexicana, "Lazaro Cárdenas," A. C., 1984.

Nora, Pierre, dir. *Realms of Memory: The Construction of the French Past. I. Conflicts and Divisions,* Arthur Goldhammer, trans. New York: Columbia University Press, 1996.

Nuñez y Domínguez, José de J., and Nicolas Rangel. *El Monumento a la Independencia: Bosquejo histórico.* México: Departamento del Distrito Federal, 1930.

Obregón Santacilia, Carlos. *50 Años de Arquitectura Mexicana.* México: Patria, 1952.

Obregón Santacilia, Carlos. *El Monumento a la Revolución: Simbolismo e historia.* México: Secretaría de Educación Pública, 1960.

O'Gorman, Edmundo. "La Historiografía." In *México: Cincuenta Años de la Revolución.* México: Fondo de Cultura Económica, 1960.

O'Gorman, Edmundo. *The Invention of America: An Inquiry into the Historical*

Nature of the New World and the Meaning of its History. Bloomington: Indiana University Press, 1961.

Oliverio Martínez, 1901–1938. Catálogo, Rafael Matos Galeria de Arte, Mexico City, julio–agosto, 1991.

O'Malley, Illene V. *The Myth of the Mexican Revolution: Hero Cults and the Institutionalization of the Mexican State, 1920–1940*. New York: Greenwood Press, 1986.

O'Neil, Daniel J. "The Cult of Juárez." *Journal of Latin American Lore* 4:1 (1978): 49–60.

Orozco, José Clemente. *An Autobiography*, Robert C. Stephenson, trans. Austin: University of Texas Press, 1962.

Ortega, Felipe de J. *La Revolución y la patria*. México: N.p., 1911.

Ortiz Monasterio, Luis. "La disputa de la escultura." *Revista de Revistas* 22:1135 (14 de febrero de 1932).

Ortiz Pinchetti, Francisco. "La Revolución descuidó su monumento, que ahora amenaza todo lo que lo rodea." *Proceso* 349 (11 de julio de 1983).

Ortiz Rubio, Pascual. *La Revolución de 1910. Apuntes históricos*. México: Herrero Editores, 1919.

Osorio Marban, Miguel, ed. *El Partido de la Revolución Mexicana*. Tomo I. México: Impresora del Centro, 1970.

Oviedo Mota, Dr. Alberto. *Paso a la verdad. Causas de la Revolución Mexicana*. New York: N.p., 1919.

Padilla, Ezequiel. *En la tribuna de la Revolución. Discursos*. México: Editorial "Cvltvra," 1929.

Padilla González, Francisco. *Perfiles Rojos*. Veracruz: Imprenta del Gobierno Constitucionalista, 1915.

Palacios, Aurelio. *Historia Verídica del célebre guerrillo del Sur, Emiliano Zapata*. Orizaba: N.p., 1924.

Palacios, Guillermo. "La idea oficial de la 'Revolución Mexicana'." Tesis de Maestria, Centro de Estudios Históricos, El Colegio de Mexico, 1969.

Palacios, Guillermo. "Postrevolutionary Intellectuals, Rural Readings and the Shaping of the 'Peasant Problem' in Mexico: El Maestro Rural, 1932–34." *Journal of Latin American Studies* 30 (1998): 309–39.

Palavicini, Félix F. *Cómo y Quienes Hicieron la Revolución Social en México*. México: Editorial "Cvltvra," 1931.

Palavicini, Félix F. *Un nuevo congreso constituyente*. Veracruz: N.p., 1915.

Palavicini, Félix F., ed. *México: Historia de su evolución constructiva*. 4 vols. México: Editorial Libro, 1945.

Palavicini, Félix F., ed. *El Primer Jefe*. México: N.p., 1916.

Palomares, Justino N., and Francisco Muzquiz. *Las Campañas del Norte (Sangre y Heroes). Narración de los Sucesos Más Culminantes Registrados en las Batallas de Torreón, Durango, Gómez Palacio y San Pedro*. México: Andrés Botas, Editor, 1914.

Pani, Alberto J. *Apuntes Autobiograficos*. Tomo II. México: Librería de Manuel Porrua, 1951.

Pani, Alberto J. *En Camino hacia la Democracia*. México: Poder Ejecutivo Federal, 1918.

Parra, Gonzalo de la. *De como se hizo revolucionario un hombre de buena fe*. México: N.p., 1915.

Paz, Octavio. "Muertes Paralelas." In *Tres revolucionarios, tres testimonios*. Tomo I, *Madero y Villa*. México: EOSA, 1986.

Paz, Octavio, "Re/Visions: Mural Painting." In Paz, *Essays on Mexican Art*. New York: Harcourt Brace and Co., 1993.

Pazuengo, General Matías. *Historia de la Revolución en Durango. De Junio de 1910 a Octubre de 1914*. México: N.p., 1915.

Peña, Manuel de la. "Greetings to the World from the New Liberal Constitutional Party in Mexico." In George H. Blakeslee, ed., *Mexico and the Caribbean*, pp. 141–46. New York: G. E. Stechert and Co., 1920.

Pérez Walters, Patricia. "Jesús F. Contreras." In *Jesús F. Contreras, 1866–1902: Escultor finisecular*, 23–45. México: CNCA, Instituto Nacional de Bellas Artes, Museo Nacional de Arte, 1990.

Perry, Laurens Ballard. *Juárez and Díaz: Machine Politics in Mexico*. DeKalb: Northern Illinois University Press, 1978.

Pfaff, William. *The Wrath of Nations: Civilization and the Furies of Nationalism*. New York: Touchstone, 1993.

Pierra-Purra [Pedro Lamicq]. *La Parra, la Perra y la Porra*. México: Editorial Azteca, 1915.

Planes de la Nación Mexicana. Vol. 7. México: Senado de la República, 1987.

Plasencia de la Parra, Enrique. *Independencia y nacionalismo a la luz del discurso conmemorativo (1825–1867)*. México: Consejo Nacional para la Cultura y las Artes, 1991.

Plenn, J. H. *Mexico Marches*. Indianapolis, IN: The Bobbs-Merrill Co., 1939.

Plumb, J. H. *The Death of the Past*. Middlesex: Penguin Books, 1973.

Popoca y Palacios, Lamberto. *Historia de El Bandalismo en el Estado de Morelos. Ayer como Ahora*. Puebla: N.p., 1912.

Popular Memory Group. *Making Histories: Studies in History Writing and Politics*. Minneapolis: University of Minnesota Press, 1982.

Portes Gil, Emilio. *En memoria de Zapata. Un balance social político del momento actual en México*. México: Partido Nacional Revolucionario, Biblioteca de Cultura Social y Política, 1936.

Potash, Robert A. "Historiography of Mexico since 1821." *Hispanic American Historical Review* 40:3 (August 1960): 381–424.

Prida, Ramón. *From Despotism to Anarchy: Facts and Commentaries about the Mexican Revolutions at the Beginning of the Twentieth Century*. New York: N.p., 1914.

Prida, Ramón. *De la dictadura a la anarquía*. San Antonio, TX: N.p., 1914.

Primer Congreso de Unificación de las Organizaciones Campesinas de la República. Celebrado en la Ciudad de México, D.F. del 15 al 20 Noviembre de 1926. Puebla: N.p., 1927.

Puente, Ramón. *La Dictadura, la Revolución y sus hombres*. México: N.p., 1938.

Puente, Ramón. *Pascual Orozco y la revuelta de Chihuahua*. México: Eusebio Gómez de la Puente, 1912.

Puente, Ramón. "Prólogo." In José T. Meléndez, ed., *Historia de la Revolución Mexicana*, pp. 7–16. México: Talleres Gráficos de la Nación, 1936.

Puig Casauranc, J. M. *La Aspiración suprema de la Revolución mexicana*. México: Imprenta de la Secretaría de Relaciones Exteriores, 1933.

Puig Casauranc, J. M. *Galatea rebelde a varios pigmaliones*. México: N.p., 1938.

Puig Casauranc, J. M. *El sentido social del proceso histórico de México*. México: Ediciones Botas, 1936.

Quirk, Robert E. *The Mexican Revolution, 1914–1915: The Convention of Aguascalientes*. Bloomington: Indiana University Press, 1960.

Quiros Martínez, Roberto. *Álvaro Obregón. Su vida y su obra*. México: N.p., 1928.

Rabasa, Emilio. *La evolución histórica de México*. México: N.p., 1920.

Rabasa, José. *Inventing America: Spanish Historiography and the Formation of Eurocentrism*. Norman: University of Oklahoma Press, 1993.

Ramírez, Rafael, et al. *La enseñanza de la historia en México*. México: Instituto Panamericano de Geografía e Historia, 1948.

Ramírez Garrido, J. D. "El por qué de esta Revista." *La Revolución Mexicana. Revista Ilustrada de Historia y Literatura* 1:1 (junio 1934): 1–3.

Ramos, Roberto. *Bibliografía de la Revolución Mexicana (Hasta Mayo de 1931)*. México: Monografías Bibliográficas Mexicanas, Imprenta de la Secretaría de Relaciones Exteriores, 1931.

Ramos Pedrueza, Rafael. *Sugerencias Revolucionarias para la Enseñanza de la Historia*. México: Universidad Nacional Autónoma de México, Sección Editorial, 1932.

Rauch, Angelika, "The Broken Vessel of Tradition." *Representations* 53 (Winter 1996): 74–96.

Reed, Alma. *Orozco*. New York: Oxford University Press, 1956.

Reed, John. *Insurgent Mexico*. 1914. Reprint. New York: Penguin Books, 1983.

Regeneración 1900–1918. La corriente más radical de la revolución mexicana de 1910 a través de su periódico de combate. Prólogo, selección y notas de Armando Bartra. México: Ediciones Era, 1977.

Renan, Ernest. "Qu'est-ce qu'une nation?" Reprinted as "What is a Nation?" in Homi K. Bhabha, *Nation and Narration*. London: Routledge, 1990.

Resendi, Salvador F. *La Revolución Actual. Sus Causas y Tendencias, Sus Triunfos y Fracasos*. México: N.p., 1912.

Resumen de Historia Patria. San Antonio, TX: Librería de Quiroga, 1916.

La Revolución libertaria y la Reacción en México. México: N.p., 1915.

La Revolución Mexicana. México: Secretaría de Educación Pública, 1954.

La Revolución Mexicana a Través de sus Documentos. México: Universidad Nacional Autónoma de México, 1987.

Reyes Aviles, Carlos. *Cartones Zapatistas.* México: N.p., 1928.

Ribot, Hector. *Las últimas revoluciones, 1910–1911.* México: N.p., 1912.

Richmond, Douglas. *Venustiano Carranza's Nationalist Struggle, 1898–1920.* Lincoln: University of Nebraska Press, 1983.

Rius. *Rius en Proceso.* México: Revista Proceso, 1983.

Rivas Coronado, Carlos. *Los horrores del Carrancismo en la Ciudad de México.* México: N.p., 1915.

Rivera de la Torre, Antonio. *Paralismo de Hombres y Caracteres. Juárez = Carranza, Asuntos Varios del Constitucionalismo.* México: Oficina Impresora de Hacienda, 1918.

Rivero, Gonzalo G. *Hacia la Verdad. Episodios de la Revolución.* México: Compañía Editora Nacional, 1911.

Robeledo, Federico P. *El Constitucionalismo y Francisco Villa a la Luz de la Verdad.* Matamoros: El Demócrata, 1915.

Rodríguez Kuri, Ariel. "El discurso del miedo: *El Imparcial* y Francisco I. Madero." *Historia Mexicana* 40:4 (1991): 697–740.

Rodríguez Prampolini, Ida. *La Crítica de Arte en México en el Siglo XIX.* Tomo I. México: Imprenta Universitaria, 1964.

Rolland, M. C. *Carta a mis conciudadanos.* México: N.p., 1916.

Romero Flores, Jesús. *Anales históricos de la Revolución Mexicana.* 4 vols. México: Ediciones Encaudernables de El Nacional, 1939.

Ross, Stanley R. *Francisco I. Madero: Apostle of Mexican Democracy.* New York: AMS Press, 1970.

Ross, Stanley R. "La protesta de los intelectuales ante México y su revolución." *Historia Mexicana* 26 (enero–marzo 1977): 412–420.

Ross, Stanley R., ed. *Is the Mexican Revolution Dead?* Second edition. Philadelphia: Temple University Press, 1975.

Ruíz, Ramón Eduardo. *The Great Rebellion: Mexico, 1905–1924.* New York: W. W. Norton, 1980.

Ruíz, Ramón Eduardo. *Triumphs and Tragedy: A History of the Mexican People.* New York: W. W. Norton, 1992.

Rutherford, John. *Mexican Society during the Revolution: A Literary Approach.* Oxford: Clarendon Press, 1971.

Ryan, Mary. "The American Parade: Representations of the Nineteenth-Century Social Order." In Lynn Hunt, ed., *The New Cultural History*, pp. 131–53. Berkeley: University of California Press, 1989.

Sáenz, Aarón. *Obregón, aspectos de su vida.* México: Editorial "Cvltvra," 1935.

Sáenz, Moisés. *Mexico: An Appraisal and a Forecast.* New York: The Committee on Cultural Relations with Latin America, 1929.

Sáenz, Moisés. *México Integro.* Lima: Imprenta Torres Aguirre, 1939.

Sáenz, Moisés. *Some Mexican Problems.* Chicago: N.p., 1926.

Salazar, Rosendo, and José G. Escobedo. *Las pugnas de la gleba, 1907–1922.* México: N.p., 1923.

Santamaria, Francisco J. *Diccionario de Mejicanismos.* Segundo edición. México: Editorial Porrua, 1974.

Santos Chocano, José. *El conflicto personal de la Revolución mexicana.* México: N.p., 1915.

Santos Chocano, José. *Los fines de la Revolución Mexicana considerados dentro del problema internacional.* Chihuahua: Imprenta del Gobierno, 1914.

Schaar, John H. "Legitimacy in the Modern State." In William Connolly, ed., *Legitimacy and the State,* pp. 104–33. New York: New York University Press, 1984.

Schavelzon, Daniel, ed. *La polémica del arte nacional en México, 1850–1910.* México: Fondo de Cultura Económica, 1988.

Schmidt, Henry C. "Power and Sensibility: Toward a Typology of Mexican Intellectuals and Intellectual Life, 1910–1920." In Roderic A. Camp, Charles A. Hale, and Josefina Zoraida Vázquez, eds., *Los intelectuales y el poder en México.* Los Angeles: El Colegio de Mexico and UCLA Latin American Center Publications, 1991.

Schmidt, Henry C. *The Roots of Lo Mexicano: Self and Society in Mexican Thought, 1900–1934.* College Station: Texas A & M University Press, 1978.

Schultz, Alfred. *Collected Papers. I. The Problem of Social Reality,* ed. Maurice Natanson. The Hague: Martinus Nijhoff, 1973.

Schwartz, Barry. "The Reconstruction of Abraham Lincoln." In David Middleton and Derek Edwards, eds., *Collective Remembering,* pp. 81–107. London: Sage, 1990.

Semo, Enrique. "La resurreción de Madero." *Proceso* 435 (4 de marzo de 1985): 38–39.

Seoane, Luis F. *Méjico y sus luchas internas.* Bilbao: Viuda e Hijos de Hernández, 1920.

Serrano, T. F. *Episodios de la Revolución en México.* El Paso, TX: Modern Printing, 1911.

Serrano, T. F., and C. del Vando. *Ratas y Rationes o Carranza y los Carrancistas.* El Paso, TX: N.p., 1914.

Sierra, Justo. *The Political Evolution of the Mexican People,* Charles Ramsdell, trans., introduction and notes by Edmundo O'Gorman. Austin: University of Texas Press, 1969.

Sierra Horcasitas, Luis. *Patria. Obra Histórico-Revolucionaria.* México: Talleres Gráficos de la Sria. de C.Y.O.P., 1916.

Silberman, Neil Asher. "Fallen Idols." *Archaeology,* January–February 1992: 26.

Simmons, Merle E. *The Mexican Corrido as a Source for Interpretive Study of Modern Mexico (1870–1950).* Bloomington: Indiana University Press, 1957.

Smith, Michael S. "Carrancista Propaganda and the Print Media in the United States: An Overview of Institutions." *The Americas* 52:2 (October 1995): 155–74.

Smith, Peter H. *Labyrinths of Power: Political Recruitment in Twentieth-Century Mexico*. Princeton: Princeton University Press, 1979.

Solís Cámara, Fernando. *La Reconstrucción de Nuestra Patria*. New York: N.p., 1915.

Sosa, Francisco. *Las Estatuas de la Reforma*. México: Colección Metropolitana, 1974.

Soto, Jesús S. *Aspectos de la nueva ideología mexicana*. México: Secretaría de Educación Pública, 1929.

Spenser, Daniela. *El Triángulo Imposible: México, Rusia Soviética y Estados Unidos en los años veinte*. México: CIESAS, 1998.

Staples, Anne. "El rechazo a la Revolución francesa." In Solange Alberro, Alicia Hernandez Chavez, and Elías Trabulse, eds., *La Revolución Francesa en México*, pp. 161–70. México: El Colegio de México, 1992.

Stevens, Donald Fithian. *Origins of Instability in Early Republican Mexico*. Durham: Duke University Press, 1991.

Tablada, José Juan. *Historia de la Campaña de la División del Norte*. México: Imprenta del Gobierno Federal, 1913.

Tamayo, J. A. *El Gral. Obregón y la Guerra*. México: N.p., 1922.

Tapia, Prof. Lucio, and Dr. Krumm Heller. *Trilogía Heróica: Historia condensada del último movimiento libertario en México*. México: Andres Botas, 1916.

Taracena, Alfonso. *Historia Extraoficial de la Revolución Mexicana*. México: Editorial Jus, 1987.

Teja Zabre, Alfonso. *Guide to the History of Mexico*. Mexico City: Press of the Ministry of Foreign Affairs, 1935.

Teja Zabre, Alfonso. *Panorama histórico de la Revolución mexicana*. México: Ediciones Botas, 1938.

Tenenbaum, Barbara A. "Streetwise History: The Paseo de la Reforma and the Porfirian State, 1876–1910." In William H. Beezley, Cheryl English Martin, and William E. French, eds., *Rituals of Rule, Rituals of Resistance: Public Celebrations and Popular Culture in Mexico*, pp. 127–150. Wilmington: SR Books, 1994.

Thomason, Burke C. *Making Sense of Reification: Alfred Schultz and Constructionist Theory*. London: The Macmillan Press, 1982.

Thomson, Guy P. C. "Bulwarks of Patriotic Liberalism: The National Guard, Philharmonic Corps and Patriotic Juntas in Mexico, 1847-1888." *Journal of Latin American Studies* 22:1 (February 1990): 31–68.

Tobler, Hans Werner. *La Revolución Mexicana: Transformación social y cambio político, 1876–1940*. México: Alianza Editorial, 1994.

Toledano, Vicente Lombardo. *Definición de la Nación Mexicana*. México: Universidad Obrera de México, 1943.

Tolosa Sánchez, Guadalupe. "Luis Ortiz Monasterio." In *La escuela mexicana de escultura. Maestros fundadores*. México: Instituto Nacional de Bellas Artes, 1990.

Tres intelectuales Hablan sobre México. México: N.p., 1916.

Tres revolucionarios, tres testimonios. Tomo I, *Madero y Villa,* Tomo II: *Zapata,* Octavio Paz, ed. México: EOSA, 1986.

Tribuna Revolucionaria. Discursos pronunciados durante la jira política del Ingeniero Pascual Ortiz Rubio. Año de 1929. México: N.p., 1930.

Tumarkin, Nina. *The Living and the Dead: Rise and Fall of the Cult of World War II in Russia.* New York: Basic Books, 1994.

Turner, Frederick C. *The Dynamic of Mexican Nationalism.* Chapel Hill: University of North Carolina Press, 1968.

Turner, Victor. "Liminality and the Performative Genres." In John J. MacAloon, ed., *Rite, Drama, Festival, Spectacle: Rehearsals Toward a Theory of Cultural Performance.* Philadelphia: Institute for the Study of Human Issues, 1984.

Urquiaga y Rivas, Vicente. "La Avenida 20 de Noviembre." *Arquitectura y Decoración* 2:7 (mayo 1938): 335–48.

Urquijo, Ygnacio. *Apuntes para la Historia de México (1910–1924).* México: N.p., 1925.

Urrea, Blas [Luis Cabrera]. *La Herencia de Carranza.* México: N.p., 1920.

Urrea, Blas [Luis Cabrera]. *Obras políticas del Lic. Blas Urrea.* México: Imprenta Nacional, 1921.

Valadés, José C. *Historia general de la Revolución Mexicana: II. Los hombres en armas.* México: Edición Conmemorativa del 75 Aniversario de la Revolución Mexicana, 1985.

Valtierra Moisés, Miranda. "Historia de un Símbolo: El Monumento a la Revolución." Unpublished paper, Museo Nacional de la Revolución, 1989.

Valverde, Custodio. *Julian Blanco y la Revolución en el Estado de Guerrero.* México: Imprenta J. Chavez, 1916.

Vanderwood, Paul. *Disorder and Progress: Bandits, Police and Mexican Development.* Lincoln: University of Nebraska Press, 1981.

Van Young, Eric. "Conclusion: The State as Vampire—Hegemonic Projects, Public Ritual, and Popular Culture in Mexico, 1600–1990." In William H. Beezley, Cheryl English Martin, and William E. French, eds., *Rituals of Rule, Rituals of Resistance: Public Celebrations and Popular Culture in Mexico,* pp. 343–74. Wilmington, DE: SR Books, 1994.

Vasconcelos, José. *La caida de Carranza, de la dictadura a la libertad.* México: N.p., 1920.

Vaughan, Mary Kay. "The Construction of the Patriotic Festival in Tecamachalco, Puebla, 1900–1946." In William H. Beezley, Cheryl English Martin, and William E. French, eds., *Rituals of Rule, Rituals of Resistance: Public Celebrations and Popular Culture in Mexico,* pp. 213–46. Wilmington, DE: SR Books, 1994.

Vaughan, Mary Kay. *Cultural Politics in Revolution: Teachers, Peasants, and Schools in Mexico, 1930–1940.* Tucson: University of Arizona Press, 1997.

Vaughan, Mary Kay. *The State, Education, and Social Class in Mexico, 1880–1928.* DeKalb: Northern Illinois University Press, 1982.

Vazquez Gómez, Emilio. *El pensamiento de la Revolución*. México: N.p., 1912.

Vazquez Santa Ana, Higinio. *Hombres Ilustres Nacionales*. México: Secretaría de Gobernación, 1920.

Vera Estañol, Jorge. *Partido Popular Evolucionista*. México: N.p., 1911.

Villegas, Gloria. "El Viraje de la Historiografía Mexicana Frente a la Crisis Revolucionaria, 1914–1916." *Anuario de Historia* 11 (1983): 213–30.

Villegas Moreno, Gloria. "La Militancia de la 'Clase Media Intelectual' en la Revolución Mexicana." In Roderic A. Camp, Charles A. Hale, and Josefina Zoraida Vázquez, eds., *Los intelectuales y el poder en México*, 211–33. Los Angeles: El Colegio de México and UCLA Latin American Center Publications, 1991.

Wahrman, Dror. *Imagining the Middle Class: The Political Representation of Class in Britain, c. 1780–1840*. Cambridge: Cambridge University Press, 1995.

Walzer, Michael. "On the Role of Symbolism in Political Thought." *Political Science Quarterly* 82:2 (June 1967): 191–204.

Weeks, Charles A. *The Juárez Myth in Mexico*. Tuscaloosa: University of Alabama Press, 1987.

Wells, Allen. "Oaxtepec Revisited: The Politics of Mexican Historiography, 1968–1988." *Mexican Studies/Estudios Mexicanos* 7:2 (Summer 1991): 311–46.

Widdifield, Stacie G. *The Embodiment of the National in Late Nineteenth-Century Mexican Painting*. Tucson: University of Arizona Press, 1996.

Wieseltier, Leon. "After Memory." *The New Republic*, May 3, 1993: 15–21.

Wilentz, Sean, ed. *Rites of Power: Symbolism, Ritual, and Politics Since the Middle Ages*. Philadelphia: University of Pennsylvania Press, 1985.

Wilson, Elizabeth Barkeley. "Jacques-Louis David: Stage Manager of the Revolution." *Smithsonian*, August 1998: 81–91.

Wolfe, Bertram D. "Art and Revolution in Mexico." *The Nation*, August 27, 1924: 207–8.

Wolfe, Bertram D. *The Fabulous Life of Diego Rivera*. New York: Stein and Day, 1963.

Womack, John, Jr. "The Mexican Revolution, 1910–1920." In Leslie Bethell, ed., *The Cambridge History of Latin America. Volume V: c. 1870–1930*, pp. 79–153. Cambridge: Cambridge University Press, 1986.

Womack, John, Jr. *Zapata and the Mexican Revolution*. New York: Vintage Books, 1969.

Wong, Oscar. "Reflexión y a la Historia: El Museo Nacional de la Revolución." *Siempre* 1953 (noviembre 28 de 1990).

. . . *Y Nos Fuimos a la Revolución*. México: Museo del Monumento a la Revolución, 1987.

Yack, Bernard. "The Myth of the Civic Nation." *Critical Review* 10:2 (Spring 1996): 193–212.

Yankelevich, Pablo. *Miradas australes. Propaganda, cabildeo y proyección de la Revolución mexicana en el Rio de la Plata, 1910–1930*. México: SRE-Instituto Nacional de Estudios Históricos de la Revolución Mexicana, 1997.

Yankelevich, Pablo. "Némesis: Mecenazgo Revolucionario y Propaganda Apologética." *Boletín* 28 (mayo–agosto de 1998): 1–32.

Yépez Solórzano, Miguel. *Mensaje al Grupo Revolucionario de México: Programa de táctica revolucionaria para obtener su solidaridad y cohesión.* México: N.p., 1924.

Young, James E. "The Biography of a Memorial Icon: Nathan Rapoport's Warsaw Ghetto Monument." *Representations* 26 (Spring 1989): 69–106.

Young, James E. *The Texture of Memory: Holocaust Memorials and Meaning.* New Haven: Yale University Press, 1993.

Los Zapatas de Diego Rivera. México and Cuernavaca: Consejo Nacional para la Cultura y las Artes, Instituto Nacional de Bellas Artes, Gobierno Constitucional del Estado de Morelos, 1989.

Zerubaval, Evitar. *Hidden Rhythms: Schedules and Calendars in Social Life.* Chicago: The University of Chicago Press, 1981.

Zerubavel, Yael. *Recovered Roots: Collective Memory and the Making of Israeli National Tradition.* Chicago: University of Chicago Press, 1995.

Index

Page numbers in italics indicate illustrations.

233

Urueta, Jesús, 50

Valadés, José C., 150
Vanderwood, Paul, 104
Van Young, Eric, 116
Vasconcelos, José, 68, 74, 95, 138, 141
Vaughan, Mary Kay, 95, 111, 137
Villa, Francisco (Pancho), 34
  in *corridos*, 56, 71
  interred in the Monument to the
    Revolution, 134
La voceros de la Revolución, 13, 31–32, 37,
    68, 157, 165
  as intellectuals, 167n2

Walzer, Michael, 21
Wells, Allen, 151
Womack, John, 159

Young, James E., 118, 162

Zapata, Emiliano, 34
  in *corridos*, 56
  in history, 145–146
  monument to, *86*, 125–126,
    128
Zapatismo (and Zapatistas)
  on revolution, 53–54
Zerubavel, Evitar, 100